Archibald Henry Sayce

Early Israel and surrounding Nations

Archibald Henry Sayce

Early Israel and surrounding Nations

ISBN/EAN: 9783743348035

Manufactured in Europe, USA, Canada, Australia, Japa

Cover: Foto ©ninafisch / pixelio.de

Manufactured and distributed by brebook publishing software (www.brebook.com)

Archibald Henry Sayce

Early Israel and surrounding Nations

EARLY ISRAEL

AND THE

SURROUNDING NATIONS

BY THE

REV. A. H. SAYCE

PROFESSOR OF ASSYRIOLOGY AT OXFORD

AUTHOR OF

"THE EARLY HISTORY OF THE HEBREWS," &c

London

SERVICE & PATON

5 HENRIETTA STREET

COVENT GARDEN

1899

INTRODUCTION

ONE of the first facts which strike the traveller in Palestine is the smallness of a country which has nevertheless occupied so large a space in the history of civilised mankind. It is scarcely larger than an English county, and a considerable portion of it is occupied by rocky mountains and barren defiles where cultivation is impossible. Its population could never have been great, and though cities and villages were crowded together on the plains and in the valleys, and perched at times on almost inaccessible crags, the difficulty of finding sustenance for their inhabitants prevented them from rivalling in size the European or American towns of to-day. Like the country in which they dwelt, the people of Palestine were necessarily but a small population when compared with the nations of our modern age.

And yet it was just this scanty population which has left so deep an impress on the thoughts and religion of mankind, and the narrow strip of territory they inhabited which formed the battle-ground of the ancient empires of the world. Israel was few in numbers, and the Canaan it conquered was limited in extent; but they became as it were the centre round which the forces of civilisation revolved, and towards which they all pointed. Palestine, in fact, was for the eastern world what Athens was for the western world; Athens and Attica were alike insignificant in area and the Athenians were but a handful of men, but we derive from them the principles of our art and philosophic speculation just as we derive from Israel and Canaan the principles of our religion. Palestine has been the mother-land of the religion of civilised man.

The geographical position of Palestine had much to do with this result. It was the outpost of western Asia on the side of the Mediterranean, as England is the outpost of Europe on the side of the Atlantic; and just as the Atlantic is the highroad of commerce and trade for us of to-day, so the Mediterranean was the seat of maritime enterprise and the source of maritime wealth for the generations of the past. Palestine, moreover, was the meeting-place of Asia and Africa. Not only was the way open for its merchants by sea to the harbours and products of Europe, but the desert which formed its southern boundary sloped away to the frontiers of Egypt, while to the north and east it was in touch with the great kingdoms of western Asia, with Babylonia and Assyria, Mesopotamia and the Hittites of the north. In days of which we are just beginning to have a glimpse it had been a pro-

INTRODUCTION vii

vince of the Babylonian empire, and when Egypt threw off the yoke of its Asiatic conquerors and prepared to win an empire for itself, Canaan was the earliest of its spoils. In a later age Assyrians, Babylonians, and Egyptians again contended for the mastery on the plains of Palestine; the possession of Jerusalem allowed the Assyrian king to march unopposed into Egypt, and the battle of Megiddo placed all Asia west of the Euphrates at the feet of the Egyptian Pharaoh.

Palestine is thus a centre of ancient Oriental history. Its occupation by Babylonians or Egyptians marks the shifting of the balance of power between Asia and Africa. The fortunes of the great empires of the eastern world are to a large extent reflected in its history. The rise of the one meant the loss of Palestine to the other.

The people, too, were fitted by nature and circumstances for the part they were destined to play. They were Semites with the inborn religious spirit which is characteristic of the Semite, and they were also a mixed race. The highlands of Canaan had been peopled by the Amorites, a tall fair race, akin probably to the Berbers of northern Africa and the Kelts of our own islands; the lowlands were in the hands of the Canaanites, a people of Semitic blood and speech, who devoted themselves to the pursuit of trade. Here and there were settlements of other tribes or races, notably the Hittites, who had descended from the mountain-ranges of the Taurus and spread over northern Syria. Upon all these varied elements the Israelites flung themselves, at first in hostile invasion, afterwards in friendly admixture. The Israelitish conquest of Palestine was a slow process, and it was only in its earlier stages that it was accompanied by the storming of cities and the massacre of their inhabitants. As time went on the invaders intermingled with the older population of the land, and the heads of the captives which surmount the names of the places captured by the Egyptian Pharaoh Shishak in the kingdom of Judah all show the Amorite and not the Jewish type of countenance. The main bulk of the population, in fact, must have continued unchanged by the Israelitish conquest, and conquerors and conquered intermarried together. The genealogies given by the Hebrew writers prove how extensive this intermingling of racial elements must have been; even David counted a Moabitess among his ancestors, and surrounded himself with guards of foreign nationality. Solomon's successor, the first king of Judah, was the son of an Ammonite mother, and we have only to read a few pages of the Book of Judges to learn how soon after the invasion of Canaan the Israelites adopted the gods and religious practices of the older population, and paid homage to the old Canaanite shrines.

A mixed race is always superior to one of purer descent. It possesses more enterprise and energy, more originality of thought and purpose. The virtues and failings of the different elements it embodies are alike intensified in it. We shall probably not go far wrong if we ascribe to this mixed character of the Israelitish people the originality which marks their history and finds its expression in the rise of prophecy. They were a race, moreover, which was moulded in different directions by the nature of the country in which it lived. Palestine was partly mountainous; the great block of limestone known as the mountains of Ephraim formed its backbone, and was that part of it which was first occupied by the invading Israelites. But besides mountains there were fertile plains and valleys, while on the sea-coast there were harbours, ill adapted, it is true, to the requirements of modern ships, but sufficient for the needs of ancient navigation. The Israelites were thus trained on the one hand to the habits of hardy warriors, living a life of independence and individual freedom in the fastnesses of the hills, and on the other hand were tempted to become agriculturists and shepherds wherever their lot was cast in the lowlands. The sea-coast was left to the older population, and to the Philistines, who had settled upon it about the time of the Hebrew exodus from Egypt; but the Philistines eventually became the subject-vassals of the Jewish kings, and friendly intercourse with the Phœnicians towards the north not only brought about the rise of a mixed people, partly

Canaanite and partly Israelitish, but also introduced among the Israelites the Phœnician love of trade.

Alike, therefore, by its geographical position, by the characteristics of its population, and by the part it played in the history of the civilised East, Palestine was so closely connected with the countries and nations which surrounded it that its history cannot be properly understood apart from theirs. Isolated and alone, its history is in large measure unintelligible or open to misconception. The keenest criticism is powerless to discover the principles which underlie it, to detect the motives of the policy it describes, or to estimate the credibility of the narratives in which it is contained, unless it is assisted by testimony from without. It is like a dark jungle where the discovery of a path is impossible until the sun penetrates through the foliage and the daylight streams in through the branches of the trees.

Less than a century ago it seemed useless even to hope that such external testimony would ever be forthcoming. There were a few scraps of information to be gleaned from the classical authors of Greece and Rome, which had been so sifted and tortured as to yield almost any sense that was required; but even these scraps were self-contradictory, and, as we now know, were for the most part little else than fables. It was impossible to distinguish between the true and the false; to determine whether the Chaldæan fragments

INTRODUCTION xi

of Berossos were to be preferred to the second and third hand accounts of Herodotus, or whether the Egyptian chronology of Manetho was to be accepted in all its startling magnitude. And when all was said and done, there was little that threw light on the Old Testament story, much less that supplemented it.

But the latter part of the nineteenth century has witnessed discoveries which have revolutionised our conceptions of ancient Oriental history, and illuminated the pages of the Biblical narrative. While scholars and critics were disputing over a few doubtful texts, the libraries of the old civilised world of the East were lying underground, waiting to be disinterred by the excavator and interpreted by the decipherer. Egypt, Assyria, and Babylonia have yielded up their dead; Arabia, Syria, and Asia Minor are preparing to do the same. The tombs and temples of Egypt, and the papyri which have been preserved in the sandy soil of a land where frost and rain are hardly known, have made the old world of the Egyptians live again before our eyes, while the clay books of Babylonia and Assyria are giving us a knowledge of the people who wrote and read them fully equal to that which we have of Greece or Rome. And yet we are but at the beginning of discoveries. What has been found is but an earnest of the harvest that is yet in store. It is but two years since that the French excavator, de Sarzec, discovered a library of 30,000 tablets at Tello in southern Chaldæa, which had already been formed when Gudea ruled over the city in B.C. 2700, and was arranged in shelves one above the other. At Niffer, in the north of Babylonia, the American excavators have found an even larger number of tablets, some of which go back to the age of Sargon of Akkad, or 6000 years ago, while fresh tablets come pouring into the museums of Europe and America from other libraries found by the Arabs at Bersippa and Babylon, at Sippara and Larsa. The Babylonia of the age of Amraphel, the contemporary of Abraham, has, thanks to the recent finds, become as well known to us as the Athens of Periklês; the daily life of the people can be traced in all its outlines, and we even possess the autograph letters written by Amraphel himself. The culture and civilisation of Babylonia were already immensely old. The contracts for the lease and sale of houses or other estate, the documents relating to the property of women, the reports of the law cases that were tried before the official judges, all set before us a state of society which changed but little down to the Persian era. Behind it lie centuries of slow development and progress in the arts of life. The age of Amraphel, indeed, is in certain respects an age of decline. The heyday of Babylonian art lay nearly two thousand years before it, in the epoch of Sargon and his son Naram-Sin. It was then that the Babylonian empire was established throughout western Asia as far as the Mediterranean, that a postal

INTRODUCTION   xiii

service was organised along the highroads which led from one city of the empire to another, and that Babylonian art reached its climax. It was then, too, that the Babylonian system of writing practically took its final form.

The civilisation of western Asia is, as has been said, immensely old. That is the net result of modern discovery and research. As far back as excavation can carry us there is still culture and art. We look in vain for the beginnings of civilised life. Even the pictures out of which the written systems of the ancient East were developed belong to a past of which we have but glimpses. Of savagery or barbarism on the banks of the lower Euphrates there is not a trace. So far as our materials enable us to judge, civilised man existed from the beginning in "the land of Shinar." The great temples of Babylonia were already erected, the overflow of the rivers controlled, and written characters imprinted on tablets of clay. Civilisation seems to spring up suddenly out of a night of darkness, like Athena from the head of Zeus.

This is one of the chief lessons that have been taught us by Oriental archæology. Culture and civilisation are no new thing, at all events in the East; long before the days of classical Greece, long before the days even of Abraham, man was living in ease and comfort, surrounded by objects of art and industry, acquainted with the art of writing, and carrying on intercourse with distant lands. We must rid ourselves once for all of the starveling ideas of chronology which a classical training once encouraged, and of the belief that history, in the true sense of the word, hardly goes back beyond the age of Darius or Periklês. The civilisations of Babylonia and Egypt were already decrepid when the ancestors of Periklês were still barbarians.

Another lesson is the danger of forming conclusions from imperfect evidence. Apart from the earlier records of the Old Testament, there was no literature which claimed a greater antiquity than the Homeric Poems of ancient Greece; no history of older date than that of Hellas, unless indeed the annals of China were to be included, which lay altogether outside the stream of European history. Criticism, accordingly, deemed itself competent to decide dogmatically on the character and credibility of the literature and history of which it was in possession; to measure the statements of the Old Testament writings by the rules of Greek and Latin literature, and to argue from the history of Europe to that of the East. Uncontrolled by external testimony, critical scepticism played havoc with the historical narratives that had descended to it, and starting from the assumption that the world of antiquity was illiterate, refused to credit such records of the past as dwarfed the proportions of Greek history, or could not be harmonised with the

INTRODUCTION xv

canons of the critic himself. It was quite sufficient for a fact to go back to the second millennium B.C. for it to be peremptorily ruled out of court.

The discoveries of Oriental archæology have come with a rude shock to disturb both the conclusions of this imperfectly-equipped criticism and the principles on which they rest. Discovery has followed discovery, each more marvellous than the last, and re-establishing the truth of some historical narrative in which we had been called upon to disbelieve. Dr. Schliemann and the excavators who have come after him have revealed to an incredulous world that Troy of Priam which had been relegated to cloudland, and have proved that the traditions of Mykenæan glory, of Agamemnon and Menelaos, and even of voyages to the coast of Egypt, were not fables but veritable facts. Even more striking have been the discoveries which have restored credit to the narratives of the Old Testament, and shown that they rest on contemporaneous evidence. It was not so long ago that the account of the campaign of Chedor-laomer and his allies in Canaan was unhesitatingly rejected as a mere reflection into the past of the campaigns of later Assyrian kings. Even the names of the Canaanite princes who opposed him were resolved into etymological puns. But the tablets of Babylonia have come to their rescue. We now know that long before the days of Abraham not only did Babylonian armies march to the shores of the Mediterranean, but that Canaan was a Babylonian province, and that Amraphel, the ally of Chedor-laomer, actually entitles himself king of it in one of his inscriptions. We now know also that the political condition of Babylonia described in the narrative is scrupulously exact. Babylonia was for a time under the domination of the Elamites, and while Amraphel or Khammurabi was allowed to rule at Babylon as a vassal-prince, an Elamite of the name of Eri-Aku or Arioch governed Larsa in the south. Nay more; tablets have recently been found which show that the name of the Elamite monarch was Kudur-Laghghamar, and that among his vassal allies was Tudkhula or Tidal, who seems to have been king of the Manda, or "nations" of Kurdistan. Khammurabi, whose name is also written Ammurapi, has left us autograph letters, in one of which he refers to his defeat of Kudur-Laghghamar in the decisive battle which at last delivered Babylonia from the Elamite yoke.

The story of Chedor-laomer's campaign preserved in Genesis has thus found complete verification. The political situation presupposed in it—however unlikely it seemed to the historian but a few years ago—has turned out to be in strict harmony with fact; the names of the chief actors in it have come down to us with scarcely any alteration, and a fragment of old-world history, which could not be fitted

INTRODUCTION xvii

into the scheme of the modern historian, has proved to be part of a larger story which the clay books of Babylonia are gradually unfolding before our eyes. It is no longer safe to reject a narrative as "unhistorical" simply on the ground of the imperfection of our own knowledge.

Or let us take another instance from the later days of Assyrian history, the period which immediately precedes the first intercourse between Greece and the East. We are told in the Books of the Chronicles that Manasseh of Judah rebelled against his Assyrian master and was in consequence carried in chains to Babylon, where he was pardoned and restored to his ancestral throne. The story seemed at first sight of doubtful authenticity. It is not even alluded to in the Books of the Kings; Nineveh and not Babylon was the capital of the Assyrian empire, and the Assyrian monarchs were not in the habit of forgiving their revolted vassals, much less of sending them back to their own kingdoms. And yet the cuneiform inscriptions have smoothed away all these objections. Esar-haddon mentions Manasseh among the subject princes of the West, and it was just Esar-haddon who rebuilt Babylon after its destruction by his father, and made it his residence during a part of the year. Moreover, other instances are known in which a revolted prince was reinstated in his former power. Thus Assur-bani-pal forgave the Egyptian prince of Sais when, like Manasseh, he had been sent in chains to Assyria after an unsuccessful rebellion, and restored him to his old principality. What was done by Assur-bani-pal might well have been done by the more merciful Esar-haddon, who showed himself throughout his reign anxious to conciliate the conquered populations. It is even possible that Assur-bani-pal himself was the sovereign against whom Manasseh rebelled and before whom he was brought. In this case Manasseh's revolt would have been part of that general revolt of the Assyrian provinces under the leadership of Babylon, which shook the empire to its foundations, and in which the Assyrian king expressly tells us Palestine joined. The Jewish king would thus have been carried to Babylon after the capture of that city by the Assyrian forces of Assur-bani-pal.

But the recent history of Oriental archæology is strewn with instances of the danger of historical scepticism where the evidence is defective, and a single discovery may at any moment throw new and unexpected light on the materials we possess. Who, for instance, could have supposed that the name of the Israelites would ever be found on an Egyptian monument? They were but a small and despised body of public slaves, settled in Goshen, on the extreme skirts of the Egyptian territory. And yet in 1886 a granite stela was found by Professor Flinders Petrie containing a hymn of victory in honour of Meneptah the son of Ramses II., and declaring how, among other triumphs, "the

INTRODUCTION xix

Israelites" had been left "without seed." The names of all the other vanquished or subject peoples mentioned in the hymn have attached to them the determinative of place; the Israelites alone are without it; they alone have no fixed habitation, no definite locality of their own, so far at least as the writer knew. It would seem that they had already escaped into the desert, and been lost to sight in its recesses. Who could ever have imagined that in such a case an Egyptian poet would have judged it worth his while even to allude to the vanished serfs?

Still more recently the tomb of Menes, the founder of the united Egyptian monarchy, and the leader of the first historical dynasty, has been discovered by M. de Morgan at Negada, north of Thebes. It was only a few months previously that the voice of historical criticism had authoritatively declared him to be "fabulous" and "mythical." The "fabulous" Menes, nevertheless, has now proved to be a very historical personage indeed; some of his bones are in the museum of Cairo, and the objects disinterred in his tomb show that he belonged to an age of culture and intercourse with distant lands. The hieroglyphic system of writing was already complete, and fragments of obsidian vases turned on the lathe indicate commercial relations with the Ægean Sea.

If we turn to Babylonia the story is the same. Hardly had the critic pronounced Sargon of Akkad to be a creature of myth, when at Niffer and Telloh monuments both of himself and of his son were brought to light, which, as in the case of Menes, proved that this "creature of myth" lived in an age of advanced culture and in the full blaze of history. At Niffer he and his son Naram-Sin built a platform of huge bricks, each stamped with their names, and at Telloh clay *bullæ* have been discovered, bearing the seals and addresses of the letters which were conveyed during their reigns by a highly organised postal service along the highroads of the kingdom. Numberless contract-tablets exist, dated in the year when Sargon "conquered the land of the Amorites," as Syria and Canaan were called, or accomplished some other achievement; and a cadastral survey of the district in which Telloh was situated, made for the purpose of taxation, incidentally refers to "the governor" who was appointed over "the Amorites."

Perhaps, however, the discovery which above all others has revolutionised our conceptions of early Oriental history, and reversed the critical judgments which had prevailed in regard to it, was that of the cuneiform tablets of Tel el-Amarna. The discovery was made in 1887 at Tel el-Amarna on the eastern bank of the Nile, midway between the modern towns of Minia and Siût. Here is the site of the city built by Khu-n-Aten, the "Heretic" Pharaoh, when the dissensions between himself and the Theban priesthood became too acute to allow him to remain any longer in the capital of his fathers. He migrated northward, accordingly, with his court and the adherents of the new creed which he sought to impose upon his subjects, carrying with him the archives of the kingdom and the foreign correspondence of the empire. It was this foreign correspondence which was embodied in the cuneiform tablets. They make it clear that even under Egyptian rule the Babylonian language and the Babylonian system of writing continued to be the official language and script of western Asia, and that the Egyptian government itself was forced to keep Babylonian secretaries who understood them. The fact proves the long and permanent influence of Babylonian culture from the banks of the Euphrates to the shores of the Mediterranean, and is intelligible only in the light of the further fact that the empire of Sargon of Akkad had been founded more than two thousand years before. Nothing but a prodigiously long lapse of time could explain the firm hold thus obtained by a foreign language, and a system of writing the most complex and difficult to learn that has ever been invented.

The tablets further prove the existence throughout the Oriental world of schools and libraries where the Babylonian language and characters could be taught and learned and its voluminous literature stored and studied. The age of Khu-n-Aten, which is also the age of Moses, was essentially a literary age; a know-

dealt out to such of their kinsfolk as still remained in the land. The free-born sons of Israel in the district of Goshen were turned into public serfs, and compelled to work at the buildings with which Ramses II. was covering the soil of Egypt, and their "seed" was still further diminished by the destruction of their male offspring, lest they should join the enemies of Egypt in any future invasion of the country, or assist another attempt from within to subvert the old faith of the people and the political supremacy of the Theban priests. That the fear was not without justification is shown by the words of Meneptah, the son of Ramses, at the time when the very existence of the Egyptian monarchy was threatened by the Libyan invasion from the west and the sea-robbers who attacked it from the Greek seas. The Asiatic settlers, he tells us, had pitched "their tents before Pi-Bailos" (or Belbeis) at the western extremity of the land of Goshen, and the Egyptian "kings found themselves cut off in the midst of their cities, and surrounded by earthworks, for they had no mercenaries to oppose to" the foe. It would seem that the Israelites effected their escape under cover of the Libyan invasion in the fifth year of Meneptah's reign, and on this account it is that their name is introduced into the pæan wherein the destruction of the Libyan host is celebrated and the Pharaoh is declared to have restored peace to the whole world.

If the history of Israel thus receives light and explanation on the one side from the revelations of Oriental archæology, on the other side it sometimes clears up difficulties in the history of the great nations of Oriental antiquity. The Egyptologist, for instance, is confronted by a fact towards the explanation of which the monuments furnish no help. This is the curious change that passed over the tenure of land in Egypt during the period of Hyksos rule. When the Fourteenth dynasty fell, a large part of the soil of Egypt was in the hands of private holders, many of whom were great feudal landowners whose acknowledgment of the royal supremacy was at times little more than nominal. When, however, the Hyksos were at last driven back to Asia, and Ahmes succeeded in founding the Eighteenth dynasty, these landowners had disappeared. All the landed estate of the country had passed into the possession of the Pharaoh and the priests, and the old feudal aristocracy had been replaced by a bureaucracy, the members of which owed their power and position to the king. The history of Joseph accounts for this, and it is the only explanation of the fact which is at present forthcoming. Famine compelled the people to sell their lands to the king and his minister, and a Hyksos Pharaoh and his Hebrew vizier thus succeeded in destroying the older aristocracy and despoiling the natives of their estates. It was probably at this period also that the public granaries, of which we hear so much in the age of the Eighteenth dynasty, were first established in Egypt, in imitation of those of Babylonia, where they had long been an institution, and a superintendent was appointed over them who, as in Babylonia, virtually held the power of life and death in his hands.

One of the main results, then, of recent discovery in the East has been to teach us the solidarity of ancient Oriental history, and the impossibility of forming a correct judgment in regard to any one part of it without reference to the rest. Hebrew history is unintelligible as long as it stands alone, and the attempt to interpret it apart and by itself has led to little else than false and one-sided conclusions; it is only when read in the light of the history of the great empires which flourished beside it that it can be properly understood. Israel and the nations around it formed a whole, so far as the historian is concerned, which, like the elements of a picture, cannot be torn asunder. If we would know the history of the one, we must know the history of the other also. And each year is adding to our knowledge; new monuments are being excavated, new inscriptions being read, and the revelations of to-day are surpassed by those of to-morrow. We have already learnt much, but it is only a commencement; Egypt is only now beginning to be scientifically explored, a few only of the multitudinous libraries of Babylonia have been brought to light, and the soil of Assyria has been little more than touched. Elsewhere, in Elam, in Mesopotamia, in Asia Minor, in Palestine itself, everything still remains to be done. The harvest truly is plentiful, but the labourers are few.

We have, however, learnt some needful lessons. The historian has been warned against arguing from the imperfection of his own knowledge, and rejecting an ancient narrative merely because it seems unsupported by other testimony. He has been warned, too, against making his own prepossessions and assumptions the test of historical truth, of laying down that a reported fact could not have happened because it runs counter to what he assumes to have been the state of society in some particular age. Above all, the lesson of modesty has been impressed upon him, modesty in regard to the extent of his own knowledge and the fallibility of his own conclusions. It does not follow that what we imagine ought to have happened has happened in reality; on the contrary, the course of Oriental history has usually been very different from that dreamed of by the European scholar in the quietude of his study. If Oriental archæology has taught us nothing else, it has at least taught us how little we know.

CONTENTS

CHAP.	PAGE
INTRODUCTION	v
I. THE ISRAELITES	33
II. CANAAN	67
III. THE NATIONS OF THE SOUTH-EAST	103
IV. THE NATIONS OF THE NORTH-EAST	129
V. EGYPT	145
VI. BABYLONIA AND ASSYRIA	197
VII. CONCLUSION	265
APPENDICES	271

CHAPTER I
THE ISRAELITES

EARLY ISRAEL

AND THE SURROUNDING NATIONS

CHAPTER I

THE ISRAELITES

ISRAEL traced its origin to Babylonia. It was from "Ur of the Chaldees" that Abraham "the Hebrew" had come, the rock out of which it was hewn. Here on the western bank of the Euphrates was the earliest home of the Hebrews, of whom the Israelites claimed to be a part.

But they were not the only nation of the ancient Oriental world which derived its ancestry from Abraham. He was the father not only of the Israelites, but of the inhabitants of northern and central Arabia as well. The Ishmaelites who were settled in the north of the Arabian peninsula, the descendants of Keturah who colonised Midian and the western coast, were also his children. Moab and Ammon, moreover, traced their pedigree to his nephew, while Edom was the elder brother of Israel. Israel, in fact, was united by the closest ties of blood to all the populations which in the historic age dwelt between the borders of Palestine and the mountain-ranges of south-eastern Arabia. They formed a single family which claimed descent from a common ancestor.

Israel was the latest of them to appear on the scene of history. Moab and Ammon had subjugated or absorbed the old Amorite population on the eastern side of the Jordan, Ishmael and the Keturites had made themselves a home in Arabia, Edom had possessed itself of the mountain-fastnesses of the Horite and the Amalekite, long before the Israelites had escaped from their bondage in Egypt, or formed themselves into a nation in the desert. They were the youngest member of the Hebrew family, though but for them the names of their brethren would have remained forgotten and unknown. Israel needed the discipline of a long preparation for the part it was destined to play in the future history of the world.

The Hebrews belonged to the Semitic race. The race is distinguished by certain common characteristics, but more especially by the possession of a common type of language, which is markedly different from the other languages of mankind. Its words are built on what is termed the principle of triliteralism; the skeleton, as it were, of each of them consisting of three consonants, while the vowels, which give flesh and life to the skeleton, vary according to the grammatical signification of the word. The relations of grammar are thus expressed for the most part by changes of vocalic sound, just as in English the plural of "man" is denoted by a change in the vowel. The verb is but imperfectly developed; it is, in fact, rather a noun than a verb, expressing relation rather than time. Compound words, moreover, are rare, the compounds of our European languages being replaced in the Semitic dialects by separate words.

Perhaps one of the most remarkable characteristics of the Semitic family of speech is its conservatism and resistance to change. As compared with the other languages of the world, its grammar and vocabulary have alike undergone but little alteration in the course of the centuries during which we can trace its existence. The very words which were used by the Babylonians four or five thousand years ago, can still be heard, with the same meaning attached to them, in the streets of Cairo. *Kelb* is "dog" in modern Arabic as *kalbu* was in ancient Babylonian, and the modern Arabic *ṭayyib*, "good," is the Babylonian *ṭâbu*. One of the results of this unchangeableness of Semitic speech is the close similarity and relationship that exist between the various languages that represent it. They are dialects rather than distinct languages, more closely resembling one another than is the case even with the Romanic languages of modern Europe, which are descended from Latin.

Most of the Semitic languages—or dialects if we like so to call them—are now dead, swallowed up by the Arabic of Mohammed and the Qorân. The Assyrian which was spoken in Assyria and Babylonia is extinct; so, too, are the Ethiopic of Abyssinia, and the Hebrew language itself. What we term Hebrew was originally "the language of Canaan," spoken by the Semitic Canaanites long before the Israelitish conquest of the country, and found as late as the Roman age on the monuments of Phœnicia and Carthage. The Minæan and the Sabæan dialects of southern Arabia still survive in modern forms; Arabic, which has now overflowed the rest of the Semitic world, was the language of central Arabia alone. In northern Arabia, as well as in Mesopotamia and Syria, Aramaic dialects were used, the miserable relics of which are preserved to-day among a few villagers of the Lebanon and Lake Urumîyeh. These Aramaic dialects, it is now believed, arose from a mixture of Arabic with "the language of Canaan."

On the physical side, the Semitic race is not so homogeneous as it is on the linguistic side. But this is due to intermarriage with other races, and where it is purest it displays the same general characteristics. Thick and fleshy lips, arched nose, black hair and eyes, and white complexion, distinguish the pure-blooded Semite. Intellectually he is clever and able, quick to learn and remember, with an innate capacity for trade and finance. Morally he is intense but sensuous, strong in his hate and in his affections, full of a profound belief in a personal God as well as in himself.

When Abraham was born in Ur of the Chaldees the power and influence of Babylonia had been firmly established for centuries throughout the length and breadth of western Asia. From the mountains of Elam to the coast of the Mediterranean the Babylonian language was understood, the Babylonian system of writing was taught and learned, Babylonian literature was studied, Babylonian trade was carried on, and Babylonian law was in force. From time to time Syria and Canaan had obeyed the rule of the Babylonian kings, and been formed into a Babylonian province. In fact, Babylonian rule did not come to an end in the west till after the death of Abraham; Khammurabi, the Amraphel of Genesis, entitles himself king of "the land of the Amorites," as Palestine was called by the Babylonians, and his fourth successor still gives himself the same title. The loss of Canaan and the fall of the Babylonian empire seem to have been due to the conquest of Babylon by a tribe of Elamite mountaineers.

The Babylonians of Abraham's age were Semites, and the language they spoke was not more dissimilar from Canaanitish or Hebrew than Italian is from Spanish. But the population of the country had not always been of the Semitic stock. Its first settlers—those who had founded its cities, who had invented the cuneiform system of writing and originated its culture—were of a wholly different race, and spoke an agglutinative language which had no resemblance to that of the Semites. They had, however, been conquered and their culture absorbed by the Semitic Babylonians and Assyrians of later history, and the civilisation and culture which had spread throughout western Asia was a Semitic modification and development of the older culture of Chaldæa. Its elements, indeed, were foreign, but long before it had been communicated to the nations of the west it had become almost completely Semitic in character. The Babylonian conquerors of Canaan were Semites, and the art and trade, the law and literature they brought with them were Semitic also.

In passing, therefore, from Babylonia to Canaan, Abraham was but passing from one part of the Babylonian empire to another. He was not migrating into a strange country, where the government and civilisation were alike unknown, and the manners and customs those of another world. The road he traversed had been trodden for centuries by soldiers and traders and civil officials, by Babylonians making their way to Canaan, and by Canaanites intending to settle in Babylonia for the sake of trade. Harran, the first stage on his journey, bore a Babylonian name, and its great temple of the Moon-god had been founded by Babylonian princes after the model of the temple of the

Moon-god at Ur, the birthplace of the patriarch. Even in Canaan itself the deities of Babylonia were worshipped or identified with the native gods. Anu the god of the sky, Rimmon the god of the air, Nebo the interpreter and prophet of Bel-Merodach, were all adored in Palestine, and their names were preserved to later times in the geography of the country. Even Ashtoreth, in whom all the other goddesses of the popular cult came to be merged, was of Babylonian origin.

Abraham took with him to the west the traditions and philosophy of Babylonia, and found there a people already well acquainted with the literature, the law, and the religion of his fatherland. The fact is an important one; it is one of the most striking results of modern discovery, and it has a direct bearing on our estimate of the credibility of the narratives contained in the Book of Genesis. Written and contemporaneous history in Babylonia went back to an age long anterior to that of Abraham—his age, indeed, marks the beginning of the decline of the Babylonian power and influence; and consequently, there is no longer any reason to treat as unhistorical the narratives connected with his name, or the statements that are made in regard to himself and his posterity. His birth in Ur, his migration to Harran and Palestine, have been lifted out of the region of doubt into that of history, and we may therefore accept without further questioning all that we are told of his relationship to Lot or to the tribes of north-western Arabia.

In Canaan, however, Abraham was but a sojourner. Though he came there as a Babylonian prince, as an ally of its Amoritish chieftains, as a leader of armed troops, even as the conqueror of a Babylonian army, his only possession in it was the burial-place of Machpelah. Here, in the close neighbourhood of the later Hebron, he bought a plot of ground in the sloping cliff, wherein a twofold chamber had been excavated in the rock for the purposes of burial. The sepulchre of Machpelah was the sole possession in the land of his adoption which he could bequeath to his descendants.

Of these, however, Ishmael and the sons of Keturah moved southward into the desert, out of the reach of the cultured Canaanites and the domination of Babylonia. Isaac, too, the son of his Babylonian wife, seemed bent upon following their example. He established himself on the skirts of the southern wilderness, not far on the one hand from the borders of Palestine, nor on the other from the block of mountains within which was the desert sanctuary of Kadesh-barnea. His sons Esau and Jacob shared the desert and the cultivated land between them. Esau planted himself among the barren heights of Mount Seir, subjugating or assimilating its Horite and Amalekite inhabitants, and securing the road which carried the

THE ISRAELITES

trade of Syria to the Red Sea; while Jacob sought his wives among the settled Aramæans of Harran, and, like Abraham, pitched his tent in Canaan. At Shechem, in the heart of Canaan, he purchased a field, not, as in the case of Abraham, for the sake of burial, but in order that he might live upon it in tent or house, and secure a spring of water for his own possession.

In Jacob the Israelites saw their peculiar ancestor. His twelve sons became the fathers and representatives of the twelve tribes of Israel, and his own name was changed to that of Israel. The inscribed tablets of early Babylonia have taught us that both Israel and Ishmael were the names of individuals in the Patriarchal age, not the names of tribes or peoples, and consequently the Israelites, like the Ishmaelites, of a later day must have been the descendants of an individual Israel and Ishmael as the Old Testament records assert. Already in the reign of the Babylonian king Ammi-zadok, the fourth successor of Amraphel, the contemporary of Abraham, a high-priest in the district of northern Chaldæa assigned to "Amorite" settlers from Canaan, bore the name of Sar-ilu or Israel.[1]

[1] See Pinches in the *Journal* of the Royal Asiatic Society, July 1897. In a tablet belonging to a period long before that of Abraham, Isma-ilu or Ishmael is given as the name of an "Amorite" slave from Palestine (Thureau-Dangin, *Tablettes chaldéennes inédites*, p. 10).

The fuller and older form of Jacob is Jacob-el We find it in contracts drawn up in Babylonia in the time of Abraham; we also find it as the name of an Egyptian king in the period when Egypt was ruled by Asiatic conquerors. The latter fact is curious, taken in connection with the further fact, that the son of the Biblical Jacob — the progenitor of the Israelites — was the viceroy of an Egyptian Pharaoh, and that his father died in the Egyptian land of Goshen. Goshen was the district which extends from Tel el-Maskhuta or Pithom near Ismailîya to Belbeis and Zagazig, and includes the modern Wadi Tumilât; the traveller on the railway passes through it on his way from Ismailîya to Cairo. It lay outside the Delta proper, and, as the Egyptian inscriptions tell us, had from early times been handed over to the nomad Bedâwin and their flocks. Here they lived, separate from the native agriculturists, herding their flocks and cattle, and in touch with their kinsmen of the desert. Here, too, the children of Israel were established, and here they multiplied and became a people.

The growth of a family into a tribe or people is in accordance with Arab rule. There are numerous historical instances of a single individual becoming the forefather of a tribe or a collection of tribes which under favourable conditions may develop into a nation. The tribe or people is known as the "sons" of their ancestor; his name is handed down from generation to generation, and the names of his leading descendants, the representatives of the tribe, are handed down at the same time. Where we speak of the population of a country, the Arab speaks of the "children" of a certain man. Such a mode of expression is in harmony with Semitic habits of thought. The genealogical method prevails alike in history and geography; a colony is the "daughter" or "son" of its mother-city, and the town of Sidon is the "first-born" of Canaan.

Jacob had twelve sons, and his descendants were accordingly divided into twelve tribes. But the division was an artificial one; it never at any time corresponded exactly with historical reality. Levi was not a tribe in the same sense as the rest of his brethren; no territory was assigned to him apart from the so-called Levitical cities; and he represented the priestly order wherever it might be found and from whatever ancestors it might be derived. Simeon and Dan hardly existed as separate tribes except in name; their territories were absorbed into that of Judah, and it was only in the city of Laish in the far north that the memory of Dan survived. The tribe of Joseph was split into two halves, Ephraim and Manasseh, while Judah was a mixture of various elements—of Hebrews who traced their origin alike to Judah, to Simeon, and to Dan; of Kenites and Jerahmeelites from the desert of Arabia; and of Kenizzites from Edom. Benjamin or Ben-Oni was, as a tribe, merely the southern portion of the house of Joseph, which had settled around the sanctuary of Beth-On or Beth-el. Benjamin means the "Southerner," and Ben-Oni "the inhabitant of Beth-On." It is even questionable whether the son of Jacob from whom the tribe was held to be descended bore the name of Benjamin. Had the name of Esau not been preserved we should not have known the true name of the founder of Edom, and it may be that the name of the tribe of Benjamin has been reflected back upon its ancestor.

In Goshen, at all events, the tribes of Israel would have been distinguished by the names of their actual forefathers. They would have been "the sons" of Reuben or Judah, of Simeon or Gad. But they were all families within a single family. They were all "Israelites" or "sons of Israel," and in an inscription of the Egyptian king Meneptah they are accordingly called *Israelu*, "Israelites," without any territorial adjunct. They lived in Goshen, like the Bedâwin of to-day, and their social organisation was that of Arabia.

The immediate occasion of the settlement of Israel on the outskirts of Egypt was that which has brought so many Bedâwin herdsmen to the valley of the Nile both before and since. The very district of Goshen in which they settled was occupied again, shortly after their desertion of it, by nomads from Edom who had besought the Pharaoh for meadow-land on which to feed their flocks. The need of pasturage from time immemorial has urged the pastoral tribes of the desert towards the fertile land of the Nile. When want of rain has brought drought upon Canaan, parching the grass and destroying the corn, the nomad has invariably set his face toward the country which is dependent for its fertility, not upon the rains of heaven, but upon the annual overflow of its river. It was a famine in Canaan, produced by the absence of rain, which made Jacob and his sons "go down into Egypt."

But besides this immediate cause there was yet another. They were assured of a welcome in the kingdom of the Nile and the gift of a district in which they might live. One of the sons of Jacob had become the Vizier of the Egyptian Pharaoh. Joseph, the Hebrew slave who had been sold into bondage by his brothers, had risen to be the first minister of the king and the favourite of his sovereign. He had foretold the coming years of plenty and dearth; but he had done more—he had pointed out how to anticipate the famine and make it subserve the interests of despotism. He was not a seer only, he was a skilful administrator as well. He had taken advantage of the years of scarcity to effect a revolution in the social and political constitution of Egypt. The people had been obliged to sell their lands and even themselves to the king for bread, and become from henceforth a population of royal slaves. The lands of Egypt were divided between the king and the priests; the peasantry tilled them for the state and for the temples, while the upper classes owed their wealth and position to the offices which they received at court.

It would seem that the Israelites entered Egypt when the country was governed by the last of those foreign dynasties from Asia which had conquered the kingdom of the Pharaoh, and are known by the name of the Hyksos or Shepherd kings. The Egyptian monuments have shown us that during their dominion its internal constitution underwent precisely the change which is described in the history of Joseph. Before the Hyksos conquest there was a great feudal aristocracy, rich in landed estates and influence, which served as a check upon the monarch, and at times even refused to obey his authority. When the Hyksos conquerors are finally expelled, we find that this feudal aristocracy has disappeared, and its place has been taken by a civil and military bureaucracy. The king has become a supreme autocrat, by the side of whom the priests alone retain any power. The land has passed out of the hands of the people; high and low alike are dependent for what they have on the favour of the king.

The Hyksos dynasties were allied in race and sympathies with the settlers from Asia. Joseph must have died before their expulsion, but it is probable that he saw the outbreak of the war which ended in it, and which after five generations of conflict restored the

THE ISRAELITES 47

Egyptians to independence. The Eighteenth dynasty was founded by the native princes of Thebes, and the war against the Asiatic stranger which had begun in Egypt was carried into Asia itself. Canaan was made an Egyptian province, and the Egyptian empire was extended to the banks of the Euphrates.

But the conquest of Asia brought with it the introduction of Asiatic influences into the country of the conqueror. The Pharaohs married Asiatic wives, and their courts became gradually Asiatised. At length Amenophis IV., under the tutelage of his mother, attempted to abolish the national religion of Egypt, and to substitute for it a sort of pantheistic monotheism, based on the worship of the Asiatic Baal as represented by the Solar Disk. The Pharaoh transferred his capital from Thebes to a new site farther north, now known as Tel el-Amarna, changed his own name to Khu-n-Aten, "the Glory of the Solar Disk," and filled his court with Asiatic officials and the adherents of the new cult. The reaction, however, soon came. The native Egyptians rose in revolt; the foreigner fled from the valley of the Nile, and the capital of Khu-n-Aten fell into ruin. A new dynasty, the Nineteenth, arose under Ramses I., whose grandson, Ramses II., reigned for sixty-seven years, and crowded Egypt with his buildings and monuments.

One of the cities he built has been shown by the excavations of Dr. Naville to have been Pa-Tum, the

D

Pithom of the Old Testament. Ramses II., therefore, must have been the Pharaoh of the Oppression. The picture set before us in the first chapter of Exodus fits in exactly with the character of his reign. The dynasty to which he belonged represented the reaction against the domination and influence of the foreigner from Asia, and the oppression of the Israelites would naturally have been part of its policy. Such of the Asiatics as still remained in Egypt were turned into public serfs, and measures were taken to prevent them from multiplying so as to be dangerous to their masters. The free spirit of the Bedâwin was broken by servitude, and every care was used that they should be unable to help their brethren from Asia in case of another "Hyksos" invasion. The incessant building operations of Ramses needed a constant supply of workmen, and financial as well as political interests thus suggested that merciless *corvée* of the Israelites which rendered them at once politically harmless and serviceable to the state.

In spite of all repression, however, the oppressed people continued to multiply, and eventually escaped from their "house of bondage." The stela of Meneptah, on which the name of "Israelites" occurs, implies that they had already been lost to sight in the desert. The other nationalities over whom Meneptah is said to have triumphed all have the term "country" attached to their names; the "Israelites" alone are without local habitation. Egyptian legend, as reported by the native historian Manetho, placed the Exodus in the reign of Meneptah, and as Meneptah was the son and successor of Ramses II., the correctness of the statement is antecedently probable. It was in the fifth year of his reign that the Delta was attacked by a formidable combination of foes. The Libyans threatened it on the west: on the north, bands of sea-pirates from the coasts of Asia Minor and the islands of the Mediterranean attacked it by sea and land. A mutilated inscription of Meneptah tells us how the tents of the invaders had been pitched on the outskirts of the land of Goshen, within reach of the Bedâwin shepherds who fed their flocks there, and how the troops of the Pharaoh, pressed at once by the enemy and by the disaffected population of Goshen, had been cooped up within the walls of the great cities, afraid to venture forth. The fate of the invasion was sealed, however, by a decisive battle in which the Egyptians almost annihilated their foes. But the land of Goshen was left empty and desolate; the foreign tribes who had dwelt in it fled into the wilderness under the cover of the Libyan invasion. The pressure of the invasion had forced the Pharaoh to allow his serfs a free passage out of Egypt, quite as much as the "signs and wonders" which were wrought by the hand of Moses. Egypt was protected on its eastern side by a line of fortifications, and through these permission was given that the Israelites should pass. But the permission was hardly given before it was recalled. A small body of cavalry, not more than six hundred in number, was sent in pursuit of the fugitives, who were loaded with the plunder they had carried away from the Egyptians. They were a disorganised and unwarlike multitude, consisting partly of serfs, partly of women and children, partly of stragglers from the armies of the Libyan and Mediterranean invaders. Six hundred men were deemed sufficient either to destroy them or to reduce them once more to captivity.

But the fugitives escaped as it were by miracle. A violent wind from the east drove back the shallow waters at the head of the Gulf of Suez, by the side of which they were encamped, and the Israelites passed dryshod over the bed of "the sea." Before their pursuers could overtake them, the wind had veered, and the waters returned on the Egyptian chariots. The slaves were free at last, once more in the wilderness in which Isaac had tended his flocks, and in contact with their kinsmen of Edom and Midian.

Moses had led them out of Egypt, and Moses now became their lawgiver. The laws which he gave them formed them into a nation, and laid the foundations of the national faith. Henceforth they were to be a separate people, bound together by the worship of one God, who had revealed Himself to them under the name of Yahveh. First at Sinai, among the mountains of Seir and Paran, and then at Kadesh-barnea, the modern 'Ain Qadîs, the Mosaic legislation was promulgated. The first code was compiled under the shadow of Mount Sinai; its provisions were subsequently enlarged or modified by the waters of En-Mishpat, "the Spring of Judgment."

The Israelites lay hidden, as it were, in the desert for many long years, preparing themselves for the part they were afterwards to play in the history of mankind. But from the moment of their departure from Egypt their goal had been Canaan. They were not mere Bedâwin; they belonged to that portion of the Semitic race which had made settlements and founded kingdoms in Moab and Ammon and Edom, and their residence in the cultured land of the Nile had made it impossible for them ever to degenerate into the lawless robbers of the wilderness. They were settled Bedâwin, not Bedâwin proper; not Bedâwin by blood and descent, but Semites who had adopted the wandering and pastoral habits of the Bedâwin tribes. They were like their brethren of Edom, who, though they came to Egypt seeking pasturage for their cattle, had nevertheless founded at home an elective monarchy. The true Bedâwin of the Old Testament are the Amalekites, and between the Israelite and the Amalekite there was the difference that there is between the peasant and the gypsy. The fact is important, and the forgetfulness of it has led more than one historian astray.

The first attempt to invade Canaan failed. It was made from the south, from the shelter of the block of mountains within which stood the sanctuary of Kadesh-barnea. The Israelitish forces were disastrously defeated at Zephath, the Hormah of later days, and the invasion of the Promised Land was postponed. The desert life had still to continue for a while. In the fastness of 'Ain Qadîs the forces of Israel grew and matured, and a long series of legislative enactments organised it into a homogeneous whole. At length the time came when the Israelites felt strong enough once more to face an enemy and to win by the sword a country of their own. It was from the east that they made their second attack. Aaron the high-priest was dead, but his brother Moses was still their leader. The Edomites refused them a passage along the high-road of trade which led northward from the Gulf of Aqaba; skirting Edom accordingly, they marched through a waterless desert to the green wadis of Moab, and there pitched their camp. The Amorite kingdoms of Sihon and Og fell before their assault. The northern part of Moab, which Sihon had conquered, was occupied by the invaders, and the plateau of Bashan, over which Og had ruled, fell into Israelitish hands. The invaders now prepared to cross the Jordan and advance into the highlands of Canaan. Moses died on the summit of a Moabite mountain, and his place was taken by Joshua.

Joshua was a general and not a legislator. He could

win battles and destroy cities, but he could not restore what he had destroyed, or organise his followers into a state. Jericho, which commanded the ford across the Jordan, fell into his hands; the confederate kings of southern Canaan were overthrown in battle, and the tribe of Ephraim, to which Joshua belonged, was established in the mountainous region which afterwards bore its name. Henceforward the mountains of Ephraim formed the centre and the stronghold of Israelitish power in Palestine, from whence the invading tribes could issue forth to conquest, or to which they could retreat for shelter in case of need.

Beyond leading his people into Canaan and establishing them too firmly in its midst to be ever dislodged, Joshua personally did but little. The conquest of Canaan was a slow process, which was not completed till the days of the monarchy. Jerusalem was not captured till the reign of David, Gezer was the dowry received by Solomon along with his Egyptian wife. At first the Canaanites were treated with merciless ferocity. Their cities were burned, the inhabitants of them massacred, and the spoil divided among the conquerors. But a time soon came when tribute was accepted in place of extermination, when leagues were made with the Canaanitish cities, and the Israelites intermarried with the older population of the country. As in Britain after the Saxon conquest, the invaders settled in the country rather than in the towns, so that while the peasantry was Israelite the townsfolk either remained Canaanite or were a mixture of the two races.

The mixture introduced among the Israelites the religion and the beliefs, the manners and the immoralities, of the Canaanitish people. The Mosaic legislation was forgotten; the institutions prescribed in the wilderness were ignored. Alone at Shiloh, in the heart of Ephraim, was a memory of the past observed; here the descendants of Aaron served in the tabernacle, and kept alive a recollection of the Mosaic code. Here alone no image stood in the sanctuary of the temple; the ark of the covenant was the symbol of the national God.

But the influence of Shiloh did not extend far. The age that succeeded the entrance into Canaan, was one of anarchy and constant war. Hardly had the last effort of the Canaanites against their invaders been overthrown on the banks of the Kishon, when a new enemy appeared in the south. The Philistines, who had planted themselves on the sea-coast shortly before the Israelites had invaded the inland, now turned their arms against the new-comers, and contended with them for the possession of the country. The descendants of Jacob were already exhausted by struggle after struggle with the populations which surrounded them. Moabites and Midianites, Ammonites and Bedâwin, even the king of distant Mesopotamia, had sacked their villages, had overrun their fields, and exacted tribute from the Israelitish tribes. The tribes themselves had lost coherence; they had ranged themselves under different "judges" or "deliverers," had forgotten their common origin and common faith, and had even plunged into interfraternal war. Joshua was scarcely dead before the tribe of Benjamin was almost exterminated by its brethren; and a few generations later, the warriors of Ephraim, the stalwart champion of Israel, were massacred by the Israelites east of the Jordan. In the south, a new tribe, Judah, had arisen out of various elements—Hebrew, Kenite, and Edomite; and it was not long before there was added to the cleavage between the tribes on the two banks of the Jordan, the further and more lasting cleavage between Judah and the tribes of the north. Israel was a house divided against itself, and planted in the midst of foes.

It needed a head, a leader who should bring its discordant elements into peace and order, and lead its united forces against the common enemy. Monarchy alone could save it from destruction. The theocracy had failed, the authority of the high-priests and of the Law they administered was hardly felt beyond Shiloh; an age of war and anarchy required military rather than religious control. The Israelites were passing through the same experience as other kindred members of the Semitic race. In Assyria the high-priests of Assur had been succeeded by kings; in southern Arabia the high-priest had similarly been superseded by the king, and the kings of Edom had but recently taken the place of *alûphim* or "dukes."

The first attempt to found a monarchy was made by the northern tribes. Jerubbaal, the conqueror of the Midianites, established his power among the mixed Hebrew and Canaanite inhabitants of Ophrah and Shechem, and his son Abimelech by a Canaanitish wife received the title of king. But the attempt was premature. The kingdom of Manasseh passed away with Abimelech; the other tribes were not yet ready to acknowledge the supremacy of a chieftain who was not sprung from themselves, and Abimelech, moreover, was half-Canaanitish by descent.

The pressure of Philistine conquest at last forced the Israelites with a common voice to "demand a king." Reinforced by bodies of their kinsfolk from Krete and the islands of the Greek seas, the Philistines poured over the frontier of Judah, plundering and destroying as they went. At first they were contented with raids; but the raids gradually passed into a continuous warfare and a settled purpose to conquer Canaan, and reduce it to tribute from one end to the other. The Israelitish forces were annihilated in a decisive battle, the ark of the covenant was taken by the heathen, and the two sons of the high-priest perished on the field of battle. The Philistine army marched northward into the heart of the mountains

THE ISRAELITES 57

of Ephraim, the sanctuary of Shiloh was destroyed and its priesthood dispersed. It was not long before the Philistine domination was acknowledged throughout the Israelitish territory on the western side of the Jordan, and Canaan became Palestine, "the land of the Philistines."

In the more inaccessible parts of Benjamin, indeed, a few Israelites still maintained a fitful independence, and Samuel, the representative of the traditions of Shiloh, was allowed to judge his own people, and preside over a Naioth or "monastery" of dervish-like prophets under the eye of a Philistine garrison. Israel seemed about to disappear from among the nations of the world.

But it had not yet wholly forgotten that it was a single people, the descendants of a common forefather, sharers in a common history, and above all, worshippers of the same God. In their extremity the Israelites called for a king. Saul, the Benjamite of Gibeah, was elected, and events soon proved the wisdom of the choice. Jabesh-gilead was rescued from the Ammonite king, the Philistine garrisons were driven out of the centre of the country, and, for a time at least, a large part of the Israelitish territory was cleared of its enemies. Saul was able to turn his arms against the Amalekite marauders of the desert, as well as the princes of Zobah to the north-east of Ammon.

But the Philistine war still continued. Saul had incorporated in his body-guard a young shepherd of Beth-lehem in Judah of the name of David. David showed himself a brave and skilful soldier, and quickly rose to high command in the Hebrew army, and to be the son-in-law of Saul. His victories over the Philistines were celebrated in popular songs, and the king began to suspect him of aiming at the throne. He was forced to fly for his life, and to hide among the mountain fastnesses of Judah, where his boyhood had been spent. Here he became a brigand-chief, outlaws and adventurers gathering around him, and exacting food from the richer landowners. Saul pursued him in vain; David slipped out of his hands time after time, thanks to the nature of the country in which he had taken refuge; and the only result of the pursuit was to open the road once more to Philistine invasion. Meanwhile David and his followers had left the Israelitish territory, and offered their services to Achish of Gath; the Philistine prince enrolled them in his body-guard and settled them in the town of Ziklag.

Saul and the priests were now at open war. Samuel, perhaps naturally, had quarrelled with the king who had superseded his authority, and had espoused the cause of David. We are told, indeed, that he had anointed David as king in the place of Saul. When, therefore, David escaped from the court, Saul accused the Shilonite priests who were established at Nob of intentionally aiding the rebel. The high-priest vainly protested their innocence, but the furious king refused to listen, and the priests were massacred in cold blood. Abiathar, the son of the murdered high-priest, alone escaped to David to tell the tale. He carried with him the sacred ephod through which the will of Yahveh was made known, and from henceforth the influence of the priesthood was thrown against the king.

Saul had lost his best general, who had gone over to the enemy; he had employed his troops in hunting a possible rival through the Judæan wilds when they ought to have been guarding the frontier against the national foe, and the whole force of Israelitish religion had been turned against him. There was little cause for wonder, therefore, that the Philistine armies again marched into the Israelitish kingdom, and made their way northward along the coast into the plain of Jezreel. A battle on the slopes of Jezreel decided the fate of Israel. The Hebrew army was cut to pieces, and Saul and his sons were slain. One only survived, Esh-baal, too young or too feeble to take part in the fight. Eshbaal was carried across the Jordan by Abner and the relics of the Israelitish forces, and there proclaimed king at Mahanaim. The Philistines became undisputed masters of Israel west of the Jordan, while their tributary vassal, David, was proclaimed King of Judah at Hebron. His nephew Joab was made commander-in-chief.

War soon broke out between David and Esh-baal. Esh-baal grew continually weaker, and his general Abner intrigued with David to betray him into the hands of the Jewish king. Abner, however, was slain by Joab while in the act of carrying out his treason, but Esh-baal was murdered shortly afterwards by two of his servants. David declared himself his successor, and claimed rule over all Israel.

This brought him into conflict with his Philistine overlords. It was equivalent to revolt, and the Philistine army swept the lowlands of Judah. David fled from Hebron and took refuge in his old retreat. Here he organised his forces; the Philistines were defeated in battle after battle, and David not only succeeded in driving them out of Judah and Israel, but in carrying the war into their own country. The Philistine cities were conquered, and soldiers from Gath, where David had himself once served as a mercenary, were drafted into the body-guard of the Hebrew sovereign.

Before the Philistine war was over, Jerusalem had fallen into David's hands. The stronghold of the Jebusites was one of the last of the Canaanitish cities to surrender to the Israelites. Its older inhabitants were allowed to live in it side by side with colonists from Judah and Benjamin. The city itself was made the capital of the kingdom. Its central position, its natural strength, and its independence of the history of any special tribe, all combined to justify the choice.

Here David built his palace, and planned the erection of a temple to Yahveh.

Meanwhile the kingdom of Israel was passing into an empire. Joab and his veterans gained victory after victory, and the Hebrew army became what the Assyrian army was in later days, the most highly disciplined and irresistible force in western Asia. Moab and Ammon were subdued; the Aramaic kinglets to the north-east were made tributaries, and the kingdom of Zobah, which had risen on the ruins of the Hittite power, was overthrown. The limits of David's rule were extended to the banks of the Euphrates, and the Syrians on either side of the river were utterly crushed. Even Edom, which had successfully defied the Pharaohs in the days of Egyptian greatness, was compelled to submit to the Jewish conqueror; its male population was mercilessly massacred, and its ports on the Gulf of Suez fell into Israelitish hands. In the north Hamath made alliance with the new power that had arisen in the Oriental world, while Hiram of Tyre was glad to call himself the friend of the Israelitish king, and to furnish him with skilled workmen and articles of luxury.

The latter years of David were troubled by revolts which had their origin partly in the polygamy in which he had indulged, partly in the discontent of a people still imperfectly welded together, and restless under military conscription. His son Solomon secured his throne by putting to death all possible rivals or opponents, including the grey-haired Joab. Solomon was cultured and well-educated, but his culture was selfish, and his extravagance knew no bounds. Palaces were built at Jerusalem in imitation of those of Phœnicia or Egypt, and Phœnician architects and artisans erected there a sumptuous temple in honour of the national God. Trade was encouraged and developed: the possession of the Edomite seaports gave Solomon the command of the Arabian trade, while his alliance with Hiram opened to him the harbours of the Mediterranean coast. But the wealth which David had accumulated, the tribute of the conquered provinces, and the trading monopolies of the king himself did not suffice for the extravagance of his expenditure, and heavy fiscal burdens had to be laid on the Israelitish tribes. Disaffection grew up everywhere except in Judah, where the king resided, and where the wealth raised elsewhere was spent.

Revolts broke out in Edom and the north. Garrisons, indeed, were planted in Zobah, which secured the caravan road through Tadmor or Palmyra to the Euphrates; but Damascus was lost, and became in a few years a formidable adversary of Israel. The death of Solomon was the signal for a revolt in Palestine itself. The northern tribes under Jeroboam separated from Judah and established a kingdom of their own, while Judah and Benjamin remained faithful to the house of David and to the capital, which lay on the frontier of both. The Levites also naturally attached themselves to the kingdom which contained the great national sanctuary, and to the royal family whose chapel it was. The disruption of the monarchy necessarily brought with it the fall of the empire; Moab, however, continued to be tributary to the northern kingdom and Edom to that of Judah.

Five years after the accession of Rehoboam, the son of Solomon, the kingdom of Judah seemed in danger of perishing altogether. Shishak, the Egyptian Pharaoh, invaded the country and sacked Jerusalem itself. But Jeroboam lost the opportunity thus afforded him of extending his rule over the south; his own territories had been partially overrun by the Egyptians, and he was probably not in a position to commence a war. Judah had time to recover; the walls of Jerusalem were rebuilt, and the Arabian trade soon supplied it with fresh resources.

The long and prosperous reign of Asa, the grandson of Rehoboam, placed the line of David on a solid foundation. The Jewish kingdom was compact; its capital was central, and was not only a strongly-fortified fortress, but also an ancient and venerable sanctuary. As time went on feelings of respect and affection gathered round the royal house; the people of Judah identified it with themselves, and looked back with pride and regret to the glorious days of David and Solomon. Religion, moreover, lent its sanction to the

Davidic dynasty. The Levitical priesthood had its centre in the temple which had been built by Solomon, and was, as it were, the private chapel of his descendants; here were preserved the rites and traditions of the Mosaic Law, and the ark of the covenant between Israel and its God. The northern kingdom, on the contrary, had none of these elements of stability. The first king was a rebel, who had no glorious past behind him, no established priesthood to support his throne, no capital even, around which all his subjects could rally. The sword had given him his crown, and the sword was henceforth the arbiter of his kingdom. The conservative forces which were strong in Judah were absent in the north; there the army became more and more powerful, and its generals dethroned princes and established short-lived dynasties. Northern Israel, moreover, was not homogeneous; the tribes on the two sides of the Jordan were never welded together like the inhabitants of Judah, and the divergence of interests that had once existed between them was never wholly forgotten.

Israel perished while Judah survived. Dynasty after dynasty had arisen in it; its capital had been shifted from time to time; it did not even possess a religious centre. Before a line of kings had time to win the loyalty of the people they were swept away by revolution, and the army became the dominating power in the state. There was no body of priests to preserve

THE ISRAELITES 65

the memory of the Mosaic Law and insist upon its observance, and the prophets who took their place protested in vain against the national apostasy. Alliance with the neighbouring kingdom of Phœnicia brought with it the worship of the Phœnician Baal, and Yahveh was forsaken for a foreign god. In B.C. 722 Samaria, the later capital of the country, was taken by the Assyrian king Sargon, and northern Israel ceased to be a nation.

Judah, on the other hand, successfully defied the Assyrian power. The invasion of Sennacherib was rolled back from the walls of Jerusalem, and though the Jewish kings paid tribute to Nineveh, they were left in possession of their territories. Edom, indeed, had long since been lost, and with it the trade with the Arabian seas, but the Philistines continued to acknowledge the supremacy of Judah, and commercial relations were kept up with Egypt. It was not until the Babylonian empire of Nebuchadrezzar had arisen on the ruins of that of Assyria that Jerusalem and its temple were destroyed, and the Davidic dynasty passed away. But they had accomplished their work; a nation had been created which through exile and disaster still maintained its religion and its characteristics, and was prepared, when happier days should come, to return again to its old home, to rebuild the temple, and carry out all the ordinances of its faith. From henceforth Judah realised its mission as a peculiar people, separated from the rest of the world, whose instructor in religion it was to be. More and more it ceased to be a nation and became a race—a race, moreover, which had its roots in a common religious history, a common faith, and a common hope. Israel according to the flesh became Israel according to the spirit.

CHAPTER II
CANAAN

CHAPTER · II

CANAAN

CANAAN was the inheritance which the Israelites won for themselves by the sword. Their ancestors had already settled in it in patriarchal days. Abraham "the Hebrew" from Babylonia had bought in it a burying-place near Hebron; Jacob had purchased a field near Shechem, where he could water his flocks from his own spring. It was the "Promised Land" to which the serfs of the Pharaoh in Goshen looked forward when they should again become free men and find a new home for themselves.

Canaan had ever been the refuge of the Asiatic population of Egypt, the goal at which they aimed when driven out of the land of the Nile. The Hyksos conquerors from Asia had retreated to Jerusalem when the native Egyptians recovered their independence and had expelled them from their seats in the Delta. Though Moses had assured the Pharaoh that all the Israelites needed was to go a short journey of three days into the wilderness, and there sacrifice to their God, it was well understood that the desert was not to be the end of their pilgrimage. Canaan, and Canaan only, was the destined country they had in view.

In the early inscriptions of Babylonia, Canaan is included in the rest of Syria under the general title of "the land of the Amorites." The Amorites were at the time the dominant population on the Mediterranean coast of western Asia, and after them accordingly the whole country received its name. The "land of the Amorites" had been overrun by the armies of Babylonia at a very remote period, and had thus come under the influence of Babylonian culture. As far back as the reigns of Sargon of Akkad and his son Naram-Sin (B.C. 3800), three campaigns had laid it at the feet of the Chaldæan monarch, and Palestine and Syria became a province of the Babylonian empire. Sargon erected an image of himself by the shore of the sea, and seems even to have received tribute from Cyprus. Colonies of "Amorite" or Canaanitish merchants settled in Babylonia for the purposes of trade, and there obtained various rights and privileges; and a cadastral survey of southern Babylonia made at the time mentions "the governor of the land of the Amorites."

The Amorites, however, though they were the dominant people of Syria, were not its original inhabitants; nor, it is probable, did they even form the largest part of its population. They were essentially the inhabitants of the mountains, as we are told in the Book of

CANAAN 71

Numbers (xiii. 29), and appear to have come from the west. We have learnt a good deal about them from the Egyptian monuments, where the " Amurru " or Amorites are depicted with that fidelity to nature which characterised the art of ancient Egypt. They belonged to the white race, and, like other members of the white race, were tall in stature and impatient of the damp heat of the plains. Their beard and eyebrows are painted red, their hair a light red-brown, while their eyes are blue. The skin is a sunburnt white, the nose straight and regular, the forehead high, and the lips thin. They wore whiskers and a pointed beard, and dressed in long robes furnished with a sort of cape. Their physical characteristics are those of the Libyan neighbours of the Egyptians on the west, the forefathers of the fair-skinned and blue-eyed Kabyles or Berbers who inhabit the mountains of northern Africa to-day. Anthropologists connect these Libyans with the Kelts of our own islands. At one time, it would seem, a Kelto-Libyan race existed, which spread along the northern coast of Africa to western Europe and the British Isles. The Amorites would appear to have been an eastern offshoot of the same race.

Wherever they went, the members of the race buried their dead in rude stone cairns or cromlechs, the dolmens of the French antiquarians. We find them in Britain and France, in the Spanish peninsula, and the north of Africa. They are also found in Palestine, more especially in that portion of it which was the home of the Amorites. The skulls found in the cairns are for the most part of the dolichocephalic or long-headed type; this too is the shape of skull characteristic of the modern Kabyle, and it has been portrayed for us by the Egyptian artists in the pictures of their Amorite foes.

In the days of the Egyptian artists—the age of the Eighteenth and two following dynasties (B.C. 1600–1200) —the special seat of the Amorites was the mountainous district immediately to the north of Palestine. But Amorite kingdoms were established elsewhere on both sides of the Jordan. Not long before the Israelitish invasion, the Amorite king Sihon had robbed Moab of its territory and founded his power on the ruins of that of the Egyptian empire. Farther north, in the plateau of Bashan, another Amorite king, Og, had his capital, while Amorite tribes were settled on the western side of the Jordan, in the mountains of southern Canaan, where the tribe of Judah subsequently established itself. We even hear of Amorites in the mountain-block of Kadesh-barnea, in the desert south of Canaan; and the Amorite type of face, as it has been depicted for us on the monuments of Egypt, may still be often observed among the Arab tribes of the district between Egypt and Palestine.

Jerusalem, Ezekiel tells us, had an Amorite as well

as a Hittite parentage, and Jacob declares that he had taken his heritage at Shechem out of the hand of the Amorite with his sword and bow. It must be remembered, however, that the term "Amorite" is sometimes used in the Old Testament in its Babylonian sense, as denoting an inhabitant of Canaan, whatever might be the race to which he belonged; we cannot always infer from it the nationality or race of those to whom it is applied. Moreover, individual branches of the Amorite stock had names of their own. In the north they were known as Hivites, at Hebron they were called Anakim, at Jerusalem they were Jebusites. The Amorite kings of Bashan are described as Rephaim, a word which the Authorised Version translates "giants." It was only on the northern frontier of Palestine and in the kingdom of Sihon that the name of "Amorite" alone was used.

The Babylonian conquests introduced into Canaan the government and law, the writing and literature, of Babylonian civilisation. The Babylonian language even made its way to the west, and was taught, along with the script, in the schools which were established in imitation of those of Chaldæa. Babylonian generals and officials lived in Palestine and administered its affairs, and an active trade was carried on between the Euphrates and the Mediterranean coast. The traderoad ran through Mesopotamia past the city of Harran, and formed a link between the Mediterranean and the Persian Gulf.

From an early date libraries had existed in Babylonia stored with the literature of the country. Similarly, libraries now grew up in "the land of the Amorites," and the clay tablets with which they were filled made known to the west the legends and records of Chaldæa. Amorite culture was modelled on that of Babylonia.

Babylonian influence lasted for centuries in western Asia. In the age of Abraham the Amorites still obeyed the suzerainty of the Babylonian kings. Khammurabi, the Amraphel of the Book of Genesis, calls himself king of the country of the Amorites as well as of Babylon, and his great-grandson does the same. At a later date Babylonia itself was conquered by a foreign line of kings, and Canaan recovered its independence. But this was of no long duration. Thothmes III., of the Eighteenth Egyptian dynasty (B.C. 1503–1449), made it a province of Egypt, and the Amorites were governed by Egyptian prefects and commissioners. The cuneiform tablets found at Tel el-Amarna in Upper Egypt give us a vivid picture of its condition at the close of the Eighteenth dynasty. The Egyptian power was falling to pieces, and Palestine was threatened by Hittite invaders from the north. The native governors were fighting with one another or intriguing with the enemies of Egypt, while all the time protesting their loyalty to the Pharaoh. Ebed-Asherah and his son Aziru governed the Amorites in the north, and the

CANAAN 75

prefect of Phœnicia sends bitter complaints to the Egyptian court of their hostility to himself and their royal master. Aziru, however, was an able ruler. He succeeded in clearing himself from the charge of complicity with the Hittites against whom he had been sent, as well as in getting the better of his Phœnician rival. The latter disappears from history, while the Amorites are allowed to settle undisturbed in Zemar and other cities of inland Phœnicia.

Under Ramses II. of the Nineteenth dynasty, Canaan still yielded a reluctant obedience to Egypt. In the troubles which had followed the fall of the Eighteenth dynasty, it had shaken itself free from foreign authority, but had been reconquered by Seti I., the father of Ramses. Egyptian authority was re-established even on the eastern side of the Jordan; but it did not continue for long. Ramses was hardly dead before Egypt was invaded by Libyans from the west and robber hordes from the Greek seas, and though the invasion was ultimately beaten back, its strength had been exhausted in the struggle. The Egyptian empire in Canaan passed away for ever, and the Canaanites were left free to govern themselves.

The kingdom of Sihon was one of the results of this ending of Egyptian rule. The Amorites became a power once more. A few years later Egypt was again attacked by armed invaders from the north. The assailants poured into it both by sea and land. Fleets of ships filled with Philistines and Achæans and other northern tribes entered the mouths of the Nile, while a vast army simultaneously attacked it by land. The army, we are told, had encamped in "the land of the Amorites," and they carried with them on their farther march recruits from the countries through which they passed. The Amorite "chief" himself was among those who followed the barbarians to Egypt, eager for the spoils of the wealthiest country in the ancient world.

Ramses III. of the Twentieth dynasty was now on the throne. He succeeded in rolling back the wave of invasion, in gaining a decisive victory over the combined military and naval forces of the enemy, and in pursuing them to the frontiers of Asia itself. Gaza, the key to the military road which ran along the seaboard of Palestine, fell once more into Egyptian hands; and the Egyptian troops overran the future Judah, occupying the districts of Jerusalem and Hebron, and even crossing the Jordan. But no permanent conquest was effected; Ramses retired again to Egypt, and for more than two centuries no more Egyptian armies found their way into Canaan. Gaza and the neighbouring cities became the strongholds of the Philistine pirates, and effectually barred the road to Asia.

The campaign of Ramses III. in southern Palestine must have taken place when the Israelites were still in the desert. Between the two invasions of Egypt by the barbarians of the north, there was no great interval of time. The Exodus, which had been due in part to the pressure of the first of them in the reign of Meneptah, was separated by only a few years from the capture of Hebron by Caleb, which must have occurred after its evacuation by the Egyptian troops. The great movement which brought the populations of Asia Minor and the Greek islands upon Canaan and the Nile, and which began in the age of the Exodus, was over before the children of Israel had emerged from the wilds of the desert.

In the Old Testament the Amorites are constantly associated with another people, the Hittites. When Ezekiel ascribes an Amorite parentage to Jerusalem, he ascribes to it at the same time a Hittite parentage as well. The same interlocking of Amorite and Hittite that meets us in the Bible, meets us also on the monuments of Egypt. Here, too, we are told that Kadesh on the Orontes, the Hittite capital, was "in the land of the Amorites." It was, in fact, on the shores of the Lake of Homs, in the midst of the district over which the Amorites claimed rule.

The Hittites were intruders from the north. The Egyptian monuments have shown us what they were like. Their skin was yellow, their eyes and hair were black, their faces were beardless. Square and prominent cheeks, a protrusive nose, with retreating chin and forehead and lozenge-shaped eyes, gave them a Mongoloid appearance. They were not handsome to look upon, but the accuracy of their portraiture by the artists of Egypt is confirmed by their own monuments. The heads represented on the Egyptian monuments are repeated, feature by feature, in the Hittite sculptures. Ugly as they were, they were not the caricatures of an enemy, but the truthful portraits of a people whose physical characteristics are still found, according to Sir Charles Wilson, in the modern population of Cappadocia.

The Hittites wore their hair in three plaits, which fell over the back like the pigtail of a Chinaman. They dressed in short tunics over which a long robe was worn, which in walking left one leg bare. Their feet were shod with boots with turned-up ends, a sure indication of their northern origin. Such boots, in fact, are snow-shoes, admirably adapted to the inhabitants of the mountain-ranges of Asia Minor, but wholly unsuited for the hot plains of Syria. When, therefore, on the walls of the Ramesseum we find the Theban artists depicting the defenders of Kadesh on the Orontes with them, we may conclude that the latter had come from the colder north just as certainly as we may conclude, from the use of similar shoes among the Turks, that they also have come from a northern home. In the Hittite system of hieroglyphic writing, the boot with upturned end occupies a prominent place.

CANAAN

When the Tel el-Amarna tablets were written (B.C. 1400), the Hittites were advancing on the Egyptian province of Syria. Tunip, or Tennib, near Aleppo, had fallen, and both Amorites and Canaanites were intriguing with the invader. The highlands of Cappadocia and the ranges of the Taurus seem to have been the cradle of the Hittite race. Here they first came into contact with Babylonian culture, which they adopted and modified, and from hence they poured down upon the Aramæan cities of the south. Carchemish, now Jerablûs, which commanded the chief ford across the Euphrates, fell into their hands, and for many centuries remained one of their capitals. But it was not until the stormy period which signalised the overthrow of the Eighteenth Egyptian dynasty, that the Hittites succeeded in establishing themselves as far south as Kadesh on the Orontes. The long war, however, waged with them by Ramses II. prevented them from advancing farther; when peace was made at last between them and the Egyptians, both sides had been exhausted by the struggle, and the southern limit of Hittite power had been fixed.

The kings of Kadesh had, however, been at the head of a veritable empire; they were able to summon allies and vassals from Asia Minor, and it is probable that their rule extended to the banks of the Halys in Cappadocia, where Hittite remains have been found. Military roads connected the Hittite cities of Cappadocia with the rest of Asia Minor, and monuments of Hittite conquest or invasion have been met with as far west as the neighbourhood of Smyrna. These monuments are all alike distinguished by the same peculiar style of art, and by the same system of pictorial writing. The writing, unfortunately, has not yet been deciphered, but as the same groups of characters occur wherever an inscription in it is found, we may infer that the language concealed beneath it is everywhere one and the same.

When the Assyrians first became acquainted with the West, the Hittites were the ruling people in Syria. As, therefore, the Babylonians had included all the inhabitants of Syria and Palestine, whatever might be their origin, under the general name of Amorites, the Assyrians included them under the name of Hittites. Even the Israelites and Ammonites are called "Hittites" by an Assyrian king. It is possible that traces of this vague and comprehensive use of the name are to be met with in the Old Testament; indeed, it has been suggested that the Hittites, or "sons of Heth," from whom Abraham bought the cave of Machpelah, owed their name to this cause. In the later books of the Hebrew Scriptures the Hittites are described as a northern population, in conformity with the Egyptian and Assyrian accounts.

The Hittites of Hebron, however, may really have been an offshoot of the Hittite nations of the north.

The "king of the Hittites" accompanied the northern barbarians when they invaded Egypt in the reign of Ramses III., and Hittite bands may similarly have followed the Hyksos conquerors of Egypt several centuries before. One of these bands may easily have settled on its way at Hebron, which, as we are told, was built seven years before Zoan, the Hyksos capital. At Karnak, moreover, an Egyptian artist has represented the people of Ashkelon with faces of a Hittite type, while Ezekiel bears witness to the presence of a Hittite element in the founders of Jerusalem. But the fact that Thothmes III. in the century before Moses calls the Hittite land of the north "the Greater," is the best proof we can have that there was a Hittite colony elsewhere, which was well known to the Egyptian scribes. The "Greater" implies the Less, and the only Lesser Hittite land with which we are acquainted is that of which the Book of Genesis speaks.

So far as we can judge from the evidence of proper names, the Hittites belonged to a race which was spread from the Halys in Asia Minor to the shores of Lake Urumiyeh. The early inhabitants of Armenia, who have left us inscriptions in the cuneiform character, also belonged to it. So also did the people of Comagênê, and it seems probable that the ruling class in northern Mesopotamia did the same. Here there existed a kingdom which at one time exercised a considerable amount of power, and whose princesses were married to the Pharaohs of the Eighteenth dynasty. This was the kingdom of Aram Naharaim, called Naharina in the Egyptian texts, Mitanni by its own inhabitants. The language of Mitanni was of a very peculiar type, as we learn from the tablets of Tel el-Amarna, one or two of which are written in it. Like the Hittites in Syria, the Mitannians appear to have descended from the north upon the cities of the Semites, and to have established themselves in them. Mitanni was at the height of its influence in the sixteenth and fifteenth centuries before our era; its armies made their way even into Canaan, and the Canaanite princes intrigued from time to time against their Egyptian masters, not only with the Babylonians and Hittites, but also with the kings of Mitanni.

Before the time of David the power and almost the name of Mitanni had passed away. The Hittite empire also had been broken up, and henceforth we hear only of "the kings of the Hittites" who ruled over a number of small states. The Semites of Syria had succeeded in rolling back the wave of Hittite conquest, and in absorbing their Hittite conquerors. The capture of Carchemish by Sargon of Assyria in B.C. 717 marks the end of Hittite dominion south of the Taurus.

But the Hittite invasion had produced lasting results. It had severed the Semites of Assyria and Babylonia from those of the West, and planted the barrier of a foreign population on the highroad that ran from Nineveh to the Mediterranean. The tradition of Babylonian culture in western Asia was broken; new influences began to work there, and the cuneiform system of writing to be disused. Room was given for the introduction of a new form of script, and the Phœnician alphabet, in which the books of the Old Testament were written, made its way into Canaan. When Joshua crosses the Jordan there is no longer any trace in Palestine of either Babylonian or Egyptian domination.

Like the Amorites and the Amorite tribe of Jebusites at Jerusalem, the Hittites were mountaineers.[1] The hot river-valleys and the sea-coast were inhabited by Canaanites. Canaan is supposed to mean "the lowlands" of the Mediterranean shore; here the Canaanites had built their cities, and ventured in trading ships on the sea. But they had also settled in the inland plains, and more especially in the valley of the Jordan. The plain of Jezreel formed, as it were, the centre of the Canaanitish kingdoms.

The Canaanites were Semites in speech, if not in blood. The language of Canaan is what we term Hebrew, and must have been adopted either by the Israelites or by the patriarchs their forefathers. Between the dialect of the Phœnician inscriptions and that of the Old Testament the difference is but slight,

[1] Numb. xiii. 29.

and the tablets of Tel el-Amarna carry back the record of this Canaanitish speech to the century before the Exodus.

In person, as we learn from the Egyptian monuments, the Canaanites resembled their descendants, the modern inhabitants of Palestine. They belonged to the white race, but had black hair and eyes. They dressed in brilliantly-coloured garments, stained with that purple or scarlet dye in search of which they explored the coasts of the Greek seas, and which was extracted from the shell of the murex. On their feet they wore high-laced sandals; their hair was bound with a fillet. Their skill as sailors was famous throughout the Oriental world; the cities of the Phœnician coast already possessed fleets of ships in the age of the Eighteenth Egyptian dynasty, and their merchants carried on a maritime trade with the islands of the Ægean and the coast of Africa. Before the time of Solomon their vessels had found their way to Tartessus in Spain, perhaps even to Cadiz, and the alliance between Hiram and the Israelitish king enabled the Tyrians to import gold and other precious things from Africa and Arabia through the ports of southern Edom. The Tel el-Amarna letters refer to the riches of Tyre, and excavations on the site of Lachish have brought to light amber beads of the same age, which indicate intercourse with the Baltic. It is possible that the tin which was needed in such large quantities for the bronze tools and weapons of the ancient East was derived from Cornwall; if so, it would have been brought, like the amber, across Europe along the road which ended at the extremity of the Adriatic Gulf.

The wealth of the Canaanitish merchants was great. The spoils carried away to Egypt by Thothmes III. after his conquest of Palestine are truly astonishing. Beautiful vases of gold and silver, artistically moulded bronzes, furniture carved out of ebony and cedar and inlaid with ivory and precious stones, were among the booty. Iron, which was found in the hills, was freely used, and made into armour, weapons, and chariots. It was "the chariots of iron" which prevented the Israelites from capturing and sacking the cities of the plains. Wealth brought with it a corresponding amount of luxury, which to the simpler Hebrews of the desert seemed extravagant and sinful. It was associated with a licentiousness which Canaanitish religion encouraged rather than repressed.

The religion was a nature-worship. The supreme deity was addressed as Baal or "Lord," and was adored in the form of the Sun. And as the Sun can be baleful as well as beneficent, parching up the soil and blasting the seed as well as warming it into life, so too Baal was regarded sometimes as the friend and helper of man, sometimes as a fierce and vengeful deity who could be appeased only by blood. In times of national or individual distress his worshippers were called upon to sacrifice to him their firstborn; nothing less costly could turn away from them the anger of their god. By the side of Baal was his colourless wife, a mere reflection of the male divinity, standing in the same state of dependence towards him as the woman stood to the man. It was only the unmarried goddess, Ashêrah as she was called by the Canaanites, who had a personality of her own. And since Ashêrah came in time to be superseded by Ashtoreth, who was herself of Babylonian origin, it is probable that the idea of separate individuality connected with Ashêrah was due to the influence of Babylonian culture. Ashêrah was the goddess of fertility, and though the fertility of the earth depends upon the Sun, it was easy to conceive of it as an independent principle.

The name Baal was merely a title. It was applied to the supreme deity of each city or tribe, by whatever special name he might otherwise be known. There were as many Baals or Baalim as there were states or cults. Wherever a high-place was erected, a Baal was worshipped. His power did not extend beyond the district in which he was adored and to which he was territorially attached. The Baal of Lebanon was distinct from the Baal of Tyre or Sidon, though in every case the general conception that was formed of him was the same. It was the attributes of particular Baalim which differed; Baal was everywhere the Sungod, but in one place he showed himself under one shape, in another place under another. The goddesses followed the analogy of the gods. Over against the Baalim or Baals stood the Ashtaroth or Ashtoreths. The Canaanitish goddess manifested herself in a multitude of forms.

As the firstborn was sacrificed to the god, so chastity was sacrificed to the goddess. The temples of Ashtoreth were crowded with religious prostitutes, and the great festivals of Canaan were orgies of licentious sin. It was a combination of nature-worship with the luxury that was born of wealth.

The Canaanites of Phœnicia believed that they had originally migrated from the Persian Gulf. In Canaan, at all events, according to the Book of Genesis, the "Fishers" city of Sidon was the first that was built. But Tyre also, a few miles to the north of it, claimed considerable antiquity. The temple of Melkarth or Melek-Kiryath, "the King of the City," the name under which the Baal of Tyre was worshipped, had been built on the island-rock twenty-three centuries before the time of Herodotus, or B.C. 2700. Gebal or Byblos, still farther to the north, had been renowned for its sanctity from immemorial times. Here stood the sanctuary of Baalith, the "lady" of Gebal, of whom we hear in the tablets of Tel el-Amarna. Still farther north were other cities, of which the most famous was Arvad, with its harbour and fleet. Southward were Dor and Joppa, the modern Jaffa, while inland were

Zemar and Arqa, mentioned in the Book of Genesis and the Tel el-Amarna correspondence, but which ceased to be remembered after the age of the Exodus. Before the Israelites entered Canaan they had been captured by the Amorites, and had passed into insignificance.

Between the Canaanites of the coast and the Canaanites of the interior a difference grew up in the course of centuries. This was caused by the sea-trade in which the cities on the coast engaged. The "Phœnicians," as they were termed, on the coast became sailors and merchants, while their brethren farther inland were content to live on the products of agriculture and import from abroad the luxuries they required. While Tyre and Sidon were centres of manufacture and maritime trade, Megiddo and Hazor remained agricultural. After the Hebrew invasion the difference between them became greater: Phœnicia continued independent; the Canaanites of the interior were extirpated by the Israelites or paid tribute to their conquerors. Little by little the latter amalgamated with the conquered race; towns like Shechem contained a mixed population, partly Hebrew and partly native; and the Israelites adopted the manners and religion of the Canaanites, worshipping at the old high-places of the country, and adoring the Baalim and Ashtaroth. The Amorite heads depicted at Karnak above the names of the places captured by Shishak in Judah show how little the population of southern Palestine had changed up to the time of Solomon's death.

Canaan was ruined by its want of union. The Canaanitish cities were perpetually fighting with one another; even the strong hand of the Pharaoh in the days of Egyptian supremacy could not keep them at peace. Now and again, indeed, they united, generally under a foreign leader, but the union was brought about by the pressure of foreign attack, and was never more than temporary. There was no lack of patriotism among them, it is true; but the patriotism was confined to the particular city or state to which those who were inspired by it belonged. The political condition of Canaan resembled its religious condition; as each district had its separate Baal, so too it had its separate political existence. If there were many Baals, there were also many kinglets.

The fourteenth century B.C. was a turning-point in the history of Canaan. It witnessed the fall of the Egyptian supremacy which had succeeded the supremacy of Babylonia; it also witnessed the severance of western Asia from the kingdoms on the Euphrates and Tigris, and the consequent end of the direct influence of Babylonian culture. The Hittites established themselves in Syria "in the land of the Amorites," while at the same time other invaders threatened Canaan itself. The Israelites made their way across the Jordan; the Philistines seized the southern portion of the coast.

The Philistine invasion preceded that of the Israelites by a few years. The Philistines were sea-robbers, probably from the island of Krete. Zephaniah calls them "the nation of the Cherethites" or Kretans, and their features, as represented on the Egyptian monuments, are of a Greek or Aryan type. They have the straight nose, high forehead, and thin lips of the European. On their heads they wear a curious kind of pleated cap, fastened round the chin by a strap. They are clad in a pair of drawers and a cuirass of leather, while their arms consist of a small round shield with two handles, a spear, and a short but broad sword of bronze. Greaves of bronze, like those of the Homeric heroes, protected their legs in battle.

The Philistines formed part of the host which invaded Egypt in the reign of Ramses III. Along with their kinsfolk, the Zakkal, they had already made themselves formidable to the coast of the Delta and of southern Canaan. The sea had long been infested by their ships, bent on plunder and piracy; the Zakkal had attacked Egypt in the time of Meneptah, and the road from Egypt to Asia which skirted the sea had long been known as "the way of the Philistines." When Ramses III. overran southern Canaan, Gaza still belonged to Egypt, as it had done for the three preceding centuries; but it is probable that the Philistines were already settled in its neighbourhood. At all events, it was not long before they made themselves

CANAAN 91

masters of Gaza, and thus closed for Egypt the way to Asia. Henceforward Gaza and its four companion cities became the strongholds of the Philistines (B.C. 1200). The southern coast as far north as Mount Carmel fell into their hands: the Zakkal established themselves at Dor, and the port of Joppa was lost to the Phœnicians.

Hardly were the Israelites planted in the Promised Land before they were confronted by the Philistines. Shamgar, we are told, one of the earliest of the Judges, slew six hundred of them "with an ox-goad." But it was not until the close of the period of the Judges that they became really formidable to Israel. Judah had become a distinct and powerful tribe, formed out of Hebrew, Kenite, and Edomite elements, and its frontier adjoined Philistia. At first there was desultory warfare; the Philistines made raids into Judæan territory, and the Jews retaliated whenever the opportunity occurred. But the Philistines were a nation of warriors, and their forces were recruited from time to time by fresh arrivals from Krete or other parts of the eastern Mediterranean. Year by year, therefore, the Philistine attack became more formidable; the raids of the enemy were no longer confined to Judah, but extended into Benjamin and Mount Ephraim. The Philistines began to dream of conquering the whole of Canaan, which was henceforth to bear the name of Palestine, "the land of the Philistines."

The Israelitish army was shattered in a decisive battle, the ark of the covenant between Israel and its national God was taken by the heathen, and the priests of Shiloh, the central sanctuary, were slain. The victors marched unresisted through the country, burning and spoiling, and securing the passes by means of permanent garrisons. Shiloh and its temple were destroyed, and its priesthood scattered abroad.

The Philistine supremacy lasted for several years. A few outlaws maintained a guerilla warfare in the mountains of Benjamin, and the prophet Samuel, the representative of Shiloh, was allowed to declare the oracles of Yahveh to his countrymen. But the vanquished population was deprived of the means for revolt. The Israelites were forbidden the use of arms, and no itinerant smith was permitted to enter their territory. The Hebrew who wished to sharpen his ploughshare or axe was forced to go to a Philistine city.

The condition of Israel became intolerable. There was but one remedy: the people needed a leader who should organise them into an army and a nation, and lead them forth against their foes. Saul was elected king, and the choice was soon justified by the results. The Philistines were driven out of the country, and Saul set up his court in the very spot where a Philistine garrison had stood.

But the Philistines were not yet subdued. Civil war broke out in Israel between Saul and his son-in-law

David; the troops which should have been employed in resisting the common enemy were used in pursuing David, and David himself took service as a mercenary under Achish, King of Gath. Saul and his sons fell in battle on Mount Gilboa; the relics of the Israelitish army fled across the Jordan, and the Philistine again ruled supreme on the western side of the Jordan. David was allowed to govern Judah as a tributary vassal of the Philistine "lords."

The murder of the feeble scion of Saul's house who had the name of king on the eastern side of the Jordan put an end to all this. David threw off his allegiance to the Philistines, and was crowned King of Israel. This act of open defiance was speedily followed by the invasion of Judah. At first the war went against the Israelitish king; he was forced to fly from his capital, Hebron, and take refuge in an inaccessible cavern. Here he organised his forces, and at last ventured into the field. The Philistine forces were defeated in battle after battle; the war was carried into their own territory, and their cities were compelled to surrender. Philistia thus became a part of the Israelitish kingdom, and never again made any serious attempt to recover its independence. At the division of the Israelitish kingdom it fell to Judah, and its vassal princes duly paid their tribute to the Jewish kings. It would seem from the Assyrian inscriptions that they were played off one against the other, and that signs of disaffection in any one of them were speedily followed by his imprisonment in Jerusalem. At all events, the Philistine cities remained in the possession of Judah down to the time of the overthrow of the monarchy, and the most devoted of David's body-guard were the Philistines of Gath.

It has been said above that Judah was a mixture of Hebrew, Kenite, and Edomite elements. Kenite means "smith," and the tribe furnished those itinerant smiths who provided Canaan with its tools and arms. Reference is made to one of them in the *Travels of a Mohar*, a sarcastic description of a tourist's misadventures in Palestine which was written by an Egyptian author in the reign of Ramses II., and of which a copy on papyrus has been preserved to us. The horses of the hero of the story, we are told, ran away and broke his carriage to pieces; he had accordingly to betake himself to "the iron-workers" and have it repaired. Similar itinerant ironsmiths wandered through Europe in the Middle Ages, handing down from father to son the secrets of their craft.

The Kenites came from the desert, and were apparently of Midianitish descent. Balaam had looked down upon their rocky strongholds from the heights of Moab; and they had accompanied their Hebrew comrades of Judah from their first camping-ground near Jericho to the wilderness south of Arad. Here they lived among the Amalekite Bedâwin down to

CANAAN 95

the days of Saul. To the last they maintained their nomadic habits, and the Kenite family of Rechab still dwelt in tents and avoided wine in that later age when the kingdom of Judah was about to fall.[1]

The Edomite element in Judah was stronger than the Kenite. It consisted of the two clans of Jerahmeel and Kenaz, or the house of Caleb as it was called in the time of David.[2] Kenaz was a grandson of Esau, and the fact that the Kenizzites shared with the Israelitish tribes in the conquest of Canaan throws light on the law of Deuteronomy[3] which gave the Edomite of "the third generation" all the rights and privileges of a Jew. Caleb, the conqueror of Hebron, was a Kenizzite; so also was Othniel, the first of the Judges of Israel. Edomites, rather than Hebrews, were the founders of the future Judah.

This accounts for the comparatively late appearance of Judah as a separate tribe in the history of Israel, as well as for the antagonism which existed between it and the more pure-blooded tribes of the north. In the Song of Deborah and Barak, Judah is not mentioned; Ephraim and Benjamin, and not Judah, are still regarded as forming the bulwark of Israel against the Amalekite marauders of the southern wilderness. It was the Philistine wars which first created the Judah of later days. They forced Hebrews, Edomites, and

[1] 1 Chr. ii. 55; Jer. xxxv. 3-10.
[2] 1 Sam. xxx. 14.
[3] Deut. xxiii 8.

Kenites to unite against the common enemy, and welded them into a single whole. Though the three peoples still continued to be spoken of separately, this was but a survival of ancient modes of speech, and after the accession of David all distinction between them disappears. From this time forward the kingdom of Judah is one undivided community.

But the Amalekites were ever on its borders. The Amalekite of the Old Testament is the Bedâwi of to-day. Now, as ever, he is the scourge of his more settled neighbours, whose fields he harries and whose families he murders. He lives by robbery and theft; too idle to work himself, he plunders those who do. A strong government forces him to hide himself in the depth of the wilderness; when the countries that skirt the desert fall into decay he emerges from his retreat like a swarm of flies. The ancient Oriental world saw in Amalek "the firstborn of nations;" he was for them the representative of the primitive savage who had survived in the wilds of the desert. Untamed and untamable, his hand was against every man, and every man's hand against him.

Before Babylonian culture had been brought to the West, Amalek already existed. He was older than the oldest of the civilised kingdoms of the earth. But civilisation had raised a barrier against him which he was ever on the watch to break through. He never lost the opportunity of raiding the inhabitants of the cultivated lands, and escaping again into the desert with his booty before he could be overtaken and punished. The desert between Palestine and Egypt was his chief camping-ground. He had occupied the wadis of Mount Seir before the Edomites had entered them, and a part of the later population of the country traced its descent from a mixture of the Bedâwi with the Edomite. The Egyptians had many names for the Bedâwin hordes. Sometimes they were the Herusha or "Lords of the Sands," sometimes the Shasu or "Plunderers," sometimes again the Sutê or "Archers." The third name was borrowed from the Babylonians; in return, as we learn from the tablets of Tel el-Amarna, the Babylonians adopted the second.

Hardly had the Israelites escaped from Egypt when they were called upon to dispute with the Amalekites the possession of the desert. At Rephidim the Bedâwin robbers fell upon the Israelitish camp. But they were beaten off with slaughter, and never again ventured to molest the people of Yahveh during their wanderings in the wilderness. The attack, however, was never forgotten, and vengeance was exacted for it in the reign of Saul. Then the Amalekites were pursued into their desert domain and mercilessly slaughtered. They had their home, it is said, in the desert which extended from Shur to Havilah. Shur was the line of fortification which defended the eastern frontier of Egypt, and ran pretty much where the Suez Canal has been dug to-day; Havilah was the "sandy" desert of northern Arabia. Here was the "city" of tents of which Agag was shêkh, and which the troops of the Israelitish king burnt and spoiled.

But the remembrance of the expedition did not last long. When civil war had weakened the power of Saul, and the march of the Philistine army to the north had left the south of Canaan without defenders, an Amalekite tribe again poured into Judah and sacked the Philistine town of Ziklag. The wives and property of David and his followers were carried off into the wilderness. But the marauders were overtaken by the Israelites they had robbed, and summary vengeance taken upon them. Men, women, and children were alike put to the sword; four hundred only escaped through the fleetness of their camels.

In the Tel el-Amarna tablets we find the Bedâwin and their shêkhs playing a part in the politics of Canaan. Their services were hired by the rival princes of Palestine, and from time to time we hear of their seizing or plundering its cities on their own account. They have never ceased indeed to infest the land. Amalekite bands joined with the Midianites in devastating the villages of central Israel in the days of Gideon, and the Amalekite who brought to David the news of Saul's death was one of those who had hovered on the skirts of the contending armies, eager when the fight was over to murder the wounded and strip the slain. In a later age the "Arabs" who, according to the inscriptions of Sennacherib, formed the body-guard of Hezekiah were probably Bedâwin, and Geshem the Arabian in the time of Nehemiah seems to have represented the Amalekite chieftain of an earlier epoch. The Bedâwin still haunt the plains and unfrequented paths of Palestine, waylaying the traveller and robbing the peasant of his flocks.

The peasantry or fellahin are the Perizzites of the Hebrew Scriptures. "Perizzite," in fact, means "villager," and the word is a descriptive title rather than the name of a people or a race. It denotes the agricultural population, whatever their origin may have been. Another word of similar signification is Hivite. If any distinction is to be drawn between them, it is that the term Perizzite was specially applied to the fellahin of southern Canaan, while the term Hivite was restricted to the inhabitants of the north. In two passages, it is true, "Hivite" seems to be used with an ethnic meaning. Esau is said in one of them to have married the granddaughter of "Zibeon the Hivite," while in the other we read of "the Hivite" who dwelt under Mount Hermon. But a comparison of the first passage with the later verses of the same chapter shows that "Hivite" must be corrected into "Horite," and in the second passage it is probable that "Hittite" instead of "Hivite" should be read.

Amorite and Hittite, Canaanite and Philistine, were all alike emigrants from other lands. The Hittites had come from the mountains of Asia Minor, the Amorites had probably wandered from the northern coast of Africa, the Canaanites traced their ancestry to the Persian Gulf, the Philistines had sailed from the harbours of the Greek seas. Canaan had been inhabited, however, before any of them had found their way to it, and this prehistoric population of the country was known to the Hebrews by the name of Rephaim. In the English translation of the Bible the word is usually rendered "giants;" it seems, however, to have been a proper name, which survived in the name of one of the cities of Bashan. Doubtless it often included other elements besides that to which it was properly applied. At times it was extended to the Amorites, whose occupation of Palestine went back to a remote past, just as in the Babylonian inscriptions the name of Amorite itself was extended to the aboriginal population. Among the Philistines this older population was called Avvim, the people of "the ruins."

Such then were the races who lived in Canaan, and with whom the invading Israelites had to contend. There was firstly the primitive population of the country, whose rude rock-sculptures may still be seen in the Wadi el-Qana near Tyre. Then there were the intrusive Amorites and Canaanites, the Amorites with their fair skins and blue eyes who made themselves a home in the mountains, and the Semitic Canaanites who settled on the coast and in the plains. The Amorite migration went back to an epoch long before that of the first Babylonian conquests in the West; the Canaanitish migration may have been coeval with the latter event. Next came the Hittites, to whom the Jebusites of Jerusalem may have belonged; then the Philistines, who seized the southern coast but a few years previously to the Israelitish invasion. Canaan was a land of many races and many peoples, who had taken shelter in its highlands, or had found their further progress barred by the sea. Small as it was, it was the link between Asia and Africa, the battle-ground of the great kingdoms which arose on the Euphrates and the Nile. It formed, in fact, the centre of the ancient civilised world, and the mixture of races within it was due in great measure to its central position. The culture of Babylonia and Egypt met there and coalesced.

CHAPTER III
THE NATIONS OF THE SOUTH-EAST

CHAPTER III

THE NATIONS OF THE SOUTH-EAST

ISRAEL was cut in two by the Jordan. The districts east of the Jordan were those that had first been conquered; it was from thence that the followers of Joshua had gone forth to possess themselves of Canaan. But this division of the territory was a source of weakness. The interests of the tribes on the two sides of the river were never quite the same; at times indeed they were violently antagonistic. When the disruption of the monarchy came after the death of Solomon, Judah was the stronger for the fact that the eastern tribes followed those of the north. The eastern tribes were the first to lose their independence; they were carried into Assyrian captivity twelve years before the fall of Samaria itself.

The eastern side of Jordan, in fact, belonged of right to the kinsfolk of the Israelites, the children of Lot. Ammon and Moab derived their origin from the nephew of Abraham, not from the patriarch himself, the ancestor of Ammon being Ben-Ammi, "the Son of Ammi," the national god of the race. It was said that the two peoples were the offspring of incest, and the cave was pointed out where they had been born. Ammon occupied the country to the north which in earlier days had been the home of the aboriginal Zuzim or Zamzummim. But they had been treated as the Canaanites were treated by the Israelites in later days; their cities were captured by the invading Ammonites, and they themselves massacred or absorbed into the conquerors.

To the north the territory of Ammon was bounded by the plateau of Bashan and the Aramaic kingdoms of Gilead. Southward it extended towards the frontier of Moab, if indeed the borders of the two nations did not at one time coincide. When the Israelitish invasion, however, took place, the Amorites under Sihon had thrust themselves between, and had carved for themselves a kingdom out of the northern half of Moab. The land north of the Arnon became Amorite; but the Ammonite frontier was too well defended to be broken through.

The kingdom of Ammon maintained itself down to the time of David. At one time, in the days of the Judges, the Ammonites had made the Israelitish tribes on the eastern side of the Jordan tributary to them, and had even crossed the river and raided the highlands of Ephraim. Under Saul, Ammon and Israel were at constant feud. Saul had begun his reign by rescuing Jabesh in Gilead from the Ammonite king

Nahash, who had threatened to treat its inhabitants with innate Semitic barbarity. When civil war broke out in Israel, Nahash naturally befriended David, and the alliance continued after David's accession to the throne. Common interests brought them together. Esh-Baal, the successor of Saul in Gilead, was the enemy of both: his frontier adjoined that of Ammon, while between him and the King of Judah there was perpetual war. David had strengthened himself by marrying the daughter of the king of the Aramaic district of Geshur, which bounded Gilead on the north, and Ammonites and Aramæans were in close alliance with each other.

As long as Nahash lived, there was peace between him and David. But with the accession of his son Hanun came a change. The King of Judah had become King of Israel, and his general, Joab, had subdued the neighbouring kingdom of Moab, and was looking out for a fresh field of fame. Hanun determined to forestall the war which he believed to be inevitable, and, in alliance with the Aramæans, to crush the rising power of David. Family quarrels also probably conspired to bring about this resolution. In the after days of Absalom's rebellion we find David entertained in Gilead by Shobi the brother of Hanun;[1] it may be, therefore, that Hanun had had a rival in his brother, who had received shelter and protection at David's

[1] 2 Sam. xvii. 27.

court. At all events the Israelitish ambassadors were grossly insulted, and a long war with Ammon began. Campaign followed upon campaign; the City of Waters, Rabbah, the "capital" of Ammon, was closely invested, and the Aramaic allies of Hanun were put to flight. Rabbah fell at last; its defenders were tortured and slain, and the kingdom of Ammon annexed to the Israelitish empire.

When it recovered its independence we do not know. In the days of Assyrian conquest in the West it was already again governed by its own kings. One of them, Baasha, the son of Rehob, was, like Ahab of Samaria, an ally of Damascus against the Assyrian invader, and we hear of two others, one of whom bears the same name as "Shinab, King of Admah." The storm of Babylonian conquest which overwhelmed Judah spared Ammon; after the destruction of Jerusalem Baalis was still king of the Ammonites, and ready to extend his power over the desolated fields of Judah.[1]

The language of Ammon, if we may argue from the proper names, was, like that of Moab, a mere dialectal variety of that of Israel. The "language of Canaan" must have been adopted by the Ammonites and Moabites just as it was by the Israelitish tribes. The Moabite Stone has proved this conclusively. Moabite and Ammonite, Phœnician and Hebrew, were all alike

[1] Jer. xl. 14.

THE NATIONS OF THE SOUTH-EAST 109

dialects of one language, which differed from one another merely as one English dialect differs from another. Hebrew had retained a few "Arabisms," a few traces of its ancient contact with Arabic-speaking tribes; that was all. In other respects it was the same as "the language of Canaan" on either side of the Jordan.

The Ammonites believed themselves to be the children of the national god Ammi. But Ammi was usually worshipped under the title of Malcham or Milcom, "the King." It was to Milcom that Solomon erected an altar at Jerusalem, in honour of that Ammonite wife whose son Rehoboam succeeded him on the throne, and it was from the head of his image at Rabbah that his crown of gold and precious stones, 131 pounds in weight, was removed to grace the triumph of David.[1]

Moab was more exposed to the inroads of its nomadic neighbours from the wilderness than its sister-kingdom of Ammon. It lay along the eastern shores of the Dead Sea, and was a land of lofty mountains and fertile river-plains. Its wadis were coveted by the tribes of the desert; the well-watered valley of the Arnon attracted more powerful foes. When the Israelites encamped in "the plain of Moab," Balak, the Moabite

[1] Rehoboam is an Ammonite name, compounded with that of the god Am or Ammi. Rehob, which is the first element in it, was also an Ammonite name, as we learn from the Assyrian inscriptions.

king, sent in terror to Balaam, the seer of Pethor. He had indeed cause for alarm. The Amorites had already robbed him of the fairest portion of his dominions; Moab north of the Arnon had fallen into their hands. The Amorite song of triumph has been preserved in the Book of Numbers. "Come unto Heshbon," it said; "let the city of Sihon be built and fortified. For a fire has gone forth from Heshbon, a flame from the city of Sihon; it hath consumed Ar of Moab, and the Baalim of the high-places of Arnon. Woe to thee, Moab! thou art undone, O people of Chemosh: [Chemosh] hath given his sons that escaped [the battle], and his daughters, into captivity unto Sihon, King of the Amorites."[1]

Moab was avenged by Israel. The Amorites were crushed by the Israelitish forces, though the lands they had taken from Moab were not restored to their original owners. The conquerors settled in them, and a mixed Israelitish and Moabite population was the result. The Moabites, in fact, were powerless to resist. The southern portion of the kingdom had been overrun by Midianite hordes; the enemy with whom the Israelites had to contend on Moabite soil was Midianite and not Moabite. Those who corrupted Israel on the high-place of Peor were Midianites in race.

The Midianites seem to have continued in occupation of Moabite territory for several generations. Reuben

[1] Numb. xxi. 27-29.

was enabled to pasture his flocks in peace in its valleys, and it is probable that it was not till Hadad, the King of Edom, "smote Midian in the plain of Moab" that Midianitish supremacy came finally to an end. It may be that Gideon's success against the Midianite oppressors of Gilead was one of the results of their overthrow by the Edomite prince.

At the same time, Midianitish supremacy did not mean the destruction of the Moabite kingdom. Moab was still governed by its own kings, tributary vassals though they were to the foreigner. One of them, Eglon, made himself master of southern Palestine shortly after the Israelitish conquest of the country, and was murdered by the Benjamite Ehud. Between Moab and Judah there was, as might be expected from their geographical position, constant intercourse. A Moabitess was the ancestress of David, and it was to the court of the King of Moab that David entrusted his parents when hard pressed by Saul. Possibly the Moabite prince was not ill pleased to befriend the enemy of his own enemy, the King of Israel.

It had been better for the Moabites, however, had David never lived to succeed Saul. The conquest of the Philistines by his troops was followed by the conquest of Moab. The vanquished people were decimated, every second man being mercilessly slain. So thoroughly was the country subdued that it was more than a century before it ventured to break away from

H

its Israelitish master. After the disruption of Solomon's heritage it fell to the share of the northern kingdom, though native kings once more sat upon its throne. Now and again they revolted, to be brought back to obedience, however, when Israel recovered its strength. Such was the case when Omri founded his dynasty at Samaria; Moab again became a dependency of the Israelitish monarch, and its ruler was forced to pay tribute and homage to his over-lord. The tribute consisted in sheep, or rather in their skins, which were tanned by the Israelites into leather, while the fleeces upon them were woven into cloth. In the time of Ahab, Mesha, the son of Chemosh-melech, sent each year 100,000 lambs and 100,000 rams.

Mesha subsequently succeeded in shaking off the foreign yoke. He has left us a record of his victories, the so-called Moabite Stone, which was discovered among the ruins of his capital, Dibon. The country north of the Arnon was wrested from Israelitish hands, and the King of Israel, in spite of help from Judah and Edom, failed to recover it. Moab was permanently lost to the kingdom of Samaria. The Assyrian texts mention some of its later rulers. One of them was Shalman, who may be the spoiler of Beth-Arbel referred to by Hosea;[1] another was Chemosh-nadab, the contemporary of Hezekiah.

Chemosh-nadab signifies "Chemosh is noble." Che-

[1] x. 14.

mosh was the national god of Moab, as Milcom or Ammi was of Ammon. Like Yahveh of Israel, he stood alone, with no wife to share his divinity. So entirely, in fact, had the conception of a goddess vanished from the mind of the Moabite, that, as we learn from the Moabite Stone, the Babylonian Istar, the Ashtoreth of Canaan, had been transformed into a male deity, and identified with Chemosh. It was to Ashtar-Chemosh, Mesha tells us, and not to Ashtoreth, that he devoted the captive women of Israel.

The older population, expelled or enslaved by the conquering Moabites, went by the name of Emim. It is probable that they belonged to the same stock as the Zamzummim or Zuzim whose country had been seized by the Ammonites. We may gather from the narrative in Genesis that the invaders forced their way eastward and northward from the valley of the Jordan and the shores of the Dead Sea.

South of Moab were the rugged and barren mountains of Seir, the seat of the kingdom of Edom. In prehistoric days they had been the home of the Horites, whose name may denote that they were of the "white" Amorite race or that they were dwellers in "caves." To the Egyptians it was known as "the Red Land," along with the desert that stretched westward; "Edom" is merely the Hebrew or Canaanitish translation of the Egyptian title. The title was one which well befitted the red cliffs of Seir.

Through the centre of the mountains a rift extended from the Dead Sea to the Gulf of Aqaba. In geological times it had been the channel of the Jordan; now it is called the Wadi el-Araba. It was this rift which brought wealth to Edom; through it passed the highroad of commerce which connected Syria with the harbours at the head of the gulf. The spices of Arabia, the gold of Africa, were unshipped at Elath and Ezion-gaber, and carried from thence on the backs of camels to the nations of the north. The tolls levied on the merchandise made the kingdom of Edom wealthy, and at the same time an object of envy to its poorer neighbours. In conquering Edom, David doubtless desired to secure the trade with the Red Sea and the ports through which the trade passed.

Edom was the elder brother of Israel. The two nations never forgot that they were of one blood and one parentage. Their languages were the same, as we may gather from the Edomite proper names; indeed, it would seem that the dialect of Edom agreed with Hebrew in those Arabising peculiarities which marked it off from the language of the Canaanites. Edomites took part in the Israelitish conquest of Palestine, and both Caleb and Othniel were Kenizzites by race.

The Edomite occupation of Seir was long subsequent to the settlement of the Ammonites and Moabites in the regions which bore their names, though it preceded the Israelitish settlement in Canaan. While

Israel was herding its flocks in Egypt, Edom was establishing itself in the mountains of Seir. Esau, the brother of Jacob, had already gathered around him a body of followers, and had married into the family of a Horite chief. His descendants, partly by conquest, partly by absorption, planted themselves securely in the country which was henceforth to be called Edom. Horite and Amalekite Bedâwin were alike absorbed into the new-comers, whose position in Edom resembled that of the Israelites in Canaan.

How long the work of conquest and settlement lasted we do not know. It resulted in the formation of numerous tribes, each under its chieftain, the *alûph* or "duke" as he was termed. These "dukes" corresponded with the "princes" of the tribes of Israel. But whereas the "princes" of the Israelitish tribes did not survive the life in the desert, the "dukes" of Edom give way only to kings. For this there was a good reason. The invasion of Canaan and the promulgation of the Mosaic Law changed the whole organisation of the Hebrew people. On the one hand, the Israelites required a leader who should lead them in the first instance against the Canaanites, in the second against the foreign oppressors who enslaved them from time to time. On the other hand, the high-priests at Shiloh exercised many of the functions which would naturally have belonged to the head of the tribe. Neither "judge" nor high-priest was needed in Edom. There the native population was weak and uncivilised; it possessed neither cities nor chariots of iron, and its subjugation was no difficult task. Once in possession of the fastnesses of Seir, the Edomites were comparatively safe from external attack. It was a land of dangerous defiles and barren mountains, surrounded on all sides by the desert. There was no central sanctuary, no Levitical priesthood, no Mosaic Law. The "duke" consequently had no rival; the history of Edom knows nothing of judges or high-priests.

The law of evolution, however, which governed other Semitic communities prevailed also in Edom. The dukes had to give place to a king. The tribes were united under a single leader, and the loosely federated clans became a kingdom. As in Israel, so too in Edom the kingdom was elective. But, unlike Israel, it remained elective; there was no pressure of Philistine conquest, no commanding genius like David, no central capital like Jerusalem to make it centralised and hereditary. Several generations had to pass before the Edomites were called upon to fight for their independence against a foreign invader, and when they did so the struggle ended in their subjugation. The elective principle and the want of a common centre and feeling of unity that resulted from it had much to do with the victory of David.

The song of triumph with which the Israelitish

THE NATIONS OF THE SOUTH-EAST 117

fugitives celebrated the overthrow of their Egyptian enemies mentions the *alûphîm* or "dukes" of Edom. But before the Israelites had emerged from the wilderness the dukes had been supplanted by a king. It was a king who refused a passage through his dominions to Moses and his followers, and in this king some scholars have seen the Aramæan seer Balaam the son of Beor. At all events, the first Edomite king is said to have been Bela or Balaam the son of Beor, and the name of the city of Dinhabah, from which he came, has a close resemblance to that of Dunip in northern Syria.

A list of the kings of Edom is given in the thirty-sixth chapter of Genesis, extracted from the state annals of the country. It seems to be brought down to the time when Saul was elected king over Israel. The chronicles of Edom were probably taken to Jerusalem at the time of its conquest by David; at any rate, they would then have become accessible to an Israelitish writer. The conquest was very thorough, all the male population being put to the sword, and a few only escaping to Egypt. Among these was a member of the royal house, Hadad by name, who grew up at the Egyptian court, and, after marrying the sister-in-law of the Pharaoh, returned to his native mountains, where he played the part of a bandit chief. The caravans which passed from the Gulf of Aqaba to the north were attacked and plundered, and Solomon up to the end of his reign failed to suppress the brigands. With the disruption of the Israelitish monarchy, Edom, as was natural, fell to the lot of Judah, and for many years was governed by a viceroy. It was not until after the death of Jehoshaphat that the Edomites succeeded in revolting from their masters, and in recovering their ancient independence. Three of their rulers are mentioned in the Assyrian inscriptions, from which we learn that there was a city of Edom, as well as a country of that name.

Of the religion of the Edomites we know but little. The supreme Baal was the Sun-god Hadad; another god worshipped by them was Qaus or Kos. Of goddesses we hear nothing. The Israelites, however, recognised in the Edomites brethren of their own, whose religion was not far removed from that of the descendants of Jacob. An Edomite of the third generation could enter "into the congregation of the Lord," and we hear of no rival deity in Edom to Yahveh of Israel. Indeed, in the old poetry of Israel Yahveh was said to have risen up "from Seir," and the charge brought against Edom by the prophet Obadiah is not that of idolatry or the worship of a "strange god," but of standing on the side of the "foreigners" on the day that Jerusalem was destroyed.

The southern part of Edom was known as Teman; it was to the east of Teman that the Kadmonites or "children of the East" pitched their tents. We first

THE NATIONS OF THE SOUTH-EAST 119

hear of them in an Egyptian papyrus of the age of the Twelfth dynasty (B.C. 2500). Then they received with hospitality a political fugitive from Egypt; he married one of their princesses and became one of their chiefs. Their wisdom was celebrated in Palestine like that of their Edomite neighbours of Teman, and the highest praise that could be bestowed on Solomon was that his "wisdom excelled all the wisdom of the children of the East."

Not far from the camping-places of the Kadmonites was the land of Uz, famous as the home of Job. Uz, in fact, was a province of Edom; Edomite colonists, so we are told in the Book of Lamentations,[1] inhabited it. Indeed, it has been suggested that the difficulties presented by the language of the Book of Job are due to the fact that it is the language of Edom rather than of the Jews, differing from the latter only as an English dialect may differ from that of a neighbouring county. At all events, Job was as much a hero of Hebrew as of Edomite tradition, while the last chapter of the Book of Proverbs contains the wise sayings of a king whose territory adjoined the land of Edom. Lemuel, according to the Hebrew text, which is mistranslated in the Authorised Version, ruled over Massa, and Massa, the Mash of Genesis, is described in the Assyrian inscriptions as that part of northern Arabia which spread eastward from Edom. The Hebrew of

[1] iv. 21.

Palestine doubtless included it in the country of "the children of the East."

The larger part of northern Arabia, however, was the home of the Ishmaelites. They lived, it is said, "from Havilah unto Shur," like the Amalekites or Bedâwin. But whereas the Amalekites were the wild, untamable natives of the desert, the Ishmaelites came of a cultured ancestry, half Babylonian, half Egyptian, and the traditions of it were never forgotten. They lived a settled life in fenced villages and fortified castles, as their descendants still do to-day. Like the Israelites, they were divided into twelve tribes, the eldest and most important of which were the Nabatheans, who spread from the frontiers of Babylonia to Petra in the far west. Kedar was another powerful tribe; in the days of the later Assyrian empire its kings contended in battle with the armies of Nineveh.

The name of Ishmael is met with in Babylonian contracts of the age of Abraham. It is a name which belongs to Canaan rather than to Babylonia or Arabia. The Ishmaelite tribes, in fact, spoke dialects in which Canaanitish and Arabic elements were mingled together. They are the dialects we term Aramaic, and represent a mixture of Arabic with Canaanitish or Hebrew. As we go northwards into Syria the Canaanitish element predominates; southward the Arabic element is the more pronounced.

THE NATIONS OF THE SOUTH-EAST 121

The Ishmaelites were merchants and traders. They lived on the caravan-road which brought the spices of southern Arabia to Canaan and Egypt, and the trade was largely in their hands. In the history of Joseph we hear of them carrying the balm of Gilead and the myrrh of the south on their camels to Egypt, and in the second century before the Christian era the merchant princes of Petra made their capital one of the wealthiest of Oriental cities. It was not until 105 A.D. that the Nabathean state was conquered by Rome, and the Ishmaelites of northern Arabia transformed into Roman subjects. They have left their tombs and inscriptions among the rocks of Petra, while the cliffs of the Sinaitic Peninsula are covered with the scrawls of Nabathean travellers.

Southward of the Ishmaelites came the Midianites. Midianites and Ishmaelites were alike of the same blood. Both traced their descent from Abraham; it was only on the side of the mother that their origin was different. While the Ishmaelites claimed connection with Egypt, the Midianites were more purely Arabic in race. The name of Keturah their ancestress means "incense," and points to the incense-bearing lands of the south. Midian was properly the district which stretched along the western coast of the Gulf of Aqaba towards Mecca, if not towards Yemen. But Midianite tribes had also pushed northwards and mingled with the descendants of Ishmael. "Ishmaelites" and "Midianites" seem convertible terms in the story of Joseph, and the Midianites who swarmed into the north of Israel in the days of Gideon, along with the Amalekites and "the children of the East," must have been as much Ishmaelite as Midianite in descent.

Between the Midianites and the Israelitish fugitives from Egypt there had been close affinity. Moses had found a refuge in Midian, and his wife and children were Midianite in race. His father-in-law, "the priest of Midian," had visited him under the shadow of Sinai, and had given him his first lessons in political organisation. A Midianite remained to guide the Israelites through the wilderness, and the Kenites, who took part with the tribe of Judah in the conquest of Canaan, appear to have migrated from Midian. It was not until just before the invasion of Palestine that the old bonds of friendship and mixture between Israel and Midian were broken asunder. Midianite hosts had overrun the land of Moab as at a later time they overran the land of Israel, and the Israelites had forsaken Yahveh for the worship of the Midianite Baal-Peor. This was the result of intermarriage; the Israelites had taken Midianite wives and conformed to the licentious rites of a Midianite god.

Israel, however, was saved by its Levite priests. They rallied round Yahveh and Moses, and in the struggle that ensued the forces on the side of the

THE NATIONS OF THE SOUTH-EAST 123

national God proved the stronger. The Midianitish faction was annihilated, its leaders put to death, and the Midianites themselves attacked and despoiled. Among the slain was the seer of Pethor, Balaam the son of Beor.

The Moabites must have hailed the Israelites as saviours. They had delivered them from their two assailants, the Amorites on the north, the Midianites on the east. But the Midianite power was broken only for a time. We hear at a subsequent date of the Edomite king Hadad "who smote Midian in the field of Moab," and a time came when Midianite shêkhs overran Gilead, and penetrated into the valleys and villages of Manasseh on the western side of the Jordan. After their defeat by Gideon, however, we hear of them no more. They passed out of the Israelitish horizon; henceforth their raiding bands never approached the frontiers of Israel. The land of Midian alone is mentioned as adjoining Edom; the Midianites who had traversed the desert and carried terror to the inhabitants of Canaan become merely a name.

Midian was originally governed by high-priests. This was the case among other Semitic peoples as well. In Assyria the kings were preceded by the high-priests of Assur, and recently-discovered inscriptions show that in southern Arabia, in the land of Sheba, the high-priest came before the king. Jethro, "the priest of Midian," represented a peculiarly Arabian institution.

The name of "Arab" was applied to certain tribes only of northern Arabia. We hear of them in the Old Testament as well as in the Assyrian inscriptions. In the Old Testament the name seems to include the Ishmaelite clans to the east of Edom. Their "kings," it is said, brought tribute to Solomon; a colony of them was established at Gur-Baal in the south of Judah. We learn from the Assyrian texts that they could be governed by queens; two of their queens indeed are mentioned by name.

It was also a "queen of the south," it will be remembered, who came to hear the wisdom of Solomon. Sheba, the Saba of classical antiquity, was an important kingdom of south-western Arabia, which had grown wealthy through its trade in spicery. From time immemorial Egypt had imported frankincense from the southern coasts of the Arabian peninsula, and the precious spices had been carried by merchants to the far north. The caravan-road of trade ran northward to Midian and Edom, touching on the one side on the frontier of Egypt, on the other on that of Palestine. The road and the country through which it passed were in the hands of the south Arabian kings. Their inscriptions have been discovered at Teima, the Tema of the Old Testament, not far inland from El-Wej, and in the days of Tiglath-pileser the kings of Saba claimed

THE NATIONS OF THE SOUTH-EAST 125

rule as far as the Euphrates. It was no strange thing, therefore, for a queen of Sheba to have heard of the power of Solomon, or to have sought alliance with so wealthy and luxurious a neighbour. His province of Edom adjoined her own possessions; his ports on the Gulf of Aqaba were open to her merchants, and the frankincense which grew in her dominions was needed for the temple at Jerusalem.

The people of Sheba belonged to the south Arabian stock. In both blood and language they differed considerably from the Semites of the north. Physically they bore some resemblance to the Egyptians, and it has been suggested that the Egyptians were originally emigrants from their shores. They lived in lofty castles, and terraced the slopes of the mountains for the purpose of cultivation, as they still do to-day. Civilisation among them was old; it was derived, at least in part, from Babylonia, and the dynasty which reigned over Babylon in the age of Abraham was of south Arabian descent. Some of them crossed the Red Sea and founded colonies in Africa, in the modern Abyssinia, where they built cities and introduced the culture of their former homes. Like the Egyptians and the Babylonians, they were a literary people; their inscriptions are still scattered thickly among the ruins of their towns, written in the letters of the alphabet which is usually termed Phœnician. But it is becoming a question whether it was not from south Arabia that

Phœnicia first borrowed it, and whether it would not be more truthfully called Arabian.

The religion of southern Arabia was highly polytheistic. Each district and tribe had its special god or gods, and the goddesses were almost as numerous as the gods. Along with Babylonian culture had come the adoption of several Babylonian divinities;—Sin, the Moon-god, for instance, or Atthar, the Ashtoreth of Canaan. How far westward the worship of Sin was carried may be judged from the fact that Sinai, the sacred mountain whereon the law of Israel was promulgated, took its name from that of the old Babylonian god.

In the tenth chapter of Genesis Sheba is one of the sons of Joktan, the ancestor of the south Arabian tribes. Foremost among them is Hazarmaveth, the Hadhramaut of to-day; another is Ophir, the port to which the gold of Africa was brought. But the same chapter also assigns to Sheba a different origin. It couples him with Dedan, and sees in him a descendant of Ham, a kinsman of Egypt and Canaan. Both genealogies are right. They are geographical, not ethnic, and denote, in accordance with Semitic idiom, the geographical relationships of the races and nations of the ancient world. Sheba belonged not only to south Arabia but to northern Arabia as well. The rule of the Sabæan princes extended to the borders of Egypt and Canaan, and Sheba was the brother of Hazarmaveth

THE NATIONS OF THE SOUTH-EAST

and of Dedan alike. For Dedan was a north Arabian tribe, whose home was near Tema, and whose name may have had a connection with that sometimes given by the Babylonians to the whole of the west.

Such, then, was Arabia in the days of the Hebrew writers. The south was occupied by a cultured population, whose rule, at all events after the time of Solomon, was acknowledged throughout the peninsula. The people of the north and the centre differed from this population in both race and language, though all alike belonged to the same Semitic stock. The Midianites on the western coast perhaps partook of the characteristics of both. But the Ishmaelites were wholly northern; they were the kinsmen of the Edomites and Israelites, and their language was that Aramaic which represents a mixture of Arabic and Canaanitish elements. Wandering tribes of savage Bedâwin pitched their tents in the desert, or robbed their more settled neighbours, as they do to-day; these were the Amalekites of the Old Testament, who were believed to be the first created of mankind, and the aboriginal inhabitants of Arabia. Apart from them, however, the peninsula was the seat of a considerable culture. The culture had spread from the spice-bearing lands of the south, where it had been in contact with the civilisations of Babylonia on the one side and of Egypt on the other, and where wealthy and prosperous kingdoms had arisen, and powerful dynasties of kings had held sway. It is to Arabia, in all probability, that we must look for the origin of the alphabet—in itself a proof of the culture of those who used it; and it was from Arabia that Babylonia received that line of monarchs which first made Babylon a capital, and was ruling there in the days of Abraham. We must cease to regard Arabia as a land of deserts and barbarism; it was, on the contrary, a trading centre of the ancient world, and the Moslems who went forth from it to conquer Christendom and found empires, were but the successors of those who, in earlier times, had exercised a profound influence upon the destinies of the East.

CHAPTER IV
THE NATIONS OF THE NORTH-EAST

CHAPTER IV

THE NATIONS OF THE NORTH-EAST

CANAAN is but the southern continuation of Syria, which shades off, as it were, into the waterless wilderness. The name of Syria is usually supposed to be an abbreviation of Assyria, but it is more probable that it comes from Suri, the name by which the Babylonians denoted Mesopotamia and Syria of the north, and in which Assyria itself was sometimes included. As we have seen, the Syria of our own maps, and more especially the southern half of it, was commonly known to the Babylonians as the land of the Amorites; in the later inscriptions of Assyria the place of the Amorites is taken by the Hittites. When Assyria appeared upon the scene of history the Hittites had become the dominant people in the west.

The main part of the population of Syria and Mesopotamia was Aramæan—that is to say, it consisted of Semites from Arabia who spoke Aramaic dialects. But it was exposed to constant attacks from the north, and from time to time passed under the yoke of a northern conqueror. At one time it was the Hittites who poured down the slopes of Mount Taurus and occupied the fertile plains and cities of northern Syria. At another time a kindred people from the highlands of Armenia established a kingdom in Mesopotamia known as that of Mitanni to its own subjects, as that of Aram-Naharaim to the Hebrews.

The northern invaders sundered the Semites of the West from those of the East. The kings of Mitanni held guard over the fords of the Euphrates, and intrigued in Palestine against the Egyptian Pharaohs. But this did not prevent them from marrying into the Pharaoh's family, while their daughters were sent to the harem of the Egyptian king. Towards the end of the Eighteenth dynasty the sacred blood of the Pharaohs became contaminated by these foreign alliances. For two generations in succession the queen-mother was a Mitannian princess, and a king finally sat upon the Pharaohs' throne who attempted to supplant the religion of which he was the official head by a foreign cult, and thereby brought about the fall of his house and empire.

The power of Mitanni or Aram-Naharaim—Aram of the Two Rivers—does not seem to have long survived this event. Chushan-rishathaim, we learn from the Book of Judges, held Palestine in subjection for eight years, until he was driven out by the Kenizzite Othniel, and about the same time Ramses III. of Egypt records his victory over the Mesopotamian

THE NATIONS OF THE NORTH-EAST 133

king. After this we hear no more of a king of Aram-Naharaim in Canaan or on the frontier of Egypt, and when the name of Mitanni is met with a little later in the Assyrian inscriptions it is that of a small and insignificant state.

The Hittites had grown at the expense of Mitanni, but their glory too was of no long duration. In the days of Ramses II., the Pharaoh of the Oppression, their power was at its height. From their southern capital at Kadesh on the Orontes their armies had gone forth to contend on equal terms with the forces of the Nile, and after twenty-one years of warfare, peace was made between the two combatants, neither side having gained an advantage in the long struggle. The text of the treaty is engraved on the walls of Karnak. There we may read how the two rivals swore henceforth to be friends and allies, how the existing boundaries of their respective territories in Syria were to remain unchanged for ever, and how a general amnesty was to be granted to the political fugitives on either side. It was only the criminal to whom the right of asylum in the dominions of the other was denied.

In the war they had waged with Egypt the Hittite princes of Kadesh had summoned their vassal allies from the distant coasts of Asia Minor. Lycians and Dardanians had come from the far west; and were joined by the troops of Aram-Naharaim from the east. The extension of Hittite supremacy to the shores of the Ægean Sea is testified by the monuments it has left behind. Hittite inscriptions have been found near Smyrna engraved on the rocks, as well as the figures of Hittite warriors guarding the westernmost pass of the ancient road. The summer residences of the Hittite princes were on the eastern bank of the Halys. Here the roads of Asia Minor converged, and here we still see the sculptured bas-reliefs of a Hittite palace and long rows of Hittite deities.

The Hittite empire broke up into a multitude of small principalities. Of these Carchemish, now Jerablûs, on the Euphrates, was perhaps the most important. It commanded the ford across the river, and the high-road of commerce from east to west. Its merchants grew rich, and "the mina of Carchemish" became a standard of value in the ancient world. Its capture by Sargon destroyed a rival of Assyrian trade, and opened the road to the Mediterranean to the armies of Assyria.

The decay of the Hittite and Mitannian power meant the revival of the older Aramæan population of the country. The foreigner was expelled or absorbed; Syria and Mesopotamia became more and more Semitic. Aramæan kingdoms arose on all sides, and a feeling of common kinship and interests arose among them at the same time. To the north of the Gulf of Antioch, in the very heart of the Hittite terri-

THE NATIONS OF THE NORTH-EAST 135

tory, German excavators have lately found the earliest known monuments of Aramæan art. The art, as is natural, is based on that of their Hittite predecessors; even the inscriptions in the alphabet of Phœnicia are cut in relief like the older hieroglyphs of the Hittites. But they prove that the triumph of the Aramæan was complete. The foreigner and his works were swept away; no trace has been discovered of a Hittite text, barely even of a Hittite name. The gods are all Semitic—Hadad the Sun-god and Shahr the Moon-god, the Baal of Harran, and Rekeb-el, "the Chariot of God."

Hittite inscriptions have been found at Hamath on the Orontes. But they must belong to a period earlier than that of David. The rulers of Hamath who made alliance with David bear Semitic names. The crown-prince came himself to Jerusalem, bringing with him costly vessels of gold and silver and bronze. His name was Hadoram, "Hadad is exalted;" but out of compliment to the Israelitish king, the name of Hadad was changed into that of the God of Israel, and he became known to history as Joram. A common enmity united Hamath and Israel. The war with Ammon had brought David into conflict with Zobah, an Aramaic kingdom which under Hadad-ezer was aiming at the conquest of the whole of Syria. In the reign of Saul, Zobah was divided into a number of separate clans or states; these had been welded together by Hadad-ezer, who had added to his empire the smaller Aramaic principalities of central Syria. Geshur, Maachah, Damascus all acknowledged his authority. He had secured the caravan-road which led across the desert, past the future Palmyra, to the Euphrates, and eastward of that river the Aramæan states sent him help in war. Like the Pharaohs of a former generation, he had erected a monument of his victory on the banks of the great river, marking the farthest limit of his dominions.

Hamath was threatened by the growing power of Hadad-ezer, when a new force entered the field. Joab, the commander of the Israelitish army, was a consummate general, and the veterans he led had been trained to conquer. Ammon was easily crushed, and while its capital was closely invested the Israelitish troops fell upon the Aramæans in campaign after campaign. Victory followed victory; the forces of Zobah and its allies were annihilated, and the Aramæan states as far as Hamath and even the Euphrates became the tributaries of David. Wealth flowed into the royal treasury at Jerusalem; the cities of northern Syria were plundered of their bronze, and the yearly tribute of the subject states, as well as the proceeds of the desert trade, yielded an unfailing revenue to the conqueror. The attempt of Hadad-ezer to found an Aramæan empire had failed.

But the empire of David was hardly longer lived.

THE NATIONS OF THE NORTH-EAST 137

The murder of Joab, and the unwarlike character and extravagance of Solomon, brought about its downfall. Damascus revolted under Rezon; and though in the war that ensued Solomon succeeded in keeping the cities of Zobah which kept guard over the caravan road, it never returned to Israelitish rule. When the disruption of the Israelitish kingdom came after Solomon's death, the Aramæans rallied round the successors of Rezon. Damascus increased in strength, and at times laid northern Israel under tribute. Between the two kingdoms there was indeed constant intercourse, sometimes peaceful, sometimes hostile. Syrian merchants had bazaars in Samaria, where they could buy and sell, undisturbed by tolls and exactions, and Israelitish traders had similar quarters assigned to them by treaty in Damascus. "Damask couches" were already famous, and Ahab sent a contingent of 10,000 men and 2000 chariots to the help of Ben-Hadad II. in his war against Assyria. This Ben-Hadad is called Hadad-idri or Hadad-ezer in the Assyrian texts; Ben-Hadad, in fact, was a god, who was worshipped by the Syrians by the side of his father Hadad.

In the struggle with Assyria the Aramæan forces were led by Hamath. Most of the states of western Asia contributed troops; even the "Arabs" took part in the conflict. But the confederates were overthrown with great slaughter at Karkar on the Orontes in B.C. 853, and immediately afterwards we find Ahab at war with his late ally. Hadad-idri lived only a few years longer. In B.C. 842 he was murdered by Hazael, who seized the throne. But Hazael, like his predecessor, was soon called upon to face an Assyrian army. Year after year the Assyrians invaded the territories of Damascus, and though they never succeeded in capturing the capital, the country was devastated, and a countless amount of booty carried away. The Syrian kingdom was utterly exhausted, and in no condition to resist the attacks of the Israelitish kings Jehoash and Jeroboam II. Jehoash, we are told, gained three victories over his hereditary enemy, while Jeroboam occupied its cities. When an Assyrian army once more appeared at the gates of Damascus in B.C. 797, its king Mariha was glad to purchase peace by rich presents and the offer of homage. Gold and silver, bronze and iron in large quantities were yielded up to the conqueror, and Damascus for a while was the vassal of Nineveh.

But a respite was granted it in which to recover its strength. Civil war sapped the strength of the kingdom of Israel, and Assyria fell into decay. Freed from its enemies, Damascus again amassed wealth through the trade across the desert, and was recognised as the head of the smaller Aramæan states. In conjunction with the Israelitish king Pekah, Rezon II. proposed to overthrow Judah and supplant the Davidic dynasty by a Syrian vassal-prince. The fall of Judah would have

THE NATIONS OF THE NORTH-EAST 139

meant the fall also of Edom and the submission of the Philistines, as well as that of Moab and Ammon. The strength of its capital made Judah the champion and protector of southern Canaan; with Jerusalem in their hands, the confederate rulers of Damascus and Samaria could do as they chose. Ahaz of Judah turned in his despair to the Assyrians, who had once more appeared on the scene. Tiglath-pileser III. had overthrown the older Assyrian dynasty and put new life into the kingdom. In the interests of the merchants of Nineveh he aimed at incorporating the whole of western Asia and its commerce into his empire, and the appeal of Ahaz gave him an excuse for interfering in the affairs of Palestine. Ahaz became his vassal; Pekah was put to death, and an Assyrian nominee made king in his place, while Rezon was shut up in his capital and closely besieged. For two years the siege continued; then Damascus was taken, its last king slain, and its territory placed under an Assyrian satrap.

Hamath had already fallen. A portion of its population had been transported to the north, and their places filled with settlers from Babylonia. Its king had become an Assyrian vassal, who along with the other subject princes of Asia attended the court held by Tiglath-pileser at Damascus after its capture, there to pay homage to the conqueror and swell his triumph. A few years later, on the accession of Sargon, Hamath made a final effort to recover its freedom. But the effort was ruthlessly crushed, and henceforward the last of the Aramæan kingdoms was made an Assyrian province. When an Aramæan tribe again played a part in history it was in the far south, among the rocky cliffs of Petra and the desert fortress of the Nabathean merchants.

In the Book of Genesis, Mesopotamia, the country between the Euphrates and Tigris, is called not only Aram-Naharaim, "Aram of the Two Rivers," but also Padan-Aram, "the acre of Aram." Padan, as we learn from the Assyrian inscriptions, originally signified as much land as a yoke of oxen could plough; then it came to denote the "cultivated land" or "acre" itself. The word still survives in modern Arabic. In the Egypt of to-day land is measured by *feddans*, the *feddan* (or *paddan*) being the equivalent of our acre. *Paddan* was used in the same sense in the Babylonia of the age of Abraham. Numerous contracts have been found for the lease or sale of estates in which the "acreage" or number of *paddani* is carefully stated. The application of the name to the plain of Mesopotamia was doubtless due to the Babylonians. An early Babylonian king claims rule over the "land of Padan," and elsewhere we are told that it lay in front of the country of the Arman or Aramæans.

It was in western Padan that the kingdom of Mitanni was established. Its founders, as we have

THE NATIONS OF THE NORTH-EAST 141

seen, came from the north. From the river Halys in Asia Minor to Lake Urumiyeh, east of Armenia, there was a multitude of tribes, most of whom seem to have belonged to the same race and to have spoken dialects of the same language. The Hittites of Cappadocia and the ranges of the Taurus have already been described. East of them came the Meshech and Tubal of the Bible as well as the kingdom of Comagêne, of which we often hear in the Assyrian texts. But of all these northern populations the most important—at all events in the later Old Testament age—were the inhabitants of a country called Biainas, but to which its neighbours gave the name of Ararat. Ararat corresponded to southern Armenia, Biainas being the modern Van, and the Mount Ararat of modern geography lying considerably to the north of it. In the ninth century before our era a powerful dynasty arose at Van, which extended its conquests far and wide, and at one time threatened to destroy even the Assyrian empire. It signalised its accession to power by borrowing the cuneiform writing of Nineveh, and numerous inscriptions exist recording the names and victories of its sovereigns, the buildings they erected, and the gods they served. The language of the inscriptions is strange and peculiar; it seems to be distantly related to modern Georgian, and may be akin to the dialects of the Hittites or of Mitanni.

If we may trust the representations of the Assyrian

artists, the people of Ararat did not all belong to the same race. Two ethnic types have been handed down to us—one with beardless faces, resembling that of the Hittites, the other of a people with high foreheads, curved and pointed noses, thin lips, and well-formed chin. Both, however, wear the same dress. On the head is a crested helmet like that of the Greeks, on the feet the Hittite boot with upturned end; the body is clad in a tunic which reaches to the knee, and a small round target is used in battle.

For many centuries the Semites and the people of the north contended for the possession of the Syrian plains. Horde after horde descended from the northern mountains, capturing the Aramæan cities and setting up kingdoms in their midst. At one time it seemed as if the Semites of the east and west were to be permanently sundered from one another. The decay of Babylonia and Egypt enabled the Mitannians and Hittites to establish themselves in Mesopotamia and Syria, and to gain possession of the fords of the Euphrates and the great lines of trade. But the northerner was not suited by nature for the hot and enervating climate of the south. His force diminished, his numbers lessened, and the subjugated Semite increased in strength. Mitanni perished like the Hittite empire, and with the rise of the second Assyrian empire the intruding nations of the north found themselves compelled to struggle for bare existence. Ararat

THE NATIONS OF THE NORTH-EAST 143

had become the leader among them, and in the latter days of the older Assyrian dynasty had wrested territory from the Assyrians themselves, and had imposed its dominion from the borders of Cappadocia to the shores of Lake Urumiyeh. But on a sudden all was changed. Tiglath-pileser swept the land of Ararat to the very gates of its capital, destroying and plundering as he went, and a war began between north and south which ended in the triumph of Assyria. Ararat indeed remained, though reduced to its original dimensions in the neighbourhood of Lake Van; but its allies in Comagênê and Cappadocia, in Cilicia and among the Hittites, were subjugated and dispersed. The tribes of Meshech and Tubal retreated to the coasts of the Black Sea, and Ararat and its sister-kingdom of Minni were too exhausted to withstand the invasion of a new race from new quarters of the world. The Aryan Kimmerians from Russia poured through them, settling on their way in Minni; while other Aryans from Phrygia made themselves masters of Ararat, which henceforth took the name of Armenia. The Aramæan was avenged: the invaders who in days before the Exodus had already robbed him of his lands were themselves pursued to their northern retreats. The south proved to them a land of decay and destruction; Gog and his host were given, "on the mountains of Israel," to the vulture and the beast of prey.

K

CHAPTER V
EGYPT

CHAPTER V

EGYPT

EGYPT had been the bondhouse of Israel. It was there that Israel had grown from a family into a people, which the desert was to transform into a nation. The Exodus out of Egypt was the beginning of Israelitish history, the era from which it dated. Down to the last the kingdom of the Pharaohs exercised upon it an influence more or less profound; the extravagant splendour of Solomon was modelled after that of the Egyptian monarchs, his merchants found their best market on the banks of the Nile, and the last Canaanitish city which passed into Israelitish hands was the gift to him of the Pharaoh. The invasion of the Egyptian king prevented Rehoboam from attempting to reconquer the revolted tribes, and in the days of Assyrian ascendancy it was Egypt that was played off against the Assyrian invader by the princes and statesmen of the west. The defeat of Necho at Carchemish handed Palestine over to the Babylonians, and indirectly brought about the destruction of Jerusalem; even in the age of the Ptolemies Egypt still influenced the history of Israel, and the Jews of Alexandria prepared the way for the Christian Church. For centuries Palestine was the battle-ground of the nations; but it was so because it lay between the two great powers of the ancient East, between Egypt on the one side and Assyria and Babylonia on the other.

Egypt is the creation of the Nile. Outside the Delta and the strip of land which can be watered from the river there is only desert. When the annual inundation covers the fields the land of Egypt exists no more; it becomes a watery plain, out of which emerge the villages and towns and the raised banks which serve as roads. For more than 1600 miles the Nile flows without an affluent; in the spring it falls so low that its channel becomes almost unnavigable; but in the late summer, its waters, swollen by the rains and melted snows of Central Africa, and laden with the fertilising silt of the Abyssinian mountains, spread over the cultivated country, and bring fertility wherever they go.

The waters of the inundation must have been confined by dykes, and made to flow where the cultivator needed them, at a very remote date. Recent discoveries have thrown light on the early history of the country. We find it inhabited by at least one race, possibly of Libyan origin, which for the present we must term pre-historic. Its burial-places are met with in various localities in Upper Egypt. The members of the race were not acquainted with the use of metals, but they were expert artificers in stone and clay. Stone was skilfully carved into vessels of different forms, and vases of clay were fashioned, with brightly polished surfaces. Sometimes the vases were simply coloured red and black, or adorned with patterns and pictures in incised white lines; at other times, and more especially in the later tombs, they were artistically decorated with representations of men and animals, boats, and geometrical patterns in red upon a pale drab ground.

The pre-historic race or races had already reached a fair level of civilisation—neolithic in type though it may have been—when a new people appeared upon the scene, bringing with them the elements of a high culture and a knowledge of working in metals. These were the Pharaonic Egyptians, who seem to have come from Babylonia and the coasts of southern Arabia. Cities were built and kingdoms were founded on the banks of the Nile, and the older population was forced to become the serfs of the new-comers, to cultivate their fields, to confine the Nile within artificial boundaries, and to carry out those engineering works which have made the valley of the Nile what it is to-day.

The Pharaonic Egyptians are the Egyptians of history. They were acquainted with the art of writing, they mummified their dead, and they possessed to a high degree the faculty of organisation. The gods they worshipped were beneficent deities, forms of the

Sun-god from whom their kings derived their descent. It was a religion which easily passed into a sort of pantheistic monotheism in the more cultivated minds, and it was associated with a morality which is almost Christian in its character. A belief in a future world and a resurrection of the flesh formed an integral part of it; hence came the practice of embalming the body that it might be preserved to the day of resurrection; hence too the doctrine of the dead man's justification, not only through his own good works, but through the intercession of the Sun-god Horus as well. Horus was addressed as "the Redeemer;" he had avenged the death of his father Osiris upon his enemy Set, the lord of evil, and through faith in him his followers were delivered from the powers of darkness. Horus, however, and Osiris were but forms of the same deity. Horus was the Sun-god when he rises in the morning; Osiris the Sun-god as he journeys at night through a world of darkness; and both were identical with Tum, the Sun-god of the evening. The gods who watched over the great cities of Egypt, some of which had been the capitals of principalities, were identified with the Sun-god in these his various forms. Thus Ptah of Memphis became one with Osiris; so also did Ra, the Sun-god of Heliopolis, while in those later days when Thebes rose to sovereign power its local god Amon was united with Ra.

Along with this higher and spiritual religion went

—at least in historical times—a worship of sacred animals. The anomaly can be explained only by that mixture of races of which archæology has assured us. Beast-worship must have been the religion of the prehistoric inhabitants of Egypt, and just as Brahmanism has thrown its protection over the superstitions of the aboriginal tribes of India and identified the idols of the populace with its own gods, so too in ancient Egypt a fusion of race must have brought about a fusion of ideas. The sacred animals of the older cult were associated with the deities of the new-comers; in the eyes of the upper classes they were but symbols; the lower classes continued to see in them what their fathers had seen, the gods themselves. While the Pharaonic Egyptian adored Horus, the older race knew of Horus only as a hawk. If we may trust Manetho, the Egyptian historian, it was not till the beginning of the Second historical dynasty that the sacred animals of popular worship were received into the official cult.

The Pharaonic Egyptian resembled in body and character the typical native of Central Egypt to-day. He was long-headed, with a high and intellectual forehead, straight nose, and massive lower jaw. His limbs were well-proportioned and muscular, his feet and hands were small. He belonged to the white race, but his hair and eyes were black, the hair being also straight. His artistic and intellectual faculties were highly developed, he was singularly good-tempered and light-hearted, averse to cruelty, though subject at times to fits of fanatical excitement and ferocity. At once obstinate and industrious, he never failed to carry out what he had once taken in hand. The Nile valley was reclaimed for the use of man, and swamp and jungle, the home of wild beasts and venomous serpents, were turned by his labours into a fruitful paradise.

By the side of the long-headed Egyptian of the ruling classes we find in the age of the earlier dynasties a wholly different type, of which the famous wooden statue now in the Cairo Museum, and commonly known as the "Shêkh el-Beled," may be taken as an illustration. Here the skull is round instead of long, the lips and nostrils are thick and fleshy, the expression good-humoured rather than intellectual. The type is that of a portion of the lower classes, and disappears from the monuments after the fall of the Sixth dynasty. After that epoch the races which inhabited Egypt were more completely fused together, and the rounded skull became rare.

Egyptian history begins with Menes, the founder of the united monarchy, and of the First historical dynasty. Our glimpses of the age that preceded him —the age of the followers of Horus, as the Egyptians termed it—are few and scanty. Egypt was divided into several kingdoms, which were gradually unified into two only, those of the north and the south. The northern kingdom was symbolised by the snake and papyrus, the southern kingdom by the vulture and aloe. The vulture was the emblem of Nekheb, the goddess of the great fortress whose ruins are now called El-Kab; and it is probable that the city of Nekhen, which stood opposite it on the western bank of the Nile, was once the capital of the south. However this may be, when Menes mounted the throne he was hereditary ruler of This, a city which adjoined the sacred burial-place of Osiris at Abydos, and of which Girgeh is the modern successor.

Menes made himself master of the north, and so united all Egypt under one rule. He then undertook and carried through a vast engineering work, one of the greatest the world has ever seen. The Nile was turned aside out of its old channel under the Libyan cliffs into a new channel to the east. The dyke which forced the river from its old course still remains, and two or three thousand years before the bed of the valley had risen to its present level the destruction of the dyke would have meant the return of the Nile to its former path. North of the dyke English engineers have found that the alluvial soil bears witness to interference with the natural course of the river of a far-reaching kind, and its long straight course resembles that of a canal rather than of the naturally winding stream of the Nile.

On the embankment thus won from the waters Menes built his capital, which bore the two names of Men-nefer or Memphis, "the Beautiful Place," and Hâ-ka-Ptah or Ægyptos, "the Temple of the Double of Ptah." On the north side of it, in fact, stood the temple of Ptah, the local god, the scanty remains of which are still visited by the tourist. In front of the shrine was the sacred lake across which, on days of festival, the image of the god was ferried, and which now serves as a village pond.

Menes was followed by six dynasties of kings, who reigned in all 1478 years. The tombs of the two first dynasties have been found at Abydos. Menes himself was buried on the edge of the desert near Negada, about twenty miles to the north of Thebes. His sepulchre was built in rectangular form, of crude bricks, and filled with numerous chambers, in the innermost and largest of which the corpse of the king was laid. Then wood was heaped about the walls and the whole set on fire, so that the royal body and the objects that were buried with it were half consumed by the heat. The mode of burial was peculiar to Babylonia. Here, in an alluvial plain, where stone was not procurable, and where the cemeteries of the dead adjoined the houses of the living, brick was needful instead of stone, and sanitary considerations made cremation necessary. But in the desert of Egypt, at the foot of rocky cliffs, such customs were out of place; their existence can be explained only by their importation from abroad. The use of seal-cylinders of Babylonian pattern, and of clay as a writing material, in the age of Menes and his successors, confirms the conclusion to which the mode of burial points. The culture of Pharaonic Egypt must have been derived from the banks of the Euphrates.

That Menes should have been buried at Negada, and not, like the rest of his dynasty, in the sacred necropolis of his mother-city, is strange. But we are told that he was slain by a hippopotamus, the Egyptian symbol of a foe. It may be, therefore, that he fell fighting in battle, and that his sepulchre was erected near the scene of his death. However that may be, the other monarchs of the first two dynasties were entombed at Abydos. The mode of burial was the same as in the case of Menes.

The objects found in the tombs of Menes and his successors prove that the culture of Egypt was already far advanced. The hieroglyphic system of writing was fully developed, tools and weapons of bronze were used in large quantities, the hardest stones of the Red Sea coast were carved into exquisitely-shaped vases, plaques of ivory were engraved with high artistic finish, and even obsidian was worked into vases by means of the lathe. As the nearest source of obsidian to Egypt that is known are the islands of Santorin and Melos in the Ægean Sea, there must have already been a maritime trade with the Greek seas. Art had already reached maturity; a small dog carved out of ivory and discovered in the tomb of Menes is equal to the best work of later days. Finally, the titles assumed by the Pharaohs are already placed above the double name of the king, and the symbols employed to denote them are the same as those which continued in use down to the end of the Egyptian monarchy.

The first six dynasties are known to Egyptologists as the Old Empire. Kings of the Fourth dynasty, Khufu, Khafra, and Menkaura, built the great pyramids of Giza, the largest of which is still one of the wonders of the world. Its huge granite blocks are planed with mathematical exactitude, and, according to Professor Flinders Petrie, have been worked by means of tubular drills fitted with the points of emeralds or some equally hard stone. It was left for the nineteenth century to re-discover the instrument when the Mont Cenis tunnel was half completed. The copper for the bronze tools employed by the workmen was brought from the mines of Sinai, where the Egyptian kings had kept an armed garrison for many generations; the tin mixed with the copper must have come from India and the Malayan Peninsula, or else from Spain and Britain.

While the Fifth and Sixth dynasties were reigning, exploring expeditions were sent into the lands of the Upper Nile. The two dynasties had sprung from the island of Elephantinê, opposite Assuan; it was, therefore, perhaps natural that they should take an interest in the country to the south. One expedition made its way into the land of Punt, to the north of Abyssinia, and brought back a Danga dwarf, whose tribal name still survives under the form of Dongo. Later expeditions explored the banks of the Nile as far south as the country of the Dwarfs, as well as the oases of Libya.

The Old Empire was followed by a period of decline. Egypt was overrun by barbarians, its kings lost their power, and the whole land suffered decay. The pyramid tombs of the Old Empire were entered and despoiled; the bodies of the monarchs within them were torn to pieces, and the precious objects that had been buried with them were carried away. As the power of the kings diminished, that of the great landowners and nobles increased; a feudal aristocracy grew up, which divided Egypt between its members, and treated the royal authority with only nominal respect. Memphis ceased to be the capital, and a new dynasty, the Ninth, was founded by the feudal prince of Herakleopolis, now Ahnas, south of the Fayyûm. For a time the Tenth dynasty succeeded in reducing its rebellious vassals to obedience, but the princes of Thebes steadily grew in strength, and at length one of them seized the throne of the Pharaohs and established the Eleventh dynasty. Thebes became the capital of the kingdom, and under the Twelfth dynasty was the capital of an empire.

Once more Egypt revived. The power of the aristocracy was broken, and the local princes became court officials. Temples were built, and engineering works undertaken all over the country. The ancient temple of Ra at Heliopolis was restored, and two obelisks, one of which is still standing, were planted in front of it. The depression west of the Nile, now known as the Fayyûm, was drained of its waters, and by means of embankments transformed from a pestiferous marsh into fertile fields. The Nile was brought to it by a river-like canal, and the supply of water regulated by locks. Fresh exploring expeditions were sent to the Somali coast and elsewhere. The goldmines of Hammamât were worked in the eastern desert, and Egypt became the California or Australia of the ancient world. The eastern frontier was defended against the Asiatic tribes, while campaign after campaign was carried on in the south, resulting in the conquest of the Sudân.

The Thirteenth dynasty came to an end in the midst of internal troubles. The short reigns of the kings of the dynasty that followed show that the line of the Pharaohs was again becoming feeble. It closed in disaster and overthrow. Hordes of invaders poured into Egypt from Asia and overran the whole country. They are known as the Hyksos or Shepherds, and the greater part of them were of Semitic descent. For 669 years they ruled the valley of the Nile in three dynasties, and the recollection of their hated sway never faded from the Egyptian mind. At first they burned and plundered, then they established themselves in Memphis and Zoan, and from thence governed the rest of the country. But they soon submitted to the influence of Egyptian culture. The conquered people took their conquerors captive, and the Hyksos kings became veritable Pharaohs. The manners and customs, the writing and titles of the native monarchs were adopted, and, in course of time, even the language also. The court was filled with native officials, the cities and temples were restored, and Egyptian learning was patronised. One of the few Egyptian treatises on mathematics that have come down to us is dedicated to a Hyksos sovereign. It was only in religion that the new rulers of Egypt remained foreign.

They continued to worship a form of the Semitic Baal, who was invoked under the Hittite name of Sutekh. An attempt to impose his worship upon the native Egyptians led to the war of independence which ended in the expulsion of the stranger. Apophis III., of the Seventeenth dynasty, sent messengers to Skenen-Ra, the prince of Thebes, bidding him renounce Amon of Thebes for the god of his suzerain. Skenen-Ra resisted, and a long war followed, which, after lasting through five generations, resulted in the complete triumph of the Egyptians. The Hyksos were driven back into Asia, and the prince of

Thebes was acknowledged the Pharaoh of an united Egypt (B.C. 1600).

It was while the Hyksos kings were reigning that Abraham visited the Delta. Their court was held at Zoan, now Sân, close to the Asiatic frontier, and on the frontier itself stood their fortress of Avaris, which served at once to bar the way from Asia and to overawe the conquered Egyptians. The Pharaoh of Joseph was probably Apophis III. If so, the Hebrew vizier would have witnessed the outbreak of the war of independence towards the close of the long reign of the Hyksos king. It may be that the policy which transferred the soil of Egypt from the people to the king and the priests gave its first impulse to the movement.

The Eighteenth dynasty founded an Egyptian empire. Its kings carried the war into Asia, and planted the boundaries of Egyptian dominion on the banks of the Euphrates. Thothmes III. (B.C. 1503–1449) made Canaan an Egyptian province, dividing it into districts, each under a governor or a vassal prince, who was visited from time to time by a royal commissioner. Carriage roads were constructed, with posting inns at intervals along them where food and lodging could be procured. The country east of the Jordan equally obeyed Egyptian rule. The plateau of Bashan was governed by a single prefect; Ammon and Moab were tributary; Edom alone retained its

EGYPT 161

independence, thanks to its barren mountains and inaccessible ravines. Thebes, the capital of the dynasty, was adorned with splendid buildings, and all the wealth and luxury of Asia was poured into it. Thothmes established zoological and botanical gardens, where the strange plants, birds, and animals he had collected in his campaigns could be preserved. His immediate predecessor, Queen Hatshepsu, had already revived the exploring expeditions of earlier centuries. An exploring fleet had been sent by her to Punt, the land of frankincense, and it returned home with rarities of all kinds, including apes and giraffes. The history of the expedition and the treasures it brought back were depicted on the walls of the temple built by the queen at Dêr el-Bâhari, after the design of the architect Sen-Mut.

The authority of Egypt was not extended to the Euphrates only. Cyprus sent tribute to the Pharaoh, the coasts of Asia Minor, perhaps also of Greece, were harried, and the Sudân was conquered as far south as Berber, if not Khartûm. Under Amen-hotep III., the grandson of Thothmes III., the empire underwent still farther extension. Egyptian temples were erected on the banks of the Upper Nile, and Napata, the future capital of Ethiopia, was built at Gebel Barkal, beyond Dongola.

In Asia, Mitanni was the first neighbour of Egypt that had maintained its independence. Assyria and the Mesopotamian prince of Singar or Shinar had paid tribute to Thothmes III.; so, too, had the Hittite king, and even Babylonia had been forced to acquiesce sullenly in the annexation by Egypt of her old province of Canaan, and to beg for gifts of gold from the Egyptian mines. But Mitanni was too powerful to be attacked. Her royal family accordingly married into the Solar race of Egypt. One of her princesses was the mother of Amen-hotep III.; another was probably the mother of his son and successor, Amen-hotep IV.

Amen-hotep IV. was one of the most remarkable monarchs that have ever sat upon a throne. His father died while he was still a boy, and he was brought up under the Asiatic influences of his mother Teie. But he was a philosopher by nature rather than a king. The purpose of his life was to reform the religion of Egypt, to replace it, in fact, by a pantheistic monotheism, the visible symbol of which was the solar disk. For the first time in history a religious persecution was entered on; the worship of Amon, the god of Thebes, was proscribed, and his very name erased from the monuments. Amen-hotep changed his own name to Khu-n-Aten, "the glory of the solar disk," and every effort was made to extirpate the state religion, of which he was himself the official head. But the ancient priesthood of Thebes proved too strong for the king. He left the city of his fathers, and built a new capital farther north, where its ruins are now known as Tel el-Amarna. Here he lived with the adherents of the new creed, and here he erected a temple to the god of his worship and a stately palace for himself.

Along with the reformation in religion had gone a reformation in art. The old conventionalised art of Egypt was cast aside, and an attempt was made to imitate nature exactly, even to the verge of caricature. The wall and floor paintings that have been discovered at Tel el-Amarna are marvels of realistic art. Plants and animals and birds are alike represented in them with a spirit and faithfulness to nature which is indeed astonishing. Like the houses of his followers, the palace of the king was adorned with similar frescoes. But it was also decorated with a lavish profusion of precious materials; its walls and columns were inlaid with gold and bronze and precious stones, statues almost Greek in their type stood within it, and even its stuccoed floors were covered with costly paintings. Roads were made in the desert eastward of the city, where its wealthier inhabitants took their morning drives, and the king occupied the earlier part of the day in giving lectures or sermons on the articles of his faith.

The archives of the empire had been transferred from Thebes to the new capital. Among them was the foreign correspondence, written upon clay tablets in the cuneiform characters, and (for the most part) in the language of Babylonia. We have learnt from it that the Babylonian language and script were the common means of intercommunication from the Euphrates to the Nile in the century before the Exodus. It proves how long and how profound must have been the influence and rule of Babylonia in western Asia. Throughout the civilised world of Asia the educated classes were compelled to learn a foreign writing and language, and when the empire passed from Babylonia to Egypt, Egypt itself, whose script and literature went back to immemorial times, was forced to do the same. The correspondence was active and far-reaching. There are letters in it from the kings of Babylonia and Assyria, of Mitanni and Cappadocia, as well as from the Egyptian governors in Canaan. Even Bedâwin shêkhs take part in it, and the letters are sometimes on the most trivial of subjects. It is clear that schools and libraries must have existed throughout the civilised East, where the Babylonian characters could be taught and learned, and where Babylonian literature and official correspondence could be stored up. Among the tablets found at Tel el-Amarna are some fragments of Babylonian literature, one of which has served as a lesson-book, and traces of dictionaries have also been discovered there.

The religious reforms of Khu-n-Aten resulted in the fall of the dynasty and the Egyptian empire. The letters from Canaan, more especially those from the vassal-king of Jerusalem, show that the power of Egypt in Asia was on the wane. The Hittites were advancing from the north, Mitanni and Babylonia were intriguing with disaffected Canaanites, and the Canaanitish governors themselves were at war with one another. The Pharaoh is entreated to send help speedily; if his troops do not come at once, it is repeated, they will come too late. But it would seem that the troops could not be spared at home. There, too, civil war was breaking out, and though Khu-n-Aten died before the end came, his sepulchre was profaned, his mummy rent to pieces, and the city he had built destroyed. The stones of the temple of his god were sent to Thebes, there to be used in the service of the victorious Amon; and the tombs prepared for his mother and his followers remained empty. In the national reaction against the Asiatised court and religion of Khu-n-Aten, the Canaanitish foreigners who had usurped the highest offices were either put to death or driven into exile, and a new dynasty, the Nineteenth, arose, whose policy was "Egypt for the Egyptians."

Ramses I. was regarded as the founder of the Nineteenth dynasty. His reign was short, and he was followed by his son Seti I., who once more led his armies into Asia and subdued the coast-land of Syria. Seti was succeeded by his son Ramses II., who died at a great age after a reign of sixty-seven years (B.C. 1348-1281), and whose mummy, like that of his father, is now in the Cairo Museum. He set himself to restore the Asiatic empire of Thothmes. But the

Hittites barred his way. They had established themselves at Kadesh on the Orontes, and a long war of twenty-one years ended at last in a treaty of peace in which the two combatants agreed to respect from henceforth the existing boundaries of Egypt and Kadesh. Egypt was left with Palestine on both sides of the Jordan, a possession, however, which it lost soon after Ramses' death. The treaty was cemented by the marriage of the Hittite princess with the Pharaoh.

Ramses II. was the great builder of Egypt. Go where we will, we find the remains of the temples he erected or restored, of the cities he founded, and of the statues he set up. His architectural conceptions were colossal; the temple of Abu-Simbel, hewn out of a mountain, and the shattered image of himself at Thebes, are a proof of this. But he attempted too much for the compass of a single reign, however long. Much of his work is pretentious but poor, and indicative of the feverish haste with which it was executed.

Among the cities he built in the Delta were Ramses and Pithom. Pithom, or Pa-Tum, is now marked by the mounds of Tel el-Maskhuta, on the line of railway between Ismailîa and Zagazig; it lay at the eastern extremity of Qoshem or Goshen, in the district of Succoth. Like Ramses, it had been built by Israelitish labour, for the free-born Israelites of Goshen had been turned into royal serfs. None had suffered more from the revolution which overthrew the Asiatised court of the Eighteenth dynasty and brought in a "new king which knew not Joseph." They had been settled in the strip of pasture-land which borders the Freshwater Canal of to-day, and is still a place of resort for the Bedâwin from the east. It lay apart from the cultivated lands of the Egyptian peasantry, it adjoined the desert which led to Asia, and it was near the Hyksos capital of Zoan. Meneptah, the son and successor of Ramses II., tells us that from of old it had been given by the Pharaohs to the nomad shepherds of Asia; and after the departure of the Israelitish tribes the same king is informed in a letter from one of his officials that the deserted district had been again handed over to Bedâwin from Edom. This was in the eighth year of the king's reign, three years later than that in which the Exodus must have taken place.

For 400 years the Israelites had been "afflicted" by the Egyptians. But while the Eighteenth dynasty was in power their lot could not have been hard. They still remained the free herdsmen of the Pharaoh, feeding their flocks and cattle on the royal demesne. During the reign of Khu-n-Aten, indeed, their own Semitic kinsmen from Canaan held the chief offices of state, and the Pharaoh was endeavouring to force upon his subjects a form of monotheism which had much in common with that of Israel. The language of the hymns engraved on the walls of the tombs at

Tel el-Amarna reads not unfrequently like the verses of a Hebrew Psalm.

The national reaction which found its expression in the rise of the Eighteenth dynasty swept away the power and influence of Asia, and brought back the gods and religion of Egypt. The Semites who had absorbed the government of the country were expelled or slain; their weaker brethren, the Israelites in Goshen, were enslaved. Egypt became for them a house of bondage, and they had to toil under the lash of the taskmaster at the cities and temples which the Pharaoh built. Ramses held his court at Zoan, like the Hyksos of old days, but it was to keep guard over the Asiatic frontier, not to be in touch with a kindred people in Canaan. Canaan itself was conquered afresh, and the Canaanitish captives — the "mixed multitude" of the Bible—assisted the Israelites in erecting the monuments of their conqueror.

Nevertheless, the people multiplied. The memory of the Hyksos invasion had not passed away, and the Pharaoh and his subjects alike feared the possibility of other invaders from Asia being joined by their disaffected kinsfolk in Egypt itself. That their fears were justified is shown by what happened less than a century later. When the Nineteenth dynasty fell in the midst of civil war, a Canaanite, Arisu by name, seized the throne and made himself master of Egypt. Ramses determined to prevent such a catastrophe by destroying as many as possible of the male children of the Hebrews. The men were worn down in body and mind by constant labour, the children were not allowed to live.

Egyptian testimony confirms the statement of Scripture that this policy was actually carried out. A hymn of victory addressed to Meneptah alludes to "the Israelites" to whom "no seed" had been left. But the policy was ineffectual. The opportunity came at last when the serfs could fly from their enforced labour and escape into the wilderness.

It was in the fifth year of Meneptah (B.C. 1276). Egypt was threatened by formidable enemies. The Libyans advanced against it by land, the nations of the Greek seas attacked it by water. Achæans came from the north, Lycians from Asia Minor, Sardinians and Sicilians from the islands of the west. The Delta was overrun by swarms of barbarians, who pitched their tents in front of Belbeis at the western end of the land of Goshen. Plague after plague descended upon the Egyptians, and the freedom of his serfs was wrung from the Pharaoh. They fled by night, carrying with them the spoil they had taken from their masters, only to find that the gate of the great line of fortification which protected the eastern frontier of Egypt was closed against them. Meneptah had repented of his act, and a squadron of six hundred chariots was sent in pursuit of the fugitives.

But a violent wind drove back the sea from the shallows at the southern extremity of the forts, and enabled the Israelites to cross them. While their pursuers were following in their footsteps, the dropping of the wind caused the waters to return upon them, and chariots, horses, and men were alike overwhelmed. The Israelites were saved as it were by miracle, and the Pharaoh lost his bondsmen.

But Egypt also succeeded in repelling the storm of invasion which had fallen upon it. The Libyans and their northern allies were annihilated in a decisive battle, their king, Murai, fled from the field, and a countless amount of booty and prisoners fell into the hands of the victorious Egyptians. Canaan, however, was lost, with the exception of Gaza, which defended the road from Egypt, and was still garrisoned by Egyptian troops. But Gaza, the Calais of Egypt, was not destined to remain long in their power. Already the coast-road was made dangerous by the attacks of Philistine pirates from Crete; and it was not long before the pirates took permanent possession of the southern corner of Palestine, and established themselves in its five chief towns. The Egyptian domination in Asia had passed away for ever.

After Meneptah's death the Nineteenth dynasty soon came to an inglorious end. Civil war distracted the country, and for a time it obeyed the rule of a foreign chief. Then came the rise of the Twentieth dynasty, and a third Ramses restored the prestige and prosperity of his kingdom. But once more the foreign invader was upon its soil. The nations of the north had again poured southward, partly by land, partly by sea, greedy for the wealth that was stored in the cultured lands of the Oriental world, and eager to find new settlements for an expanding population. Greek traditions spoke of the movement as a consequence of the Trojan war, and delighted to dwell on the voyages of its heroes into unknown seas, of the piratical descents to which it led, and of the colonies which were planted by it. The Philistine occupation of southern Palestine was one of its results.

As in the time of Meneptah, the Libyans took part with the northern tribes in the assault upon Egypt, and Sardinians and Sicilians followed behind them. But the main bulk of the invaders came from the Greek seas. The Danaans take the place of the Achæans, and the Philistines are among their allies. The invaders had swept through western Asia, plundering and destroying as they marched, and bringing in their train contingents from the countries through which they passed. Hittites, Mitannians, and Amorites all followed with them, and the motley host of men and ships finally reached the Egyptian frontier. Here, however, they were met by the Pharaoh. The battle raged by sea and land, and ended in a triumph of the Egyptians. The invaders were utterly overthrown, their ships burned, their kings and leaders made captive. Egypt was once more saved from destruction, and Ramses III. was free to develop its resources and repair the damage that had been done.

First came a campaign in Canaan and Syria, the object of which was not to acquire territory, but to teach the Asiatic that there was once more an army in Egypt. The Egyptian forces seem to have gone as far as Hamath; at all events, they occupied southern Palestine, capturing Gaza, Hebron, and Jerusalem, and made their way across the Jordan into Moab. Another campaign carried the Egyptian troops into Edom, where they burned the "tents" of the Bedâwin, and for the first and last time in history planted the Egyptian standard on the slopes of Mount Seir. Ramses now turned to the internal administration of his country, and the copper-mines of Sinai, like the gold-mines of the eastern desert, were worked with fresh vigour. The spoil won from the northern invaders made the Pharaoh the richest monarch of the age. Temples were built, and endowed with lavish generosity, and the priesthood must have grieved when he died at last after a reign of thirty-three years.

He was followed by a line of feeble princes. The high-priests of Amon at Thebes usurped their power, and finally dispossessed the last of them of the throne. A new dynasty arose in the Delta. In the south the government was practically in the hands of the Theban high-priests. With a divided kingdom the strength of Egypt passed away.

It was restored by a foreigner, Shishak I., the captain of the Libyan mercenaries. The Pharaoh whose daughter was married by Solomon must have been the last king of the old dynasty. Perhaps he sought to strengthen himself against his enemies in Egypt by an alliance with his powerful neighbour. At all events, the King of Israel allowed his army to march through Palestine as far as Gezer. The Egyptians flattered themselves that they had thereby asserted their old claim to sovereignty over Palestine, but the substantial gainer was the Israelitish monarch. He won the last independent Canaanite city without effort or expenditure, and was allowed to marry into the Solar race.

Shishak had no need of Israelitish alliances. On the contrary, Solomon was connected by marriage with the dethroned dynasty, and the power of Israel, if unchecked, was a menace to his own kingdom. But while Solomon lived he was afraid to move. He kept at his court, however, an Israelitish rebel, who might prove useful when the time came. Hardly was Solomon dead when Jeroboam returned to his native country, and the kingdom of David was sundered in twain. Shishak seized the opportunity of striking a blow at what remained of it. With contemptuous impartiality he overran the territories of both Judah and the revolted tribes, but it was Judah which suffered the most.

The unfinished fortifications of Jerusalem were stormed, the treasures accumulated by Solomon carried to the Nile, and the King of Judah compelled to acknowledge himself the vassal of Shishak. Judah never recovered from the blow: had it not been for the Egyptian invasion, and the consequent loss of its hoarded wealth, it might have been able to suppress the rebellion of Jeroboam, and to reduce all the tribes of Israel once more under one sceptre. The names of the captured cities of Palestine are still to be read on the walls of the temple of Karnak.

Shishak's successors of the Twenty-second dynasty did not inherit his military vigour and skill. The central authority grew gradually weaker, and Egypt again fell back into the condition from which he had rescued it. The tribes of the Sûdan could no longer be hindered from attacking the enfeebled land, and Ethiopian princes made their way to Memphis, carrying back with them to their capital of Napata the spoil and tribute of a defeated and disunited people. At last the Ethiopian raids changed into permanent conquest, and a negro dynasty—the Twenty-fifth—sat on the throne of Menes.

But the kings who belonged to it, Shabaka and Taharka, were vigorous, and for a short while there was peace in the valley of the Nile. Assyria, however, had already arisen in its strength, and was claiming the empire over western Asia which had belonged to

Babylon in the dawn of history. The states of Palestine endeavoured in vain to play off Assyria against Egypt. Again and again the Egyptian armies were defeated on the borders of Canaan, and Taharka was saved from invasion only by the disaster which befell Sennacherib during his siege of Jerusalem. But the respite was only momentary. Asia at last submitted to the dominion of Nineveh, the King of Judah became an Assyrian vassal, and Esar-haddon, the successor of Sennacherib, was now ready to march against the land of the Nile. In B.C. 674 he entered the Delta and scattered the forces of the Ethiopians. But two more campaigns were needed before the country was thoroughly subdued. At last, in June B.C. 670, he drove the Egyptian forces before him in fifteen days from the frontier to Memphis, twice defeating them with heavy loss and wounding Taharka himself. Three days later Memphis opened its gates, and Taharka fled to Egypt, leaving Egypt in the hands of the Assyrian. It was divided among twenty satraps, most of whom were Egyptians by birth.

Two years, however, were hardly past when it revolted, and while on the march to subdue it Esarhaddon fell ill, and died on the 10th of Marchesvan or October. But the revolt was quickly suppressed by his successor Assur-bani-pal, and the twenty satrapies restored. It was not long, however, before the satraps quarrelled with one another, intrigued with Taharka, and rebelled against their suzerain. Headed by Necho of Sais, they invited the Ethiopians to return; but the plot was discovered, and Necho and his fellow-conspirators sent in chains to Nineveh. Sais, Mendes, and other cities of northern Egypt were sacked, and Taharka, who had advanced as far as Thebes and even Memphis, fled to Ethiopia and there died. Meanwhile Necho had been pardoned and loaded with honours by the Assyrian king; his son, who took an Assyrian name, was made satrap of Athribis, near the modern Benha, and the satraps of the Delta henceforward remained faithful to their Assyrian master. But another Ethiopian prince, Tuant-Amon, made a last attempt to recover the dominion of his fathers. Thebes received him with acclamation, and Memphis was taken without difficulty. There the satrap of Goshen came to pay him homage on behalf of his brother-governors in the north.

His triumph, however, was short-lived. Assur-banipal determined to inflict a terrible punishment on the rebel country, and to reduce it to subjection once for all. Thebes had been the centre of disaffection; its priesthood looked with impatience on the rule of the Asiatic, and were connected by religion and tradition with Ethiopia; on Thebes and its priesthood, therefore, the punishment had to fall. The Ethiopian army retreated to Nubia without striking a blow, and Egypt was left defenceless at the mercy of the Assyrian. The

Assyrian army entered Thebes, the No or "City" of Amon, bent on the work of destruction. Its temple-strongholds were plundered and overthrown, its inhabitants carried into slavery, and two obelisks, seventy tons in weight, were sent as trophies to Nineveh. The sack of Thebes made a deep impression on the Oriental world; we find it referred to in the prophecies of Nahum (iii. 8).

Egypt now enjoyed peace, but it was the peace of exhaustion and powerlessness. Psammetikhos had succeeded his father Necho, who had been put to death by Tuant-Amon. He was a man of vigour and ability, and he aimed at nothing less than sovereignty over an united and independent Egypt. His opportunity came in B.C. 655. The Assyrian empire was shaken to its foundations by a revolt of which Babylonia was the centre and which had spread to its other provinces. For a time it was called on to struggle for bare existence. While the Assyrian armies were employed elsewhere, Psammetikhos shook himself free of its authority, and, with the help of Greek and Karian mercenaries from Lydia, overcame his rival satraps and mounted the throne of the Pharaohs. Once more, under the Twenty-sixth dynasty, Egypt enjoyed rest and prosperity; the administration was re-organised, the cities and temples restored, and art underwent an antiquarian revival. Psammetikhos even dreamed of recovering the old supremacy of Egypt in Asia; the

Assyrian empire was falling into decay, and Egypt was endeavouring to model its life after the pattern of the past. After a long siege Ashdod was taken, and the control of the road into Palestine was thus secured.

But the power of the Twenty-sixth dynasty rested upon its Greek mercenaries. The kings themselves were, it is probable, Libyans by descent, and the feelings of the native priesthood towards them do not seem to have been cordial. Their policy and ideas were European rather than Egyptian. Necho, the son and successor of Psammetikhos, cleared out the old canal which united the Red Sea with the Nile, and did all that he could to encourage trade with the Mediterranean. An exploring fleet was even sent under Phœnician pilots to circumnavigate Africa. Three years were spent on the voyage, and the ships finally returned through the Straits of Gibraltar to the mouths of the Nile. Meanwhile, the Pharaoh had marched into Palestine. Gaza was captured, and the Jewish king, Josiah, slain in his attempt to bar the way of his unexpected enemy. Jerusalem surrendered, and a nominee of the Egyptians was placed upon its throne.

The Asiatic empire of the Eighteenth dynasty was thus restored. But it lasted barely three years. In B.C. 605 the Egyptians were defeated by Nebuchadrezzar under the walls of Carchemish on the Euphrates, and Asia passed into the possession of the Babylonians.

Once more Palestine became a shuttlecock between the kingdoms of the Nile and the Euphrates. Trusting to the support of Egypt, Zedekiah of Judah revolted from his Babylonian master. His policy at first seemed successful. The Babylonian army which was besieging Jerusalem retired on the approach of Psammetikhos II., who had succeeded his father Necho, and the Jewish statesmen again breathed freely. But the respite lasted for only six years. The Babylonian troops returned with increased strength; the Egyptians retreated to their own country, and Jerusalem fell in B.C. 588, one year after the death of the Egyptian king.

His son Hophra or Apries had made a vain attempt to rescue Zedekiah. His fleet had held the sea, while his army marched along the coast of Palestine and occupied Tyre and Sidon. But the fall of Jerusalem obliged it to retire. The dream of an Asiatic empire was over, and the Pharaoh had more than enough to do to defend himself against his own subjects. They saw with growing impatience that the power and wealth of the Greek mercenaries continually increased. The native army had already deserted to Ethiopia; now the priests complained that the revenues of the temples were sacrilegiously confiscated for the support of the foreigner. In B.C. 570 discontent reached a head; civil war broke out between Hophra and his brother-in-law Ahmes or Amasis, which ended in the defeat of Hophra and his loss of the crown.

But Amasis found the Greeks more indispensable than ever, and they were loaded with favours even more than before. They were moved to Memphis that they might be close to the king, and at the same time overawe the native Egyptians, and Amasis himself married a Greek wife. The invasion of Egypt by Nebuchadrezzar in B.C. 567 showed that the policy of Amasis had been a wise one. The Babylonians were unable to penetrate beyond the eastern part of the Delta; the Greek troops fought too well. The limits of the Babylonian empire were permanently fixed at the frontiers of Palestine.

That empire, however, was overthrown by Cyrus, and it was easy to see that the conqueror who had proved so irresistible in Asia would not allow Egypt to remain at peace. Amasis prepared himself accordingly for the coming storm. Cyprus was occupied, and therewith the command of the sea was assured. The maritime policy of the Twenty-sixth dynasty was an indication of Greek influence; in older days the sea had been to the Egyptian a thing abhorred.

Kambyses carried out the invasion which his father, Cyrus, had planned. Unfortunately for the Egyptians, Amasis died while the Persian army was on its march, and the task of opposing it fell to his young and inexperienced son. The Greek mercenaries fought bravely, but to no purpose: the battle of Pelusium gave Egypt to the invader, Memphis was taken, and the Pharaoh put to death. In the long struggle between Asia and Egypt, Asia had been finally the victor.

The Egyptians did not submit tamely to the Persian yoke. Kambyses indeed seemed inclined to change himself into an Egyptian Pharaoh; he took up his residence at Memphis and sent an expedition to conquer the Sudân. But under Darius and his successors, whose Zoroastrian monotheism was of a sterner description, there was but little sympathy between the conquered and their conquerors. Time after time the Egyptians broke into revolt, once against Xerxes, once again against Artaxerxes I., and a third time against Artaxerxes II. The last insurrection was more successful than those which had preceded it, and Egypt remained independent for sixty-five years. Then the crimes and incompetence of its last native king, Nektanebo II., opened the way to the Persian, and the valley of the Nile once more bowed its neck under the Persian yoke. Its temples were ruined, the sacred Apis slain, and an ass set up in mockery in its place.

A few years later Egypt welcomed the Macedonian Alexander as a deliverer, and recognised him as a god. The line of the Pharaohs, the incarnations of the Sun-god, had returned in him to the earth. It was not the first time that the Egyptian and the Greek had stood side by side against the common Persian foe. Greek troops had disputed the passage of Kambyses into Egypt. The first revolt of Egypt had saved Greece from the impending invasion of Darius, and postponed it to the reign of his feebler son, and during its second revolt Athenian ships had sailed up the Nile and assisted the Egyptians in the contest with the Persians. If Egypt could not be free, it was better that its master should be a Greek.

Alexander was followed by the Ptolemies. They were the ablest of his successors, the earlier of them being equally great in war and in peace. Alexandria, founded by Alexander on the site of the village of Rakotis, became the commercial and literary centre of the world; thousands of books were collected in its Library, and learned professors lectured in the halls of its Museum. An elaborate fiscal system was devised and carefully superintended, and enormous revenues poured into the treasury of the king. As time passed on, the Ptolemies identified themselves more and more with their subjects; the temples were rebuilt or restored, and the Greek king assumed the attributes of a Pharaoh. The Jews flocked into the country, where special privileges were granted to them, and where many of them were raised to offices of state. A rival temple to that of Jerusalem was built at Onion near Heliopolis, the modern Tel el-Yahudîya, or

"Mound of the Jews," and the books of the Hebrew Scriptures were translated into Greek. A copy of the Septuagint, as the Greek translation was called, was needed for the Alexandrine Library.

Egypt, once the house of bondage, thus became a second house of Israel. It gave the world a new version of the Hebrew Bible which largely influenced the writers of the New Testament; it gave it also a new Canon which was adopted by the early Christian Church. The prophecy of Isaiah was fulfilled: "The Lord shall be known to Egypt, and the Egyptians shall know the Lord."

In the course of centuries, however, the monotheistic element in Egyptian religion had grown clearer and more pronounced in the minds of the educated classes. The gods of the official cult ceased to be regarded as different forms of the same deity; they became mere manifestations of a single all-pervading power. As M. Grébaut puts it: they were "the names received by a single Being in his various attributes and workings. . . . As the Eternal, who existed before all worlds, then as organiser of the universe, and finally as the Providence who each day watches over his work, he is always the same being, reuniting in his essence all the attributes of divinity." It was the hidden God who was adored under the name whatever the latter might be, the God who is described in the texts as "without form" and "whose name is a mystery," and of whom it is said that He is the one God, "beside whom there is no other." In Ptah of Memphis or Amon of Thebes or Ra of Heliopolis, the more educated Egyptian recognised but a name and symbol for the deity which underlay them all.

Along with this growth in a spiritual conception of religion went, as was natural, a growth in scepticism. There was a sceptical as well as a believing school, such as finds its expression in the festal Dirge of King Antef of the Eleventh dynasty. Here we read in Canon Rawnsley's versified translation—

> "What is fortune? say the wise.
> Vanished are the hearths and homes,
> What he does or thinks, who dies,
> None to tell us comes.
>
> Eat and drink in peace to-day,
> When you go, your goods remain;
> He who fares the last, long way,
> Comes not back again."

A curious work of much later date that has come down to us is in the form of a discussion between an Ethiopian cat and the unbelieving jackal Kufi, in which the arguments of a sceptical philosophy are urged with such force and sympathy as to show that they were the author's own. But such scepticism was confined to the few; the Egyptian enjoys this life too much, as a rule, to be troubled by doubts about another, and he has always been distinguished by an intensity of religious belief.

With his religion there were associated ideas and beliefs some of which have a strangely Christian ring. He was a believer in the resurrection of the body; hence the care that was taken from the time of the Third dynasty onwards to preserve it by embalmment, and to place above the heart the scarab beetle, the symbol of evolution, which by its magical powers would cause it to beat again. Hence, too, the long texts from the Ritual of the Dead which enabled the deceased to pass in safety through the perils that encompassed the entrance to the next world, as well as the endeavour to place the corpse where it should not be found and injured.

The Egyptian believed also in a Messiah. Thus, in a papyrus of the time of Thothmes III., we read that "a king will come from the south, Ameni the truth-declaring by name. . . . He will assume the crown of Upper Egypt, and will lift up the red crown of Lower Egypt. . . . The people of the age of the Son of Man will rejoice, and establish his name for all eternity. They will be far from evil, and the wicked will humble their mouths for fear of him. The Asiatics will fall before his blows, and the Libyans before his flame."

Even the conception of a son who is born of a virgin and a god is met with in the temples of Hatshepsu at Dêr el-Bâhari, and of Amenophis III. at Luxor. Here

Amon-Ra is said to have "gone to" the queen, "that he might be a father through her. He made her behold him in his divine form, so that she might bear a child at the sight of his divine beauty. His charms penetrated her flesh, filling it with the odours of Punt." And the god is finally made to declare to her: " Amenhotep shall be the name of the son that is in thy womb. He shall grow up according to the words that proceed out of thy mouth. He shall exercise sovereignty and righteousness in this land unto its very end. My soul is in him, and he shall wear the twofold crown of royalty, ruling the two lands like the sun for ever."

Religious dogmas did not weaken the firm hold the Egyptian had upon morality. His moral code was very high. Even faith in Horus the "Redeemer" did not suffice by itself to ensure an entrance for the dead man into the fields of Alu, the Egyptian Paradise. His deeds were weighed in the balance, and if they were found wanting, he was condemned to the fiery pains of hell. Each man, after death, was called upon to make the "Negative Confession," to prove that he had not sinned against his fellows, that he had not oppressed or taken bribes, had not judged wrongfully, had not injured a slave or overtasked the poor man, had not murdered or stolen, lied or committed adultery, had not given short weight or robbed the gods and the dead, had made none to "hunger" or "weep." Only when all the questions of the awful judges in the underworld had been answered satisfactorily was he allowed to pass into the presence of Osiris and to cultivate the fields of Alu with his own hands.

This was the last trial demanded from the justified Egyptian, and it was a hard one for the rich and noble who had done no peasants' work in this present life. Accordingly, small images of labourers were buried with the dead, and it was supposed that their "doubles" or shadows would assist him in his labours. The supposition rested on a theory which ascribed to all things, whether animate or inanimate, a double or reflection which corresponded to the thing itself in every particular. It was like a shadow, except that it was invisible to mortal eyes, and did not perish with the object which had projected it.

The "double" was called *ka*, and the *ka* of a man was his exact representation in the other world, a spiritual representation, it is true, but nevertheless one which had the same feelings, the same needs, and the same moral nature as himself. It thus differed from the *ba* or "soul," which flew away to the gods on the dissolution of the body. It was, in fact, the Personality of the man.

From the outset the Pharaonic Egyptians were a nation of readers and writers. Nothing is more astonishing than the way in which the simplest articles of daily use are covered with inscriptions. Even the rocks on the river-bank are scribbled over by the generations who once passed beside them. Already in the time of Menes the hieroglyphic system of writing was fully developed, and before the end of the Third dynasty a "hieratic" or running hand had been formed out of it. The more cumbrous and picturesque hieroglyphics were reserved for engraving on wood or stone or metal, or for the sacred texts; the ordinary book was written in hieratic. The papyrus which grew in the marshes of the Delta was the writing material, and in spite of its apparently fragile character, it has been found to last as long as paper. When its use was at last discontinued in the tenth century of our era, the cultivation of the papyrus ceased also, and it became extinct in its ancient home. Tradition, however, asserted that leather had been employed by the scribe before papyrus, and in the time of Pepi of the Sixth dynasty a description of the plan of the temple of Dendera was discovered inscribed on parchment. Even in later ages leather was sometimes employed.

Egyptian literature covered a wide field. Two of the oldest books that have come down to us are the wise sayings of Qaqemna and Ptah-hotep, the first of whom lived under the Third, the second under the Fifth dynasty. They are moral treatises like the Proverbs of Solomon or the Discourses of Confucius. Ptah-hotep already laments that men were not as they had been. He had reached the age of a hundred and ten years, and had fallen upon degenerate days. Perhaps he was right, for it would seem that the examination system had already been introduced for the disposal of official posts. Ptah-hotep's style, too, is involved and elaborate; he writes for a *blasé* circle of readers who can no longer appreciate simplicity.

The historical novel was an Egyptian invention. Several of the works that have survived are examples of it. But light literature of every kind was much in fashion. A tale written for Seti II. when he was crown-prince contains an episode which closely resembles the history of Joseph and Potiphar's wife, and the reign of Ramses II. produced a sarcastic account of the misadventures of a tourist in Canaan, the object of which was to ridicule the style and matter of another writer. Poetry—heroic, lyrical, and religious—flourished, and a sort of Egyptian Iliad was constructed by the poet Pentaur out of a deed of personal prowess on the part of Ramses II. during the war with the Hittites.

Reference has already been made to the work on mathematics that was composed when the Hyksos were ruling Egypt. A century or two later a work on medicine was written, a copy of which is known as the Ebers Papyrus. It shows that medicine has not advanced very rapidly since the age of the Eighteenth Egyptian dynasty. Diseases were already carefully diagnosed and treated, much as they are to-day. The medical prescriptions read like those of a modern doctor; we have the same formulæ, the same admixture of various drugs.

The Egyptians were not only a people of scribes and readers, they were also a people of artists. They had the same power as the Japanese of expressing in a few outlines the form and spirit of an object; their drawing is accurate, and at the same time spirited. It is true that their canon of perspective was not the same as our own, but the greater difficulties it presented to the artist were successfully overcome. Their portraits of foreign races are marvellously true to life, and their caricatures are as excellent as their more serious drawings. It was in statuary, however, that the Egyptian artist was at his best. The hardest of stones were carved into living likenesses, or invested with a dignity and pathos which it is difficult to match. Such at least was the case with the statuary of the Old Empire, before the conventionalised art of a later day had placed restrictions on the sculptor and stifled his originality. The great statue of King Khaf-Ra of the Fourth dynasty, seated on his throne with the imperial hawk behind his head, is carved out of diorite, and nevertheless the sculptor has thrown an idealised divinity over the face, which we yet feel to be a speaking likeness of the man. The seated scribe in the Museum of Cairo, with his high forehead, sparkling eyes, and long straight hair divided in the middle, has a countenance that is the very ideal of intellectuality, and in the wooden figure of the "Shêkh el-beled," we have an inimitable portrait of the sleek and wealthy *bourgeois* as he walks about his farm. All these statues are older than the Sixth dynasty.

In disposition the Egyptian was remarkably kindly. He was affectionate to his family, fond of society, and, alone among the nations of antiquity, humane to others. His laws aimed at saving life and reclaiming the criminal. Diodoros states that punishments were inflicted not merely as a deterrent, but also with a view towards reforming the evil-doer, and Wilkinson notices that at Medinet Habu, where the artist is depicting the great naval battle which saved Egypt from the barbarians in the reign of Ramses III., he has represented Egyptian soldiers rescuing the drowning crew of an enemy's ship.

The Pharaoh derived his title from the Per-âa or "Great House" in which he lived, and where he dispensed justice. The title thus resembles that of the "Sublime Porte." Next to him, the priests were the most powerful body in the kingdom; indeed, after the close of the struggle between Khu-n-Aten and the priesthood of Thebes the latter obtained more and more power, until under the kings of the Twentieth dynasty they were the virtual rulers of the state. They stood between the labouring classes and the great army of bureaucracy which from the days of the

Eighteenth dynasty onward carried on the administration of the kingdom. The labouring classes, however, knew how to defend their own interests; the artisans formed unions and "went on strike." Curious accounts have been preserved of strikes among them at Thebes in the time of Ramses III. The free labouring population must be distinguished from the slaves, who were partly negroes, partly captives taken in war. The greater part of the latter were employed on the public works. The mines and quarries were worked by criminals.

At home the well-to-do Egyptian was artistic in his tastes. The walls and columns of his house were frescoed with pictures, and his furniture was at once comfortable and tasteful. Chairs and tables are of patterns which might well be imitated to-day, and the smallest and commonest articles of toilet were æsthetically and carefully made. Nothing can exceed the beauty of the jewellery found at Dahshur, and belonging to princesses of the Twelfth dynasty. Precious stones are so exquisitely inlaid in gold as to look like enamel, and are formed into the most beautiful of designs; small forget-me-nots, for example, alternate with plain gold crosses on one of the coronets, and the workmanship of the pectoral ornaments could hardly be equalled at the present day. In dress, however, the Egyptian was simple; his limbs were not overloaded with jewellery, and he preferred light and muslin-like linen, which was kept as scrupulously clean as his own person.

But he was fond of social entertainments, and Egyptian cookery and confectionery were famous throughout the world. Table and guests alike were adorned with fragrant flowers, and musicians and singers were called in to complete the banquet. The house was surrounded by a garden, if possible, near the river. It was open to the air and sun. The Egyptian loved the country, with its fresh air and sunshine, as well as its outdoor amusements — hunting and fishing, fowling and playing at ball. Like his descendants to-day, he was an agriculturist at heart. The wealth and very existence of Egypt depended on its peasantry, and though the scribes professed to despise them and to hold the literary life alone worth living, the bulk of the nation was well aware of the fact. Even the walls of the tombs are covered with agricultural scenes. In one of them—that of Pa-heri, at El-Kab—the songs of the labourers have been preserved. Thus the ploughmen sing at the plough: "'Tis a fine day, we are cool, and the oxen are drawing the plough; the sky is doing as we would; let us work for our master!" and of the reapers we read: "In answering chant they say: 'Tis a good day, come out to the country, the north wind blows, the sky is all we desire, let us work and take heart." The best known, however, of the songs, is that sung by the driver of the oxen who tread out the corn, which was first deciphered by Champollion—

"'Thresh away, oxen, thresh away faster,
 The straw for yourselves, and the grain for your master!'"

Such were the Egyptians and such was Egypt where the childhood of Israel was passed. It was a land of culture, it was a land of wealth and abundance, but it was also a land of popular superstition and idolatry, and the idolatry and culture were too closely associated in the minds of the Israelites to be torn apart. In turning their backs on the Egyptian idols, it was necessary that they should turn them on Egyptian civilisation as well. Hence it was that intercourse with Egypt was forbidden, and the King of Israel who began by marrying an Egyptian princess and importing horses from the valley of the Nile, ended by building shrines to the gods of the heathen. Hence, too, it was that the distinctive beliefs and practices of Egypt are ignored or disallowed. Even the doctrine of the resurrection is passed over in silence; the Pentateuch keeps the eyes of the Israelite fixed on the present life, where he will meet with his punishment or reward. The doctrine of the resurrection was part of the faith in Osiris, Isis, and Horus, and Yahveh of Israel would have no other god beside Himself.

Moreover, the Israelites saw but little of the better

EGYPT

side of the Egyptians. They lived in Goshen, on the outskirts of northern Egypt, where the native population was largely mixed with foreign elements. When they first settled there the Pharaoh and his court were Asiatic or of Asiatic descent. And in later days the rise of a purely native government meant for them a bitter bondage and the murder of their children. Between the Israelite and the Egyptian there was hostility from the first; Joseph began by confiscating the lands of both peasant and noble; the natives revenged themselves by reducing his kinsfolk to a condition of serfdom, and the last act in the drama of the Exodus was the "spoiling of the Egyptians."

CHAPTER VI
BABYLONIA AND ASSYRIA

CHAPTER VI

BABYLONIA AND ASSYRIA

WHILE the influence of Egypt upon Israel may be described as negative, that of Babylonia was positive. Abraham was a Babylonian by birth; the Asiatic world through which he wandered was Babylonian in civilisation and government, and the Babylonian exile was the final turning-point in the religious history of Judah. The Semitic Babylonians were allied in race and language to the Hebrews; they had common ideas and common points of view. Though Egyptian influence is markedly absent from the Mosaic Code, we find in it old Semitic institutions and beliefs which equally characterised Babylonia.

But the Semites were not the first occupants of Babylonia. The civilisation of the country had been founded by a race which spoke an agglutinative language, like that of the modern Finns or Turks, and which scholars have now agreed to call Sumerian. The Sumerians had been the builders of the cities, the reclaimers of the marshy plain, the inventors of the picture-writing which developed into the cuneiform or wedge-shaped characters, and the pioneers of a culture which profoundly affected the whole of western Asia. The Semites entered upon the inheritance, adopting, modifying, and improving upon it. The Babylonian civilisation, with which we are best acquainted, was the result of this amalgamation of Sumerian and Semitic elements.

Out of this mixture of Sumerians and Semites there arose a mixed people, a mixed language, and a mixed religion. The language and race of Babylonia were thus like those of England, probably also like those of Egypt. Mixed races are invariably the best; it is the more pure-blooded peoples who fall behind in the struggle for existence.

Recent excavations have thrown light on the early beginnings of Babylonia. The country itself was an alluvial plain, formed by the silt deposited each year by the Tigris and Euphrates. The land grows at the rate of about ninety feet a year, or less than two miles in a century; since the age of Alexander the Great the waters of the Persian Gulf have receded more than forty-six miles from the shore. When the Sumerians first settled by the banks of the Euphrates it must have been on the sandy plateau to the west of the river where the city of Ur, the modern Mugheir, was afterwards built. At that time the future Babylonia was a pestiferous marsh, inundated by the unchecked overflow of the rivers which flowed through it. The reclamation of the marsh was the first work of the new-comers. The rivers were banked out and the inundation regulated by means of canals. All this demanded no little engineering skill; in fact, the creation of Babylonia was the birth of the science of engineering.

Settlements were made in the fertile plain which had thus been won, and which, along with the adjoining desert, was called by the Sumerians the *Edin*, or "Plain." On the southern edge of this plain, and on what was then the coast-line of the Persian Gulf, the town of Eridu was built, which soon became a centre of maritime trade. Its site is now marked by the mounds of Abu Shahrein or Nowâwis, nearly 150 miles from the sea; its foundation, therefore, must go back to about 7500 years, or 5500 B.C. Ur, a little to the north-west, with its temple of the Moon-god, was a colony of Eridu.

In the plain itself many cities were erected, which rose around the temples of the gods. In the north was Nippur, now Niffer, whose great temple of Mul-lil or El-lil, the Lord of the Ghost-world, was a centre of Babylonian religion for unnumbered centuries. After the Semitic conquest Mul-lil came to be addressed as Bel or "Lord," and when the rise of Babylon caused the worship of its patron-deity Bel-Merodach to spread throughout the country, the Bel of Nippur became known as the "older Bel." Nippur was watered by the canal Kabaru, the Chebar of Ezekiel, and to the south of it was the city of Lagas, now Tello, where French excavators have brought to light an early seat of Sumerian power. A little to the west of Lagas was Larsa, the modern Senkereh, famous for its ancient temple of the Sun-god, a few miles to the north-west of which stood Erech, now Warka, dedicated to the Sky-god Anu and his daughter Istar.

Northward of Nippur was Bab-ili or Babylon, "the Gate of God," a Semitic translation of its original Sumerian name, Ka-Dimirra. It was a double city, built on either side of the Euphrates, and adjoining its suburb of Borsippa, once an independent town. Babylon seems to have been a colony of Eridu, and its god, Bel-Merodach, called by the Sumerians "Asari who does good to man," was held to be the son of Ea, the culture-god of Eridu. E-Saggil, the great temple of Bel-Merodach, rose in the midst of Babylon; the temple of Nebo, his "prophet" and interpreter, rose hard by in Borsippa. Its ruins are now known as the Birs-i-Nimrûd, in which travellers have seen the Tower of Babel.

In the neighbourhood of Babylon were Kish (*El-Hymar*) and Kutha (*Tel-Ibrahim*); somewhat to the north of it, and on the banks of the Euphrates, was Sippara or Sepharvaim, whose temple, dedicated to the Sun-god, has been found in the mounds of Abu-Habba. Sippara was the northern fortress of the Baby-

BABYLONIA AND ASSYRIA   203

lonian plain; it stood where the Tigris and Euphrates approached most nearly one another, and where, therefore, the plain itself came practically to an end. Upi or Opis, on the Tigris, still farther to the north, lay outside the boundaries of primæval Chaldæa.

East of Babylonia were the mountains of Elam, inhabited by non-Semitic tribes. Among them were the Kassi or Kossæans, who maintained a rude independence in their mountain fastnesses, and who, at one time, overran Babylonia and founded a dynasty there which lasted for several centuries. The capital of Elam was Susa or Shushan, the seat of an early monarchy, whose civilisation was derived from the Babylonians.

In the south the Tigris and Euphrates made their way to the region of salt-marshes, called Marratu in the inscriptions, Merathaim by the prophet Jeremiah. They were inhabited by the Semitic tribe of the Kaldâ, whose princes owned an unwilling obedience to the Babylonian kings. One of them, Merodachbaladan, succeeded in making himself master of Babylonia, and from that time forward the Kaldâ became so integral a part of the population as eventually to give their name to the whole of it. For the writers of Greece and Rome the Babylonians are Chaldæans. It is probable that Nebuchadrezzar was of Kaldâ origin; if so, this would have been a further reason for the extension of the tribal name to the whole country.

The settlement of the Kaldâ in the marshes was of comparatively late date. Indeed, in the early age of Babylonian history these marshes did not as yet exist; it was not until Eridu had ceased to be a seaport that they were reclaimed from the sea. The Kaldâ were the advance-guard of the Nabatheans and other Aramaic tribes of northern Arabia, who migrated into Babylonia and pitched their tents on the banks of the Euphrates, first of all as herdsmen, afterwards as traders. After the fall of the Babylonian monarchy their numbers and importance increased, and the Aramaic they spoke— the so-called "Chaldee"—came more and more to supersede the language of Babylonia.

When first we get a glimpse of Babylonian history, the country is divided into a number of small principalities. They are all Sumerian, and among them the principality of Kish occupies a leading place. The temple of Mul-lil at Nippur is the central sanctuary, to which they bring their offerings, and from which a civilising influence emanates. It is an influence, however, which reflects the darker side of life. Mul-lil was the lord of the dead; his priests were sorcerers and magicians, and their sacred lore consisted of spells and incantations. Supplementing the influence of Nippur, and in strong contrast with it, was the influence of Eridu. Ea or Oannes, the god of Eridu, was a god who benefited mankind. He was the lord of wisdom, and his wisdom displayed itself in delivering men from the evils that surrounded them, and in teaching them the arts of life. But he was lord also of the water, and it was told of him how he had arisen, morning after morning, from the depths of the Persian Gulf, and had instructed the people of Chaldæa in all the elements of civilisation. Eridu was the home of the hymns that were sung to the gods of light and life, and which came to be looked upon as divinely inspired.

It is clear that the myth of Oannes points to foreign intercourse as the ultimate cause of Babylonian culture. It is natural that such should have been the case. Commerce is still the great civiliser, and the traders and sailors of Eridu created tastes and needs which they sought to satisfy.

The small states of Babylonia were constantly at war with each other, even though they shared in a common civilisation, worshipped the same gods, and presented their offerings to the same sanctuary of Nippur. Southern Babylonia—or Kengi, "the land of canals and reeds," as it was often named—was already divided against the north. At times it exercised supremacy as far as Nippur. En-sakkus-ana of Kengi conquered Kis, like one of his predecessors who had dedicated the statue, the store of silver, and the furniture of the conquered prince to Mul-lil. Kis claimed sovereignty over the Bedâwin "archers," who had their home in the district now called Jokha. But Kis eventually revenged itself. One of its rulers made himself master of Nippur, and the kingdom of Kengi passed away. The final blow was struck by Lugal-zaggi-si, the son of the high-priest of the city of Opis. Lugal-zaggi-si not only conquered Babylonia, he also created an empire. On the vases of delicately-carved stone which he dedicated to the god of Nippur, a long inscription of one hundred and thirty-two lines describes his deeds, and tells how he had extended his dominion from the Persian Gulf to the Mediterranean Sea. It may be that at this time the culture of Babylonia was first brought to the west, and that his conquests first communicated a knowledge of the Sumerian language and writing to the nations of western Asia. With the spoils of his victories the walls of Ur were raised "high as heaven," and the temple of the Sun-god at Larsa was enlarged. Erech was made his capital, and doubtless now received its Sumerian title of "the City" *par excellence.*

The dynasty of Erech was supplanted by the First dynasty of Ur. Erech was captured by Lugal-kigub-nidudu of Ur, and took the second rank in the new kingdom. The position of Ur on the western bank of the Euphrates exposed it to the attacks of the Semitic tribes of northern Arabia, and thus accustomed its inhabitants to the use of arms, while at the same time its proximity to Eridu made it a centre of trade. In Abrahamic days it had long been a place of resort and settlement by Arabian and Canaanite merchants.

BABYLONIA AND ASSYRIA   207

How long the supremacy of Ur lasted we do not
know. Nor do we know whether it preceded or was
followed by the supremacy of Lagas. The kings of
Lagas had succeeded in overcoming their hereditary
enemies to the north. The so-called "Stela of the
Vultures," now in the Louvre, commemorates the overthrow of the forces of the land of Upe or Opis,
and depicts the bodies of the slain as they lie on the
battlefield devoured by the birds of prey. E-ana-gin,
the king of Lagas who erected it, never rested until
he had subjected the rest of southern Babylonia to
his sway. The whole of "Sumer" was subdued, and
the memory of a time when a king of Kis, Mesa by
name, had subjected Lagas to his rule, was finally
wiped out.

High-priests now took the place of kings in Kis
and the country of Opis. But a time came when the
same change occurred also at Lagas, doubtless in consequence of its conquest by some superior power. One
of the monuments discovered at Tello, the ancient
Lagas, describes the victories of the "high-priest"
Entemena over the ancestral foe, and the appoint-
ment of a certain Ili as "high-priest" of the land
of Opis. From henceforward Kis and Opis disappear
from history.

A new power had meanwhile appeared on the scene.
While the Sumerian princes were engaged in mutual
war, the Semites were occupying northern Babylonia,

and establishing their power in the city of Agadê or Akkad, not far from Sippara. Here, in B.C. 3800, arose the empire of Sargani-sar-ali, better known to posterity as "Sargon" of Akkad. He became the hero of the Semitic race in Babylonia. Legends told how he had been hidden by his royal mother in an ark of bulrushes daubed with pitch, and intrusted to the waters of the Euphrates, how he had been found and adopted as a son by Akki the irrigator, and how the goddess Istar had loved him and restored him to his kingly estate. At all events, the career of Sargon was a career of victories. Babylonia was united under his rule, Elam was subjugated, and three campaigns sufficed to make "the land of the Amorites," Syria and Canaan, obedient to his sway. He caused an image of himself to be carved on the shores of the Mediterranean, and demanded tribute from Cyprus, Uru-Malik or Urimelech being appointed governor of Syria, as we learn from a cadastral survey of the district of Lagas. A revolt of the Sumerian states, however, called him home, and for a time fortune seemed against him. He was besieged in Akkad, but a successful sally drove back the rebels, and they were soon utterly crushed. Then Sargon marched into Suri or Mesopotamia, subduing that country as well as the future Assyria. It was the last, however, of his exploits. His son Naram-Sin succeeded him shortly afterwards (B.C. 3750), and continued the conquests of his father. Canaan was already

BABYLONIA AND ASSYRIA 209

a Babylonian province, and Naram-Sin now carried his arms against Magan, or the Sinaitic Peninsula, where he secured the precious mines of copper and turquoise. Building stone from Magan had already been imported to Babylonia by Ur-Nina, a king of Lagas, and grandfather of E-ana-gin, but it must have been brought in the ships of Eridu.

Naram-Sin's son was Bingani-sar-ali. A queen, Ellat-Gula, seems to have sat on the throne not many years later, and with her the dynasty may have come to an end. At any rate, the empire of Akkad is heard of no more. But it left behind it a profound and abiding impression on western Asia. Henceforward the culture and art of the west was Babylonian,—Semitic Babylonian, however, and no longer Sumerian Babylonian as in the days of Lugal-zaggi-si. Sargon was a patron of literature as well as a warrior. Standard works on astronomy and astrology and the science of omens were compiled for the great library he established at Akkad, where numerous scribes were kept constantly at work. Sumerian books were brought from the cities of the south and translated into Semitic ; commentaries were written on the older literature of the country, and dictionaries and grammars compiled. It was now that that mixed language arose, or at least was admitted into the literary dialect, which made Babylonian so much resemble modern English. The lexicon was filled with Sumerian words which had put on a Semitic form, and Semitic lips expressed themselves in Sumerian idioms.

Art, too, reached a high perfection. The seal-cylinders of the reign of Sargon of Akkad represent the highest efforts of the gem-cutter's skill in ancient Babylonia, and a bas-relief of Naram-Sin, found at Diarbekr in northern Mesopotamia, while presenting close analogies to the Egyptian art of the Old Empire, is superior to anything of the kind as yet discovered in Babylonia of either an earlier or a later date. As in Egypt, so too in Babylonia, the sculpture of later times shows retrogression rather than advance. It is impossible not to believe that between the art of Egypt in the age of the Old Empire and that of Babylonia in the reigns of Sargon and Naram-Sin there was an intimate connection. The mines of the Sinaitic Peninsula were coveted by both countries.

Sumerian princes still continued to rule in Sumer or southern Babylonia, but after the era of Sargon their power grew less and less. A Second Sumerian dynasty, however, arose at Ur, and claimed sovereignty over the rest of Chaldæa. One of its kings, Ur-Bau, was a great builder and restorer of the temples, and under his son and successor Dungi (B.C. 2700), a high-priest of the name of Gudea governed Lagas, the monuments of which have given us an insight into the condition of the country in his age. His statues of hard diorite from the Peninsula of Sinai are now in the Louvre;

one of them is that of the architect of his palace, with a copy of its plan upon his lap divided according to scale. Gudea, though owning allegiance to Dungi, carried on wars on his own behalf, and boasts of having conquered "Ansan of Elam." The materials for his numerous buildings were brought from far. Hewn stones were imported from the "land of the Amorites," limestone and alabaster from the Lebanon, gold-dust and acacia-wood from the desert to the south of Palestine, copper from northern Arabia, and various sorts of wood from the Armenian mountains. Other trees came from Dilmun in the Persian Gulf, from Gozan in Mesopotamia, and from Gubin, which is possibly Gebal. The bitumen was derived from "Madga in the mountains of the river Gurruda," in which some scholars have seen the name of the Jordan, and the naphtha springs of the vale of Siddim.

The library of Gudea has been found entire, with its 30,000 tablets or books arranged in order on its shelves, and filled with information which it will take years of labour to examine thoroughly. Not long after his death, the Second dynasty of Ur gave way to a Third, this time of Semitic origin. Its kings still claimed that sovereignty over Syria and Palestine which had been won by Sargon. One of them, Inê-Sin, carried his arms to the west, and married his daughters to the "high-priests" of Ansan in Elam, and of Mer'ash in northern Syria. His grandson, Gimil-Sin, marched to the ranges of the Lebanon and overran the land of Zamzali, which seems to be the Zamzummim of Scripture.

But with Gimil-Sin the strength of the dynasty seems to have come to an end. Babylonia was given over to the stranger, and a dynasty of kings from southern Arabia fixed its seat at Babylon. The language they spoke and the names they bore were common to Canaan and the south of Arabia, and sounded strangely in Babylonian ears. The founder of the dynasty was Sumu-abi, "Shem is my father," a name in which we cannot fail to recognise the Shem of the Old Testament. His descendants, however, had some difficulty in extending and maintaining their authority. The native princes of southern Babylonia resisted it, and the Elamites harried the country with fire and sword. In B.C. 2280 Kudur-Nankhundi, the Elamite king, sacked Erech and carried away the image of its goddess, and not long afterwards we find another Elamite king, Kudur-Laghghamar or Chedor-laomer, claiming lordship over the whole of Chaldæa. The western provinces of Babylonia shared in the fate of the sovereign power, and an Elamite prince, Kudur-Mabug by name, was made "Father" or "Governor of the land of the Amorites." His son Eri-Aku, the Arioch of Genesis, was given the title of king in southern Babylonia, with Larsa as his capital. Larsa had been taken by storm by the Elamite forces, and its native king, Sin-idinnam, driven out. He fled for refuge to the court of the King of Babylon, who still preserved a semblance of authority.

Khammurabi or Amraphel, the fifth successor of Sumu-abi, was now on the throne of Babylon. His long reign of fifty-five years marked an epoch in Babylonian history. At first he was the vassal of Kudur-Laghghamar, and along with his brother vassals, Eri-Aku of Larsa and Tudghula or Tidal of Kurdistan, had to serve in the campaigns of his suzerain lord in Canaan. But an opportunity came at last for revolt, it may be in consequence of the disaster which had befallen the army of the invaders in Syria at the hands of Abram and his Amorite allies. The war lasted long, and at the beginning went against the King of Babylon. Babylon itself was captured by the enemy, and its great temple laid in ruins. But soon afterwards the tide turned. Eri-Aku and his Elamite supporters were defeated in a decisive battle. Larsa was retaken, and Khammurabi ruled once more over an independent and united Babylonia. Sin-idinnam was restored to his principality, and we now possess several of the letters written to him by Khammurabi, in which his bravery is praised on "the day of Kudur-Laghghamar's defeat," and he is told to send back the images of certain Elamite goddesses to their original seats. They had doubtless been carried to Larsa when it fell into the hands of the Elamite invaders.

As soon as Babylonia was cleared of its enemies, Khammurabi set himself to the work of fortifying its cities, of restoring and building its temples and walls, and of clearing and digging canals. The great canal known as that of "the King," in the northern part of the country, was either made or re-excavated by him, and at Kilmad, near the modern Bagdad, a palace was erected. Art and learning were encouraged, and a literary revival took place which brought back the old glories of the age of Sargon. Once more new editions were made of standard works, poets arose to celebrate the deeds of the monarch, and books became multiplied. Among the literary products of the period was the great Chaldæan Epic in twelve books, recording the adventures of the hero Gilgames, and embodying the Chaldæan story of the Deluge.

The supremacy over western Asia passed to Khammurabi, along with sovereignty over Babylonia, and he assumed the title of "King of the land of the Amorites." So too did his great-grandson, Ammi-ditana. Two generations later, with Samas-ditana the First dynasty of Babylon came to an end. It had made Babylon the capital of the country—a position which it never subsequently lost. It had raised Bel-Merodach, the god of Babylon, to the head of the pantheon, and it had lasted for 304 years. It was followed by a Sumerian dynasty from the south, which governed the country for 368 years, but of which we know little

BABYLONIA AND ASSYRIA 215

more than the names of the kings composing it and the length of their several reigns.

It fell before the avalanche of an invasion from the mountains of Elam. The Kassites poured into the Babylonian plain, and Kassite kings ruled at Babylon for 576 years and a half. During their domination the map of western Asia underwent a change. The Kassite conquest destroyed the Babylonian empire; Canaan was lost to it for ever, and eventually became a province of Egypt. The high-priests of Assur, now Kaleh Sherghat, near the confluence of the Tigris and Lower Zab, made themselves independent and founded the kingdom of Assyria, which soon extended northward into the angle formed by the Tigris and Upper Zab, where the cities of Nineveh and Calah afterwards arose. The whole country had previously been included by the Babylonians in Gutium or Kurdistan.

The population of Assyria seems to have been more purely Semitic than that of Babylonia. Such at least was the case with the ruling classes. It was a population of free peasants, of soldiers, and of traders. Its culture was derived from Babylonia; even its gods, with the exception of Assur, were of Babylonian origin. We look in vain among the Assyrians for the peace-loving tendencies of the Babylonians; they were, on the contrary, the Romans of the East. They were great in war, and in the time of the Second Assyrian empire great also in law and administration. But they were not a literary people; education among them was confined to the scribes and officials, rather than generally spread as in Babylonia. War and commerce were their two trades.

The Kassite conquerors of Babylonia soon submitted to the influences of Babylonian civilisation. Like the Hyksos in Egypt, they adopted the manners and customs, the writing and language, of the conquered people, sometimes even their names. The army, however, continued to be mainly composed of Kassite troops, and the native Babylonians began to forget the art of fighting. The old claims to sovereignty in the west, however, were never resigned; but the Kassite kings had to content themselves with intriguing against the Egyptian government in Palestine, either with disaffected Canaanites, or with the Hittites and Mitannians, while at the same time they professed to be the firm friends of the Egyptian Pharaoh. Burna-buryas in B.C. 1400 writes affectionately to his "brother" of Egypt, begging for some of the gold which in Egypt he declares is as abundant 'as the dust," and which he needs for his buildings at home. He tells the Egyptian king how his father Kuri-galzu had refused to listen to the Canaanites when they had offered to betray their country to him, and he calls Khu-n-Aten to account for treating the Assyrians as an independent nation and not as the vassals of Babylonia.

BABYLONIA AND ASSYRIA 217

The Assyrians, however, did not take the same view as the Babylonian king. They had been steadily growing in power, and had intermarried into the royal family of Babylonia. Assur-yuballidh, one of whose letters to the Pharaoh has been found at Tel el-Amarna, had married his daughter to the uncle and predecessor of Burna-buryas, and his grandson became king of Babylon. A revolt on the part of the Kassite troops gave the Assyrians an excuse for interfering in the affairs of Babylonia, and from this time forward their eyes were turned covetously towards the kingdom of the south.

As Assyria grew stronger, Babylonia became weaker. Calah, now *Nimrud*, was founded about B.C. 1300 by Shalmaneser I., and his son and successor Tiglath-Ninip threw off all disguise and marched boldly into Babylonia in the fifth year of his reign. Babylon was taken, the treasures of its temple sent to Assur, and Assyrian governors set over the country, while a special seal was made for the use of the conqueror. For seven years the Assyrian domination lasted. Then Tiglath-Ninip was driven back to Assyria, where he was imprisoned and murdered by his son, and the old line of Kassite princes was restored in the person of Rimmon-sum-uzur. But it continued only four reigns longer. A new dynasty from the town of Isin seized the throne, and ruled for 132 years and six months.

It was while this dynasty was reigning that a fresh line of energetic monarchs mounted the Assyrian throne. Rimmon-nirari I., the father of Shalmaneser I. (B.C. 1330–1300) had already extended the frontiers of Assyria to the Khabur in the west and the Kurdish mountains in the north, and his son settled an Assyrian colony at the head-waters of the Tigris, which served to garrison the country. But after the successful revolt of the Babylonians against Tiglath-Ninip the Assyrian power decayed. More than a century later Assur-ris-isi entered again on a career of conquest and reduced the Kurds to obedience.

His son, Tiglath-pileser I., was one of the great conquerors of history. He carried his arms far and wide. Kurdistan and Armenia, Mesopotamia and Comagênê, were all alike overrun by his armies in campaign after campaign. The Hittites paid tribute, as also did Phœnicia, where he sailed on the Mediterranean in a ship of Arvad and killed a dolphin in its waters. The Pharaoh of Egypt, alarmed at the approach of so formidable an invader, sent him presents, which included a crocodile and a hippopotamus, and on the eastern bank of the Euphrates, near Carchemish and Pethor, he hunted wild elephants, as Thothmes III. had done before him. His son still claimed supremacy in the west, as is shown by the fact that he erected statues in "the land of the Amorites." But the energy of the dynasty was now exhausted, and Assyria for a time passed under eclipse. This was the period when David established his empire; there was no other great power to oppose him in the Oriental world, and it seemed as if Israel was about to take the place that had once been filled by Egypt and Babylon. But the opportunity was lost; the murder of Joab and the unwarlike character of Solomon effectually checked all dreams of conquest, and Israel fell back into two petty states.

The military revival of Assyria was as sudden as had been its decline. In B.C. 885, Assur-nazir-pal II. ascended the throne. His reign of twenty-five years was passed in constant campaigns, in ferocious massacres, and the burning of towns. In both his inscriptions and his sculptures he seems to gloat over the tortures he inflicted on the defeated foe. Year after year his armies marched out of Nineveh to slaughter and destroy, and to bring back with them innumerable captives and vast amounts of spoil. Western Asia was overrun, tribute was received from the Hittites and from Phœnicia, and Armenia was devastated by the Assyrian forces as far north as Lake Van. The policy of Assur-nazir-pal was continued by his son and successor Shalmaneser II., with less ferocity, but with more purpose (B.C. 860-825). Assyria became dominant in Asia; its empire stretched from Media on the east to the Mediterranean on the west. But it was an empire which was without organisation or permanency. Every year a new campaign was needed to suppress the revolts which broke out as soon as the Assyrian army was out of sight, or to supply the treasury with fresh spoil. The campaigns were in most cases raids rather than the instruments of deliberately planned conquest. Hence it was that the Assyrian monarch found himself checked in the west by the petty kings of Damascus and the neighbouring states. Ben-Hadad and Hazael, it is true, were beaten again and again along with their allies, while Omri of Israel offered tribute to the invader, like the rich cities of Phœnicia; but Damascus remained untaken and its people unsubdued.

The war with Assyria, however, saved Israel from being swallowed up by its Syrian neighbour. Hazael's strength was exhausted in struggling for his own existence; he had none left for the conquest of Samaria. Shalmaneser himself, towards the end of his life, was no longer in a position to attack others. A great revolt broke out against him, headed by his son Assur-dain-pal, the Sardanapallos of the Greeks, who established himself at Nineveh, and there reigned as rival king for about seven years. His brother Samas-Rimmon, who had remained faithful to his father, at last succeeded in putting down the rebellion. Nineveh was taken, and its defenders slain. Henceforth Samas-Rimmon reigned with an undisputed title.

BABYLONIA AND ASSYRIA 221

But Assyria was long in recovering from the effects of the revolt, which had shaken her to the foundations. The dynasty itself never recovered. Samas-Rimmon, indeed, at the head of the army which had overcome his brother, continued the military policy of his predecessors; the tribes of Media and southern Armenia were defeated, and campaigns were carried on against Babylonia, the strength of which was now completely broken. In B.C. 812 Babylon was taken, but two years later Samas-Rimmon himself died, and was succeeded by his son Rimmon-nirari III. His reign was passed in constant warfare on the frontiers of the empire, and in B.C. 804 Damascus was surrendered to him by its king Mariha, who became an Assyrian tributary. In the following year a pestilence broke out, and when his successor, Shalmaneser III., mounted the throne in B.C. 781, he found himself confronted by a new and formidable power, that of Ararat or Van. The eastern and northern possessions of Assyria were taken from her, and the monarchy fell rapidly into decay. In B.C. 763 an eclipse of the sun took place on the 15th of June, and was the signal for the outbreak of a revolt in Assur, the ancient capital of the kingdom. It spread rapidly to other parts of the empire, and though for a time the government held its own against the rebels, the end came in B.C. 745. Assur-nirari, the last of the old dynasty, died or was put to death, and Pulu or Pul, one of his generals, was proclaimed king on the 13th of Iyyar or April under the name of Tiglath-pileser III.

Tiglath-pileser III. was the founder of the Second Assyrian empire, which was based on a wholly different principle from that of the first. Occupation and not plunder was the object of its wars. The ancient empire of Babylonia in western Asia was to be restored, and the commerce of the Mediterranean to be diverted into Assyrian hands. The campaigns of Tiglath-pileser and his successors were thus carried on in accordance with a deliberate line of policy. They aimed at the conquest of the whole civilised world, and the building up of a great organisation of which Nineveh and its ruler were the head. It was a new principle and a new idea. And measures were at once adopted to realise it.

The army was made an irresistible engine of attack. Its training, discipline, and arms were such as the world had never seen before. And the army was followed by a body of administrators. The conquered population was transported elsewhere or else deprived of its leaders, and Assyrian colonies and garrisons were planted in its place. The administration was intrusted to a vast bureaucracy, at the head of which stood the king. He appointed the satraps who governed the provinces, and were responsible for the taxes and tribute, as well as for the maintenance of order. The bureaucracy was partly military, partly civil, the two elements acting as a check one upon the other.

But it was necessary that Ararat should be crushed before the plans of the new monarch could be carried out. The strength of the army was first tested in campaigns against Babylonia and the Medes, and then Tiglath-pileser marched against the confederated forces of the Armenian king. A league had been formed among the princes of northern Syria in connection with that of the Armenians, but the Assyrian king annihilated the army of Ararat in Comagênê, and then proceeded to besiege Arpad. Arpad surrendered after a blockade of three years; Hamath, which had been assisted by Azariah of Judah, was reduced into an Assyrian province; and a court was held, at which the sovereigns of the west paid homage and tribute to the conqueror (B.C. 738). Among these were Rezon of Damascus and Menahem of Samaria. Tiglath-pileser was still known in Palestine under his original name of Pul, and the tribute of Menahem is accordingly described by the Israelitish chronicler as having been given to Pul.

The Assyrian king was now free to turn the full strength of his forces against Ararat. The country was ravaged up to the very gates of its capital, the modern Van, and only the strong walls of the city kept the invader out of it. The Assyrian army next moved eastward to the southern shores of the Caspian, striking terror into the Kurdish and Median tribes, and so securing the lowlands of Assyria from their raids. The affairs of Syria next claimed the attention of the conqueror. Rezon and Pekah, the new king of Samaria, had attempted to form a league against Assyria; and, with this end in view, determined to replace Ahaz, the youthful king of Judah, by a creature of their own. Ahaz turned in his extremity to Assyrian help, and Tiglath-pileser seized the opportunity of accepting the vassalage of Judah, with its strong fortress of Jerusalem, and at the same time of overthrowing both Damascus and Samaria. Rezon was closely besieged in his capital, while the rest of the Assyrian army was employed in overrunning Samaria, Ammon, Moab, and the Philistines (B.C. 734). Pekah was put to death, and Hosea appointed by the Assyrians in his place. After a siege of two years, Damascus fell in B.C. 732, Rezon was slain, and his kingdom placed under an Assyrian satrap. Meanwhile Tyre was compelled to purchase peace by an indemnity of 150 talents.

Syria was now at the feet of Nineveh. A great gathering of the western kings took place at Damascus, where Tiglath-pileser held his court after the capture of the city, and the list of those who came to do homage to him includes Jehoahaz or Ahaz of Judah, and the kings of Ammon, Moab, Edom, and Hamath. Hosea, it would seem, was not yet on the Israelitish throne.

BABYLONIA AND ASSYRIA

The old empire of Babylonia was thus restored as far as the Mediterranean. All that remained was for the Assyrian usurper to legitimise his title by occupying Babylon itself, and there receiving the crown of Asia. In B.C. 731, accordingly, he found a pretext for invading Babylonia and seizing the holy city of western Asia. Two years later he "took the hands" of Bel-Merodach, and was thereby adopted by the god as his own son. But he did not live long to enjoy the fruits of his victories. He died December B.C. 727, and another usurper, Ululâ, possessed himself of the throne, and assumed the name of Shalmaneser IV. His reign, however, was short. He died while besieging Samaria, which had revolted after the death of its conqueror, and in December B.C. 722, a third general seized the vacant crown. He took the name of the old Babylonian monarch, Sargon, and the court chroniclers of after-days discovered that he was a descendant of the legendary kings of Assyria. His first achievement was the capture of Samaria. Little spoil, however, was found in the half-ruined city; and the upper classes, who were responsible for the rebellion, were carried into captivity to the number of 27,280 persons. The city itself was placed under an Assyrian governor.

Sargon found that the empire of Tiglath-pileser had in great measure to be re-conquered. Neither Tiglath-pileser nor his successor had been able to leave the throne to their children, and the conquered provinces had taken advantage of the troubles consequent on their deaths to revolt. Babylonia had been lost. Merodach-baladan, the Chaldæan prince, had emerged from the marshes of the south and occupied Babylon, where he was proclaimed king immediately after Shalmaneser's death. For twelve years he reigned there, with the help of the Elamites, and one of the first tasks of Sargon was to drive the latter from the Assyrian borders. Sargon had next to suppress a revolt in Hamath, as well as an invasion of Palestine by the Egyptians. The Egyptian army, however, was defeated at Raphia, and the Philistines with whom it was in alliance returned to their allegiance to the Assyrian king.

Now came, however, a more serious struggle. Ararat had recovered from the blow it had received at the hands of Tiglath-pileser, and had organised a general confederacy of the northern nations against their dangerous neighbour. For six years the struggle continued. But it ended in victory for the Assyrians. Carchemish, the Hittite stronghold which commanded the road across the Euphrates, was taken in B.C. 717, and the way lay open to the west. The barrier that had existed for seven centuries between the Semites of the east and west was removed, and the last relic of the Hittite conquests in Syria passed away. In the following year Sargon overran the territories of

BABYLONIA AND ASSYRIA 227

the Minni between Ararat and Lake Urumiyeh, and two years later the northern confederacy was utterly crushed. The fortress of Muzazir, under Mount Rowandiz, was added to the Assyrian dominions, its gods were carried into captivity, and the King of Ararat committed suicide in despair. From henceforward Assyria had nothing to fear on the side of the north. The turn of the Medes came next. They were compelled to acknowledge the supremacy of Nineveh; so also was the kingdom of Ellipi, the later Ekbatana. Sargon could now turn his attention to Babylonia.

Merodach-baladan had foreseen the coming storm, and had done his best to secure allies. An alliance was made with the Elamites, who were alarmed at the conquest of Ellipi; and ambassadors were sent to Palestine (in B.C. 711), there to arrange a general rising of the population, simultaneously with the outbreak of war between Sargon and the Babylonian king. But before the confederates were ready to move, Sargon had fallen upon them separately. Ashdod, the centre of the revolt in the west, was invested and taken by the Turtannu or commander-in-chief; its ruler, a certain "Greek," who had been raised to power by the anti-Assyrian party, fled to the Arabian desert in the vain hope of saving his life, and Judah, Moab, and Edom were forced to renew their tribute. The Egyptians, who had promised to assist the rebels in Palestine, prudently retired, and the Assyrian yoke was fixed more firmly than ever upon the nations of Syria. Merodach-baladan was left to face his foe alone. In B.C. 709 he was driven out of Babylon, and forced to take refuge in his ancestral kingdom in the marshes. Sargon entered Babylon in triumph, and "took the hands of Bel." His title to rule was acknowledged by the god and the priesthood, and an Assyrian was once more the lord of western Asia.

Four years later the old warrior was murdered by a soldier, and on the 12th of Ab, or July, his son Sennacherib was proclaimed king. Sennacherib was a different man from his father. Sargon had been an able and energetic general, rough perhaps and uncultured, but vigorous and determined. His son was weak and boastful, and under him the newly-formed Assyrian empire met with its first check. It is significant that the Babylonian priests never acknowledged him as the successor of their ancient kings; he revenged himself by razing the city and sanctuary of Bel to the ground.

Merodach-baladan re-entered Babylon immediately after the death of Sargon in B.C. 705, but he was soon driven back to his retreat in the Chaldæan marshes, and an Assyrian named Bel-ibni was appointed king in his place. The next campaign of importance undertaken by Sennacherib was in B.C. 701. Palestine had revolted, under the leadership of Hezekiah of Judah.

BABYLONIA AND ASSYRIA 229

The full strength of the Assyrian army was accordingly hurled against it. The King of Sidon fled to Cyprus, and Phœnicia, Ammon, Moab, and Edom hastened to submit to their dangerous foe. Hezekiah and his Philistine vassals alone ventured to resist.

The Philistines, however, were soon subdued. A new king was appointed over Ashkelon, and Hezekiah was compelled to restore to Ekron its former prince, whom he had imprisoned in Jerusalem on account of his loyalty to Assyria. The priests and nobles of Ekron, who had given him up to Hezekiah, were ruthlessly impaled. Meanwhile Tirhakah, the Ethiopian king of Egypt, on whose help Hezekiah had relied, was marching to the assistance of his ally. Sennacherib met him at Eltekeh, and there the combined forces of the Egyptians and Arabians were defeated and compelled to retreat. Hezekiah now endeavoured to make peace by the offer of rich and numerous presents, including thirty talents of gold and 800 of silver. But nothing short of the death of the Jewish king and the transportation of his people would content the invader. Hezekiah accordingly shut himself up within the strong walls of his capital, while the Assyrians ravaged the rest of the country and prepared to besiege Jerusalem. The cities and villages were destroyed, and 200,150 persons were led away into captivity. But at this moment a catastrophe befell the Assyrians which saved Hezekiah and "the remnant" of Israel.

The angel of death smote the Assyrian army, and it was decimated by a sudden pestilence. Sennacherib fled from the plague-stricken camp, carrying with him his spoil and captives, and the scanty relics of his troops. It was the last time he marched to the west, and his rebellious vassal remained unpunished.

In the following year troubles in Babylonia called him to the south. Merodach-baladan was hunted out of the marshes, and fled with his subjects across the Persian Gulf to the opposite coast of Elam, while a son of Sennacherib was made king of Babylon. But his reign did not last long. Six years later he was carried off to Elam, and a new king of native origin, Nergal-yusezib by name, was proclaimed by the Elamites. This was in return for an attack made by Sennacherib upon the Chaldæan colony in Elam, where the followers of Merodach-baladan had found a refuge. Sennacherib had caused ships to be built at Nineveh by Phœnician workmen, and had manned them with Tyrian, Sidonian, and Ionian sailors who were prisoners of war. The ships sailed down to the Tigris and across the gulf, and then fell unexpectedly upon the Chaldæans, burning their settlement, and carrying away all who had escaped massacre.

Nergal-yusezib had reigned only one year when he was defeated and captured in battle by the Assyrians; but the Elamites were still predominant in Babylonia, and another Babylonian, Musezib-Merodach, was set

BABYLONIA AND ASSYRIA 231

upon the throne of the distracted country (B.C. 693). In B.C. 691 Sennacherib once more entered it, with an overwhelming army, determined to crush all opposition. But the battle of Khalulê, fought between the Assyrians on the one side, and the combined Babylonians and Elamites on the other, led to no definite result. Sennacherib, indeed, claimed the victory, but so he had also done in the case of the campaign against Hezekiah. Two years more were needed before the Babylonians at last yielded to the superior forces of their enemy. In B.C. 689 Babylon was taken by storm, and a savage vengeance wreaked upon it. The sacred city of western Asia was levelled with the dust, the temple of Bel himself was not spared, and the Arakhtu canal which flowed past it was choked with ruins. The Babylonian chronicler tells us that for eight years there were "no kings;" the image of Bel-Merodach had been cast to the ground by the sacrilegious conqueror, and there was none who could legitimise his right to rule.

On the 20th of Tebet, or December, B.C. 681, Sennacherib was murdered by his two sons, and the Babylonians saw in the deed the punishment of his crimes. His favourite son, Esar-haddon, was at the time commanding the Assyrian army in a war against Erimenas of Ararat. As soon as the news of the murder reached him, he determined to dispute the crown with his brothers, and accordingly marched against them. They were in no position to resist him, and after holding Nineveh for forty-two days, fled to the court of the Armenian king. Esar-haddon followed, and a battle fought near Malatiyeh, on the 12th of Iyyar, or April, B.C. 680, decided the fate of the empire. The veterans of Esar-haddon utterly defeated the conspirators and their Armenian allies, and at the close of the day he was saluted as king. He then returned to Nineveh, and on the 8th of Sivan, or May, formally ascended the throne.

Esar-haddon proved himself to be not only one of the best generals Assyria ever produced, but a great administrator as well. He endeavoured to cement his empire together by a policy of reconciliation, and one of his first actions was to rebuild Babylon, to bring back to it its gods and people, and to make it one of the royal residences. Bel acknowledged him as his adopted son, and for twelve years Esar-haddon ruled over western Asia by right divine as well as by the right of conquest.

But a terrible danger menaced Assyria and the rest of the civilised Oriental world at the very beginning of his reign. Sennacherib's conquest of Ellipi, and the wars against Ararat and Minni, had weakened the barriers which protected the Assyrian empire from the incursions of the barbarians of the north. The Gimirrâ or Kimmerians, the Gomer of the Old Testament, driven by the Scyths from their seats on the Dniester

BABYLONIA AND ASSYRIA   233

and the Sea of Azof, suddenly appeared on the horizon of western Asia. Swarming through the territories of the Minni to the east of Ararat, they swooped down upon the Assyrian frontier, along with other northern nations from Media, Sepharad, and Ashchenaz. While a body of Kimmerians under Teuspa marched westward, the rest of the allies, under Kastarit or Kyaxares of Karu-Kassi, attacked the fortresses which defended Assyria on the north-east. At Nineveh all was consternation, and public prayers, accompanied by fasting, were ordered to be offered up for a hundred days and nights to the Sun-god, that he might "forgive the sin" of his people, and avert the dangers that threatened them. The prayers were heard, and the invaders were driven into Ellipi. Then Esar-haddon marched against Teuspa, and forced him to turn from Assyria. The Kimmerians made their way instead into Asia Minor, where they sacked the Greek and Phrygian cities, and overran Lydia.

The northern and eastern boundaries of the empire were at length secured. It was now necessary to punish the Arab tribes who had taken advantage of the Kimmerian invasion to harass the empire on the south. Esar-haddon accordingly marched into the very heart of the Arabian desert—a military achievement of the first rank, the memory of which was not forgotten for years. The empire at last was secure.

The Assyrian king was now free to complete the

policy of Tiglath-pileser by conquering Egypt. Palestine was no longer a source of trouble. Judah had returned to its vassalage to Assyria, and the abortive attempts of Sidon and Jerusalem to rebel had been easily suppressed. True to his policy of conciliation, Esar-haddon had dealt leniently with Manasseh of Judah. He had been brought in fetters before his lord at Babylon, and there pardoned and restored to his kingdom. It was a lesson which neither he nor his successors forgot, like the similar lesson impressed a few years later upon the Egyptian prince Necho.

The Assyrian conquest of Egypt has been already described. The first campaign of Esar-haddon against it was undertaken in B.C. 674; and it was while on the march to put down a revolt in B.C. 668 that he fell ill and died, on the 10th of Marchesvan, or October. The empire was divided between his two sons. Assur-bani-pal had already been named as his successor, and now took Assyria, while Saul-sum-yukin became king of Babylonia, subject, however, to his brother at Nineveh. It was an attempt to flatter the Babylonians by giving them a king of their own, while at the same time keeping the supreme power in Assyrian hands.

The first few years of Assur-bani-pal's reign were spent in tranquillising Egypt by means of the sword, in suppressing insurrections, and in expelling Ethiopian invaders. After the destruction of Thebes in B.C. 661 the country sullenly submitted to the foreign rule;

its strength was exhausted, and its leaders and priesthood were scattered and bankrupt. Elam was now almost the only civilised kingdom of western Asia which remained independent. It was, moreover, a perpetual thorn in the side of the Assyrians. It was always ready to give the same help to the disaffected in Babylonia that Egypt was to the rebels in Palestine, with the difference that whereas the Egyptians were an unwarlike race, the Elamites were a nation of warriors. Assur-bani-pal was not a soldier himself, and he would have preferred remaining at peace with his warlike neighbour. But Elamite raids made this impossible, and the constant civil wars in Elam resulting from disputed successions to the throne afforded pretexts and favourable opportunities for invading it. The Elamites, however, defended themselves bravely, and it was only after a struggle of many years, when their cities had fallen one by one, and Shushan, the capital, was itself destroyed, that Elam became an Assyrian province. The conquerors, however, found it a profitless desert, wasted by fire and sword, and in the struggle to possess it their own resources had been drained and well-nigh exhausted.

The second Assyrian empire was now at the zenith of its power. Ambassadors came from Ararat and from Gyges of Lydia to offer homage, and to ask the help of the great king against the Kimmerian and Scythian hordes. His fame spread to Europe; the whole of the civilised world acknowledged his supremacy.

But the image was one which had feet of clay. The empire had been won by the sword, and the sword alone kept it together. Suddenly a revolt broke out which shook it to its foundations. Babylonia took the lead; the other subject nations followed in its train.

Saul-suma-yukin had become naturalised in Babylonia. The experiment of appointing an Assyrian prince as viceroy had failed; he had identified himself with his subjects, and like them dreamed of independence. He adopted the style and titles of the ancient Babylonian monarchs; even the Sumerian language was revived in public documents, and the son of Esarhaddon put himself at the head of a national movement. The Assyrian supremacy was rejected, and once more Babylon was free.

The revolt lasted for some years. When it began we do not know; but it was not till B.C. 648 that it was finally suppressed, and Saul-suma-yukin put to death after a reign of twenty years. Babylon had been closely invested, and was at last starved into surrender. But, taught by the experience of the past, Assur-banipal did not treat it severely. The leaders of the revolt, it is true, were punished, but the city and people were spared, and its shrines, like those of Kutha and Sippara, were purified, while penitential psalms were sung to appease the angry deities, and the daily sacrifices which had been interrupted were restored. A certain Kandalanu was made viceroy, perhaps with the title of king.

Chastisement was now taken upon the Arabian tribes who had joined in the revolt. But Egypt was lost to the empire for ever. Psammetikhos had seized the opportunity of shaking off the yoke of the foreigner, and with the help of the troops sent by Gyges from Lydia, had driven out the Assyrian garrisons and overcome his brother satraps.

Assur-bani-pal was in no position to punish him. The war with Elam and the revolt of Babylonia had drained the country of its fighting men and the treasury of its resources. And a new and formidable enemy had appeared on the scene. The Scyths had followed closely on the footsteps of the Kimmerians, and were now pouring into Asia like locusts, and ravaging everything in their path. The earlier chapters of Jeremiah are darkened by the horrors of the Scythian invasion of Palestine, and Assur-bani-pal refers with a sigh of relief to the death of that "limb of Satan," the Scythian king Tugdamme or Lygdamis. This seems to have happened in Cilicia, and Assyria was allowed a short interval of rest.

Assur-bani-pal's victories were gained by his generals. He himself never appears to have taken the field in person. His tastes were literary, his habits luxurious. He was by far the most munificent patron of learning

Assyria ever produced; in fact, he stands alone in this respect among Assyrian kings. The library of Nineveh was increased tenfold by his patronage and exertions; literary works were brought from Babylonia, and a large staff of scribes was kept busily employed in copying and re-editing them. Unfortunately, the superstition of the monarch led him to collect more especially books upon omens and dreams, and astrological treatises, but other works were not overlooked, and we owe to him a large number of the syllabaries and lists of words in which the cuneiform characters and the Assyrian vocabulary are explained.

When Assur-bani-pal died the doom of the Assyrian empire had already been pronounced. The authority of his two successors, Assur-etil-ilani-yukin and Sin-sar-iskun, or Saracos, was still acknowledged both in Syria and in Babylonia, where Kandalanu had been succeeded as viceroy by Nabopolassar. One of the contract-tablets from the north of Babylonia is dated as late as the seventh year of Sin-sar-iskun. But not long after this the Babylonian viceroy revolted against his sovereign, and with the help of the Scythian king, who had established himself at Ekbatana, defeated the Assyrian forces and laid siege to Nineveh. The siege ended in the capture and destruction of the city, the death of its king, and the overthrow of his empire. In B.C. 606 the desolator of the nations was itself laid desolate, and its site has never been inhabited again.

Nabopolassar entered upon the heritage of Assyria. It has been supposed that he was a Chaldæan like Merodach-baladan; whether this be so or not, he was hailed by the Babylonians as a representative of their ancient kings. The Assyrian empire had become the prey of the first-comer. Elam had been occupied by the Persians, the Scyths, whom classical writers have confounded with the Medes, had overrun and ravaged Assyria and Mesopotamia, while Palestine and Syria had fallen to the share of Egypt. But once established on the Babylonian throne, Nabopolassar set about the work of re-organising western Asia, and the military abilities of his son Nebuchadrezzar enabled him to carry out his purpose. The marriage of Nebuchadrezzar to the daughter of the Scythian monarch opened the road through Mesopotamia to the Babylonian armies; the Egyptians were defeated at Carchemish in B.C. 604, and driven back to their own land. From Gaza to the mouth of the Euphrates, western Asia again obeyed the rule of a Babylonian king.

The death of Nabopolassar recalled Nebuchadrezzar to Babylon, where he assumed the crown. But the Egyptians still continued to intrigue in Palestine, and the Jewish princes listened to their counsels. Twice had Nebuchadrezzar to occupy Jerusalem and carry the plotters into captivity. In B.C. 598 Jehoiachin and a large number of the upper classes were carried into exile; in B.C. 588 Jerusalem was taken after a long siege, its temple and walls razed to the ground, and its inhabitants transported to Babylonia. The fortress-capital could no longer shelter or tempt the Egyptian foes of the Babylonian empire.

The turn of Tyre came next. For thirteen years it was patiently blockaded, and in B.C. 573 it passed with its fleet into Nebuchadrezzar's hands. Five years later the Babylonian army marched into Egypt, the Pharaoh Amasis was defeated, and the eastern part of the Delta overrun. But Nebuchadrezzar did not push his advantage any further; he was content with impressing upon the Egyptians a sense of his power, and with fixing the boundaries of his empire at the southern confines of Palestine.

His heart was in Babylonia rather than in the conquests he had made. The wealth he had acquired by them was devoted to the restoration of the temples and cities of his country, and, above all, to making Babylon one of the wonders of the world. The temples of Merodach and Nebo were rebuilt with lavish magnificence, the city was surrounded with impregnable fortifications, a sumptuous palace was erected for the king, and the bed of the Euphrates was lined with brick and furnished with quays. Gardens were planted on the top of arched terraces, and the whole eastern world poured out its treasures at the feet of "the great king." His inscriptions, however, breathe a singular spirit of humility and piety, and we can understand from them the friendship that existed between the prophet Jeremiah and himself. All he had done is ascribed to Bel-Merodach, whose creation he was and who had given him the sovereignty over mankind.

He was succeeded in B.C. 562 by his son Evil-Merodach, who had a short and inglorious reign of only two years. Then the throne was usurped by Nergal-sharezer, who had married a daughter of Nebuchadrezzar, and was in high favour with the priests. He died in B.C. 556, leaving a child, whom the priestly chroniclers accuse of impiety towards the gods, and who was murdered three months after his accession. Then Nabu-nahid or Nabonidos, the son of Nabu-balasu-iqbi, another nominee of the priesthood, was placed on the throne. He was unrelated to the royal family, but proved to be a man of some energy and a zealous antiquarian. He caused excavations to be made in the various temples of Babylonia, in order to discover the memorial-stones of their founders and verify the history of them that had been handed down. But he offended local interests by endeavouring to centralise the religious worship of the country at Babylon, in the sanctuary of Bel-Merodach, as Hezekiah had done in the case of Judah. The images of the gods were removed from the shrines in which they had stood from time immemorial, and the local priesthoods attached to them were absorbed in that of the capital. The result was the rise of a powerful party opposed to the king, and a spirit of disaffection which the gifts showered upon the temples of Babylon and a few other large cities were unable to allay. The standing army, however, under the command of the king's son, Belshazzar, prevented this spirit from showing itself in action.

But a new power was growing steadily in the East. The larger part of Elam, which went by the name of Anzan, had been seized by the Persians in the closing days of the Assyrian empire, and a line of kings of Persian origin had taken the place of the old sovereigns of Shushan. Cyrus II., who was still but a youth, was now on the throne of Anzan, and, like his predecessors, acknowledged as his liege-lord the Scythian king of Ekbatana, Istuvegu or Astyages. His first act was to defeat and dethrone his suzerain, in B.C. 549, and so make himself master of Media. A year or two later he obtained possession of Persia, and a war with Lydia in B.C. 545 led to the conquest of Asia Minor. Nabonidos had doubtless looked on with satisfaction while the Scythian power was being overthrown, and had taken advantage of its fall to rebuild the temple of the Moon-god at Harran, which had been destroyed by the Scythians fifty-four years before. But his eyes were opened by the conquest of his ally the King of Lydia, and he accordingly began to prepare for a war which he saw was inevitable. The camp was fixed near Sippara, towards the northern boundary of Babylonia, and every

BABYLONIA AND ASSYRIA 243

effort was made to put the country into a state of defence.

Cyrus, however, was assisted by the disaffected party in Babylonia itself, amongst whose members must doubtless be included the Jewish exiles. In B.C. 538 a revolt broke out in the south, in the old district of the Chaldæans, and Cyrus took advantage of it to march into the country. The Babylonian army moved northward to meet him, but was utterly defeated and dispersed at Opis in the beginning of Tammuz, or June, and a few days later Sippara surrendered to the conqueror. Gobryas, the governor of Kurdistan, was then sent to Babylon, which also opened its gates "without fighting," and Nabonidos, who had concealed himself, was taken prisoner. The daily services in the temples as well as the ordinary business of the city proceeded as usual, and on the 3rd of Marchesvan Cyrus himself arrived and proclaimed a general amnesty, which was communicated by Gobryas to "all the province of Babylon," of which he had been made the prefect. Shortly afterwards, the wife—or, according to another reading, the son — of Nabonidos died; public lamentations were made for her, and Kambyses, the son of Cyrus, conducted the funeral in one of the Babylonian temples. Cyrus now took the title of "King of Babylon," and associated Kambyses with himself in the government. Conquest had proved his title to the crown, and the priests and god of Babylon hastened to confirm it.

Cyrus on his side claimed to be the legitimate descendant of the ancient Babylonian kings, a true representative of the ancient stock, who had avenged the injuries of Bel-Merodach and his brother-gods upon Nabonidos, and who professed to be their devoted worshipper. Offerings to ten times the usual amount were bestowed on the Babylonian temples, and the favour of the Babylonian priesthood was secured. The images which Nabonidos had sacrilegiously removed from their shrines were restored to their old homes, and the captive populations in Babylonia were allowed to return to their native soil. The policy of transportation had proved a failure; in time of invasion the exiles had been a source of danger to the government, and not of safety.

Each people was permitted to carry back with it its ancestral gods. The Jews alone had no images to take; the sacred vessels of the temple of Jerusalem were accordingly given to them. It was a faithful remnant that returned to the land of their fathers, consisting mostly of priests and Levites, determined henceforward to obey strictly the laws of their God, and full of gratitude to their deliverer. In Jerusalem Cyrus thus had a colony whose loyalty to himself and his successors could be trusted, and who would form, as it were, an outpost against attacks on the side of Egypt.

As long as Cyrus and his son Kambyses lived Baby-

BABYLONIA AND ASSYRIA 245

lonia also was tranquil. They flattered the religious and political prejudices of their Babylonian subjects, and the priesthood saw in them the successors of a Sargon of Akkad. But with the death of Kambyses came a change. The new rulers of the empire of Cyrus were Persians, proud of their nationality and zealous for their Zoroastrian faith. They had no reverence for Bel, no belief in the claim of Babylon to confer a title of legitimacy on the sovereign of western Asia. The Babylonian priesthood chafed, the Babylonian people broke into revolt. In October B.C. 521 a pretender appeared who took the name of Nebuchadrezzar II., and reigned for nearly a year. But after two defeats in the field, he was captured in Babylon by Darius and put to death in August 520. Once more, in B.C. 514, another revolt took place under a second pretender to the name of "Nebuchadrezzar the son of Nabonidos." The strong walls of Babylon resisted the Persian army for more than a year, and the city was at last taken by stratagem. The walls were partially destroyed, but this did not prevent a third rebellion in the reign of Xerxes, while the Persian monarch was absent in Greece. On this occasion, however, it was soon crushed, and Ê-Sagila, the temple of Bel, was laid in ruins. But a later generation restored once more the ancient sanctuary of Merodach, at all events in part, and services in honour of Bel continued to be held there down to the time when Babylon was superseded by the Greek town of Seleucia, and the city of Nebuchadrezzar became a waste of shapeless mounds.

Babylonian religion was a mixture of Sumerian and Semitic elements. The primitive Sumerian had believed in a sort of animism. Each object had its zi or "spirit," like men and beasts; the zi gave it its personality, and endowed it, as it were, with vital force. The zi corresponded with the ka or "double" of the Egyptians, which accompanied like a shadow all things in heaven and earth. The gods themselves had each his zi; it was this alone that made them permanent and personal. With such a form of religion there could be neither deities nor priests in the usual sense of the words. The place of the priest was taken by the sorcerer, who knew the spells that could avert the malevolence of the "spirits" or bring down their blessings upon mankind.

With the progress of civilisation, certain of the "spirits" emerged above the rest, and became veritable gods. The "spirit" of heaven became Ana of Erech, the Sky-god; the "spirit" of earth passed into El-lil of Nippur; and the "spirit" of the deep into Ea of Eridu. The change was hastened by contact with the Semite. The Semite brought with him a new religious conception. He believed in a god who revealed himself in the sun, and whom he addressed as Baal or "Lord." By the side of Baal stood his colourless reflection, the goddess Baalath, who owed her existence partly to the feminine gender possessed by the Semitic languages, partly to the analogy of the human family. But the Baalim were as multitudinous as their worshippers and the high-places whereon they were adored; there was little difficulty, therefore, in identifying the gods and "spirits" of Sumer with the local Baals of the Semitic creed.

El-lil became Bel of Nippur, Asari or Merodach Bel of Babylon. But in taking a Semitic form, the Sumerian divinities did not lose their old attributes. Bel of Nippur remained the lord of the ghost-world, Bel-Merodach the god who "raises the dead to life" and "does good to man." Moreover, in one important point the Semite borrowed from the Sumerian. The goddess Istar retained her independent position among the crowd of colourless female deities. Originally the "spirit" of the evening-star, she had become a goddess, and in the Sumerian world the goddess was the equal of the god. It is a proof of the influence of the Sumerian element in the Babylonian population, that this conception of the goddess was never forgotten in Babylonia; it was only when Babylonian culture was handed on to the Semitic nations of the west that Istar became either the male Atthar of southern Arabia and Moab, or the emasculated Ashtoreth of Canaan.

The official religion of Babylonia was thus the Baal-worship of the Semites engrafted on the animism of the Sumerians. It was further modified by the introduction of star-worship. How far this went back to a belief in the "spirits" of the stars, or whether it had a Semitic origin, we do not know; but it is significant that the cuneiform character which denotes "a god" is a picture of a star, and that the Babylonians were from the first a nation of star-gazers. In the astro-theology of a later date the gods of the pantheon were identified with the chief stars of the firmament, but the system was purely artificial, and must have been the invention of the priests.

The religion and deities of Babylonia were adopted by the Assyrians. But in Assyria they were always somewhat of an exotic, and even the learned class invoked Assur rather than the other gods. Assur was the personification of the old capital of the country and of the nation itself, and though the scribes found an etymology for the name in that of An-sar, the primæval god of Sumerian cosmogony, the fact was always remembered. Assur was purely Semitic in his attributes, and, like Yahveh of Israel or Chemosh of Moab, was wifeless and childless. It is true that a learned scribe now and then found a wife for him among the numerous divinities of the Babylonian cult, but the discovery was never accepted, and Assur for the mass of his worshippers remained single and alone. It was through trust in him that the Assyrian kings believed their victories were gained, and it was to punish those who disbelieved in him that their campaigns were undertaken.

In the worship of Assur, accordingly, a tendency to monotheism reveals itself. The tendency was even more pronounced in a certain literary school of thought in Babylonia. We have texts which resolve the deities of the popular faith into forms of one god; sometimes this is Anu of Erech, sometimes it is Merodach of Babylon.

Babylonian worship necessitated a large hierarchy of priests. At the head was the high-priest, who in early times possessed temporal power and in many states was the predecessor of the king. The king, in fact, inherited his priesthood from him, and was consequently qualified to perform priestly functions. Under the high-priest there were numerous classes of ministers of the gods, such as the "anointers," whose duty it was to anoint the holy images with oil, the ordinary "priests," the "seers," and the "prophets." The prophets enjoyed high consideration; they even accompanied the army to the field, and decided whether the campaign would result in victory or defeat. Quite apart from all these were the astrologers, who did not belong to the priesthood at all. On the contrary, they professed to be men of science, and the predictions of the future which they read in the stars were founded on the records and observations of former generations.

A chief part of the duty of the priests consisted in offering sacrifice and reciting the services. The sacrifices were of two kinds, as in the Jewish ritual. The same animals and the same fruits of the earth were offered by both Babylonians and Israelites, and in many cases the regulations relating to the sacrifices were similar. The services were elaborate, and the rubrics attached to the hymns and prayers which had to be recited are minute and complicated. The hymns had been formed into a sort of Bible, which had in time acquired a divine authority. So sacred were its words, that a single mispronunciation of them was sufficient to impair the efficacy of the service. Rules for their pronunciation were accordingly laid down, which were the more necessary as the hymns were in Sumerian. The dead language of Sumer had become sacred, like Latin in the Middle Ages, and each line of a hymn was provided with a translation in Semitic Babylonian.

In appearance, a Babylonian temple was not very unlike those of Canaan or of Solomon. The image of the god stood in the innermost shrine, the Holy of Holies, where also was the mercy-seat, whereon it was believed, as upon a throne, the deity was accustomed to descend at certain times of the year. In the little temple of Balawât, near Nineveh, discovered by Mr. Hormuzd Rassam, the mercy-seat was shaped like an ark, and contained two written tables of stone;

no statue of the god, however, seems in this instance to have stood beside it. In front of it was the altar, approached by steps.

In the court of the temple was a "sea" or "deep," like that which was made by Solomon. An early hymn which describes the construction of one of them, states that it was of bronze, and that it rested on the figures of twelve bronze oxen. It was intended for the ablutions of the priests and the vessels of the sanctuary, and was a representation of that primæval deep out of which it was believed that the world originated.

One peculiarity the Babylonian temples possessed which was not shared by those of the west. Each had its *ziggurat* or "tower," which served for the observation of the stars, and in the topmost storey of which was the altar of the god. It corresponded with the "high-place" of Canaan, where man imagined himself nearest to the gods of heaven. But in the flat plain of Babylonia it was needful that the high-place should be of artificial construction, and here accordingly they built the towers whose summits "reached to" the sky.

The temples and their ministers were supported partly by endowments, partly by voluntary gifts, sometimes called *kurbanni*, the Hebrew *korban*, partly by obligatory contributions, the most important of which was the *esrâ* or "tithe." Besides the fixed festivals, which were enumerated in the calendar, special days of thanksgiving or humiliation were appointed from time to time. There was also a weekly Sabattu or "Sabbath," on the 1st, 7th, 14th, 21st, and 28th days of the month, as well as on the 19th, the last day of the seventh week from the beginning of the previous month. The Sabbath is described as "a day of rest for the heart," and all work upon it was forbidden. The king was not allowed to change his dress, to ride in his chariot, or even to take medicine, while the prophet himself was forbidden to utter his prophecies.

The mass of the people looked forward to a dreary existence beyond the grave. The shades of the dead flitted like bats in the darkness of the under-world, hungry and cold, while the ghosts of the heroes of the past sat beside them on their shadowy thrones, and Allat, the mistress of Hades, presided over the warders of its seven gates. The Sumerians had called it "the land whence none return," though in the theology of Eridu and Babylon Asari or Merodach was already a god who, through the wisdom of his father Ea, "restored the dead to life." But as the centuries passed, new and less gloomy ideas grew up in regard to the future life. In a prayer for the Assyrian king the writer asks that he may enjoy an endless existence hereafter in "the land of the silver sky," and the realms of the gods of light had been peopled with the heroes of Babylonian literature at an early date.

BABYLONIA AND ASSYRIA 253

The belief in Hades went back to those primitive ages when the Sumerians of Eridu conceived of the earth as floating on the deep, which surrounded it as a snake with its coils, while the sky covered it above like an extinguisher, and was supported on the peak of "the mountain of the world," where the gods had their abode. This primitive cosmological conception underwent changes in the course of time, but the underlying idea of an abyss of waters out of which all things were shaped remained to the end. The Chaldæan Epic of the Creation declares that "in the beginning," "the chaos of the deep" had been the "mother" of both heaven and earth, out of whom first came the primæval deities Lakhmu and Lakhamu, and then An-sar and Ki-sar, the upper and lower firmament. Long ages had to elapse before the Trinity of the later theology—Anu, Ea, and Bel—were born of these, and all things made ready for the genesis of the present world. Merodach, the champion of the gods of light and law, had first to do battle with Tiamat, "the dragon" of "the deep," and her allies of darkness and disorder. He had proved his powers by creating and annihilating by means of his "word" alone, and the conflict which he waged ended in the destruction of the enemy. The body of Tiamat was torn asunder and transformed into the heaven and earth, her springs of water were placed under control, and the forces of anarchy and chaos were banished from the universe. Then followed the creation of the existing order of things. The sun and moon and stars were fixed in their places, and laws given to them which they should never transgress, plants and animals were created, and finally man.

Babylonian literature went back to a remote date. The age of Sargon of Akkad was already a highly literary one, and the library he founded at Akkad contained works which continued to be re-edited down to the latest days of Babylonian literature. Every great city had its library, which was open to every reader, and where the books were carefully catalogued and arranged on shelves. Here too were kept the public records, as well as title-deeds, law-cases, and other documents belonging to private individuals. The office of librarian was held in honour, and was not unfrequently occupied by one of the sons of the king. Every branch of literature and science known at the time was represented. Theology was naturally prominent, as well as works on omens and charms. The standard work on astronomy and astrology, in seventy-two books, had been compiled for the library of Sargon of Akkad; so too had the standard work on terrestrial omens. There was also a standard work on medicine, in which medical prescriptions and spells were mixed together. Philological treatises were numerous. There were dictionaries and grammars for explaining the Sumerian language to Semitic pupils, interlinear translations of Sumerian texts, phrase-books, lists of synonyms, and commentaries on difficult or obsolete words and passages, besides syllabaries, in which the cuneiform characters were catalogued and explained. Mathematics were diligently studied, and tables of squares and cubes have come to us from the library of Larsa. Geography was represented by descriptions of the countries and cities known to the Babylonians, natural history by lists of animals and birds, insects and plants. The Assyrians were endowed with a keen sense of history, and had invented a system of reckoning time by means of certain officers called *limmi*, who gave their names to their years of office. The historical and chronological works of the Assyrian libraries are therefore particularly important. They have enabled us to restore the chronology of the royal period of Israelitish history, and to supplement the Old Testament narrative with the contemporaneous records of the Assyrian kings. The Babylonians were less historically exact, perhaps because they had less of the Semitic element in their blood; but they, too, carefully kept the annals of their kings, and took a deep interest in the former history of their country.

Contract and other tablets relating to trade and business formed, however, the larger part of the contents of most Babylonian libraries. They have revealed to us the inner and social life of the people, so that the age of Khammurabi, or even of Sargon, in Babylonia,

R

is beginning to be as well known to us as the age of Periklês in Greece. Along with the contract-tablets must be counted the numerous legal documents and records of law-cases which have been preserved. Babylonian law was, like English law, built upon precedents, and an elaborate and carefully considered code had been formed at an early date.

Collections of letters, partly royal, partly private, were also to be found in the libraries. The autograph letters of Khammurabi, the Amraphel of Genesis, have come down to us, and we even have letters of his time from a lover to his mistress, and from a tenant to his landlord, whom he begs to reduce his rent. Boys went to school early, and learning the cuneiform syllabary was a task that demanded no small amount of time and application, especially when it is remembered that in the case of the Semitic Babylonian this involved also acquiring a knowledge of the dead language of Sumer. One of the exercises of the Sumerian schoolboy bids him "rise like the dawn, if he would excel in the school of the scribes."

Purely literary texts were numerous, especially poems, though nothing corresponding to the Egyptian novel has been met with. The epic of Gilgames, composed by Sin-liqi-unnini, has already been referred to. Its twelve books answered to the twelve signs of the Zodiac, and the eleventh accordingly contains the episode of the Deluge. Gilgames was the son of a royal mother, whose son was fated to slay his grandfather, and who was consequently confined in a tower. But an eagle carried him to a place of safety, and when he grew up he delivered Erech from its foes, and made it the seat of his kingdom. He slew the tyrant Khumbaba in the forest of cedars, and by means of a stratagem tempted the satyr Ea-bani to leave the woods and become his counsellor and friend. Istar wooed him, but he scorned her offers, and taunted her with her misdeeds to the hapless lovers who had been caught in her toils. In revenge the goddess persuaded her father Anu to create a winged bull, which should work havoc in the country of the Babylonians. But Gilgames destroyed the bull, an achievement, however, for which he was punished by Heaven. Ea-bani died of the bite of a gadfly, and his spirit mounted to the skies, while Gilgames himself was smitten by a sore disease. To heal it he sailed beyond the mouth of the Euphrates and the river of death, leaving behind him the deserts of Arabia and the twin-mountain where men in the shape of huge scorpions guard the gateways of the sun. At last he found Xisuthros, the hero of the Deluge, and learned from him how he had escaped death. Cured of his malady, he returned homeward with a leaf of the tree of life. But as he rested at a fountain by the way it was stolen by a serpent, and man lost the gift of immortality.

In Babylonia, and to a lesser extent in Assyria,

women were practically on a footing of equality with the men. They could trade in their own names, could make wills, could appear as witnesses or plaintiffs in court. We hear of a father transferring his property to his daughter, reserving only the use of it during his life. Polygamy was not common; indeed, we find it stipulated in one instance that in the case of a second marriage on the part of the husband the dowry of the first wife should be returned to her, and that she should be free to go where she would. Of course these rules did not apply to concubines, who were often purchased. Adoptions were frequent, and slaves could be adopted into the family of a freeman.

The large number of slaves caused the wages of the free labourer to be low. But the slaves were treated with humanity. From early times it was a law that if a slave were hired to another, the hirer should pay a penalty to his master whenever he was incapable of work, thus preventing "sweating" or overwork. Similarly, injuries to a slave were punished by a fine. The slave could trade and acquire property for himself, could receive wages for his work when hired to another, could give evidence in a court of law, and might obtain his freedom either by manumission, by purchase, by adoption, or by impressment into the royal service.

Farms were usually held on a sort of *métayer* system, half the produce going to the landlord as rent. Sometimes, however, the tenant received only a third, a

BABYLONIA AND ASSYRIA 259

fourth, or even a tenth part of the produce, two-thirds of the annual crop of dates being also assigned to the owner of the land. The tenant had to keep the farm-buildings in order, and to build any that were required. House-property seems to have been even more valuable than farm-land. The deeds for the lease or sale of it enter into the most minute particulars, and carefully define the limits of the estate. The house was let for a term of years, the rent being paid either twice or three times a year. At the expiration of the lease, the property had to be returned in the state in which the tenant had found it, and any infringement of the legal stipulations was punished with a heavy fine. Agents were frequently employed in the sale or letting of estates.

The cities were busy centres of trade. Commercial intercourse was carried on with all parts of the known world. Wheat was exported in large quantities, as well as dates and date-wine. The staple of Babylonian industry, however, was the manufacture of cloths and carpets. Vast flocks of sheep were kept on the western bank of the Euphrates, and placed under the charge of Bedâwin from Arabia. Their wool was made into curtains and rugs, and dyed or embroidered fabrics of various kinds. Even Belshazzar, the heir-apparent of Nabonidos, did not disdain to be a wool-merchant, and we find him lending twenty manehs, the proceeds of the sale of some of it, and taking as security for the repayment of the debt certain house-property in Babylon. It was "a goodly Babylonish garment," secreted by Achan from among the spoil of Jericho, that brought destruction upon himself and his family.

Money-lending naturally occupied a prominent place in the transaction of business. The ordinary rate of interest was 20 per cent., paid in monthly instalments; in the time of Nebuchadrezzar, however, it tended to be lower, and we find loans made at $13\frac{1}{2}$ per cent. The penalty was severe if the capital were not repaid at the specified date. The payment was occasionally in kind, but money was the usual medium of exchange. It consisted of rings or tongue-like bars of gold, silver, and copper, representing manehs and shekels. The maneh was divided into sixty shekels, and the standard used in later Babylonia had been fixed by Dungi, king of Ur. One of the standard maneh-weights of stone, from the mint of Nebuchadrezzar, is now in the British Museum. In the time of the Second Babylonian empire stamped or coined money was introduced, as well as pieces of five or more shekels. This was the period when the great banking firm of Egibi flourished, which anticipated the Rothschilds in making loans to the State.

The Babylonian cemetery adjoined the cities of the living, and was laid out in imitation of the latter.

The tombs were built of crude bricks, and were separated from one another by streets, through which flowed streams of "living water." Gardens were planted by the side of some of the tombs, which resembled the houses of the living, and in front of which offerings were made to the dead. After a burial, brushwood was heaped round the walls of the tomb and set on fire, partially cremating the body and the objects that were interred with it within. Sanitary reasons made this partial cremation necessary, while want of space in the populous plain of Babylonia caused the brick tombs to be built, like the houses of the towns, one on the top of the other.

Babylonia and Assyria were both administered by a bureaucracy, but whereas in Assyria the bureaucracy was military, in Babylonia it was theocratic. The high-priest was the equal and the director of the king, and the king himself was a priest, and the adopted child of Bel. In Assyria, on the contrary, the arbitrary power of the monarch was practically unchecked. Under him was the Turtannu or Tartan, the commander-in-chief, who commanded the army in the absence of the king. The Rab-saki, Rab-shakeh, or vizier, who ranked a little below him, was the head of the civil officials; besides him we hear of the Rab-sa-resi or Rabsaris, "the chief of the princes," the Rab-mugi or Rab-Mag, "the court physician," and an endless number of other officers.

The governors of provinces were selected from among the higher aristocracy, who alone had the privilege of sharing with the king the office of *limmu*, or eponymous archon after whom the year was named. Most of these officers seem to have been confined to Assyria; we do not hear of them in the southern kingdom of Babylonia. There, however, from an early period royal judges had been appointed, who went on circuit and sat under a president. Sometimes as many as four or six of them sat on a case, and subscribed their names to the verdict.

The main attention of the Assyrian government was devoted to the army, which was kept in the highest possible state of efficiency. It was recruited from the free peasantry of the country — a fact which, while it explains the excellence of the Assyrian veterans, also shows why it was that the empire fell as soon as constant wars had exhausted the native population. Improvements were made in it from time to time; thus, cavalry came to supersede the use of chariots, and the weapons and armour of the troops were changed and improved. Engineers and sappers accompanied it, cutting down the forests and making roads as it marched, and the commissariat was carefully attended to. The royal tent was arranged like a house, and one of its rooms was fitted up as a kitchen, where the food was prepared as in the palace of Nineveh. In Babylonia it was the fleet

BABYLONIA AND ASSYRIA

rather than the army which was the object of concern, though under Nebuchadrezzar and his successors the army also became an important engine of war. But, unlike the Assyrians, the Babylonians had been from the first a water-faring people, and the ship of war floated on the Euphrates by the side of the merchant vessel and the state barge of the king.

Such then were the kingdoms of Babylonia and Assyria. Each exercised an influence on the Israelites and their neighbours, though in a different way and with different results. The influence of Assyria was ephemeral. It represented the meteor-like rise of a great military power, which crushed all opposition, and introduced among mankind the new idea of a centralised world-empire. It destroyed the northern kingdom of Samaria, and made Palestine once more what it had been in pre-Mosaic days, the battle-ground between the nations of the Nile and the Tigris. On the inner life of western Asia it left no impression.

The influence of Babylonia, on the other hand, was that of a venerable and a widely reaching culture. The Canaan of the patriarchs and the Canaanitish conquest was a Canaan whose civilisation was derived from the Euphrates, and this civilisation the Israelites themselves inherited. Abraham was a Babylonian, and the Mosaic Law is not Egyptian but Babylonian in character, wherever it ceases to be specifically Israelite. The influence of Babylonia, moreover, continued to the last. It was the Babylonish Exile which changed the whole nature of the Jewish people, which gave it new aims and ideals, and prepared it for the coming of the Messiah. The Babylonian influence which had been working in the West for four thousand years received, as it were, a fresh impulse, and affected the religion and life of Judah in a new and special manner. Nor has the influence of Babylonian culture vanished even yet. Apart from the religious beliefs we have received from Israel, there is much in European civilisation which can be traced back to the old inhabitants of Chaldæa. It came through Canaanitish hands; perhaps, too, through the hands of the Etruscans. At all events, the system of augury which Rome borrowed from Etruria had a Babylonian origin, and the prototype of the strange liver-shaped instrument by means of which the Etruscan soothsayer divined, has been found among the relics of a Babylonian library.

CHAPTER VII

CONCLUSION

CHAPTER VII

CONCLUSION

Our task is finished. We have passed under review some of the facts which have been won by modern discovery from the monuments of the nations who helped to create the history of Israel. That history no longer stands alone like a solitary peak rising from the plain. Egypt, Babylonia, and Assyria have yielded up their dead ; Canaan and even Arabia are now beginning to do likewise. The Oriental world of the past is slowly developing before our eyes ; centuries which were deemed pre-historic but a few years ago have now become familiar to us, and we can study the very letters written by the contemporaries and predecessors of Abraham, and read the same books as those that were read by them. A new light has been poured upon the Old Testament ; its story has been supplemented and explained ; its statements tested and proved.

The Israelites were but one out of many branches of the same family. Their history is entwined around that of their brethren, their characteristics were shared by others of the same race. The Canaan they occupied was itself inhabited by more than one people, and after the first few years of invasion, its influence became strong upon them. In race, indeed, the Jew was by no means pure; at the outset a mixture of Israelite and Edomite, he was further mingled with Moabite and Philistine elements. The first king of Judah as a separate kingdom had an Ammonite mother, and bore an Ammonite name, while the portraits which surmount the names of Shishak's conquests in southern Palestine show that the old Amorite population was still predominant there. It was religion and history that made the Jew, not purity of race.

That Egypt must have exercised an influence upon Israel has long been known. The Israelites were born as a nation in the land of Goshen, and the Exodus from Egypt is the starting-point of their national history. But it is only since the decipherment of the Egyptian inscriptions that it has been possible to determine how far this influence extended, and to what extent it prevailed. And the result is to show that it was negative rather than positive; that the regulations of the Mosaic Code were directed to preventing the people from returning to Egypt and its idolatries by suppressing all reference to Egyptian beliefs and customs, and silently contradicting its ideas and practices. Even the doctrine of the future life, and the resurrection of the body, which plays so prominent a part in Egyptian religion, is carefully avoided, and the Ten Commandments have little in common with the ethical code of Egypt.

CONCLUSION 269

But while the influence of Egypt has thus been shown to be negative rather than positive, the influence of Babylonia has proved to be overwhelming. Perhaps this is one of the greatest surprises of modern research, though it might have been expected had we remembered that Abraham was a native of Babylonia, and that Israelites and Semitic Babylonians belonged to the same race. We have seen that the early culture of western Asia was wholly Babylonian, and that Babylonian influence continued undiminished there down to the days of the Exodus. The very mode of writing and the language of literature were Babylonian; the whole method of thought had been modelled after a Babylonian pattern for unnumbered generations. Israel in Goshen was no more exempt from these influences than were the patriarchs in Canaan.

Babylonian influence is deeply imprinted on the Mosaic laws. The institution of the Sabbath went back to the Sumerian days of Chaldæa; the name itself was of Babylonian origin. The great festivals of Israel find their counterparts on the banks of the Euphrates. Even the year of Jubilee was a Babylonian institution, and Gudea, the priest-king of Lagas, tells us that when he kept it the slave became "for seven days the equal of his master." It was only the form and application of the old institutions that were changed in the Levitical legislation. They were adapted to the needs of Israel, and associated with the events of its history. But in themselves they were all of Babylonian descent.

There is yet one more lesson to be learnt from the revelations of the monuments. They have made it clear that civilisation in the East is immensely old. As far back as we can go we find there all the elements of culture; man has already invented a system of writing, and has made some progress in art. It is true that by the side of all this civilisation there were still races living in the lowest barbarism of the Stone Age, just as there were Tasmanians who employed stone weapons of palæolithic shape less than sixty years ago; but between the civilised man of the Babylonian plain and the barbarians around him there existed the same gulf that exists to-day between the European and the savage. The history of the ancient East contains no record of the development of culture out of savagery. It tells us, indeed, of degeneracy and decay, but it knows of no period when civilisation began. So far as archæology can teach us, the builders of the Babylonian cities, the inventors of the cuneiform characters, had behind them no barbarous past.

APPENDICES

APPENDICES

I

EGYPTIAN CHRONOLOGY

EGYPT was originally divided into several independent principalities. Eventually these became the kingdoms of Northern (or Lower), and Southern (or Upper) Egypt. Among the kings of Northern Egypt were (1) Pu, (2) Ska, (3) Katfu (?), (4) Tau, (5) Thesh, (6) Nenan (?), and (7) Mekhâ; among the kings of Southern Egypt was Besh.

The two kingdoms were united by Men or Meni (Menes), king of This, who builds Memphis and founds the First dynasty of the united monarchy.

DYNASTY I.

(THINITE).

1. Meni.
2. Teta I.
3. Atotha.
4. Ata.
5. Husapti.
6. Mer-ba-pa, 73 years.
7. Samsu, 72 years.
8. Qabhu, 83 years.

DYNASTY II.

(THINITE).

1. Buzau or Bai-neter, 95 years.
2. Kakau.
3. Ba-neter-en, 95 years.
4. Uznas, 70 years.
5. Send, 74 years.
6. Per-ab-sen or Ka-Ra (?).
7. Nefer-ka-Ra, 70 years.

DYNASTY III.

(MEMPHITE).

1. Nefer-ka-Sokar (2) 8 years, 4 months, 2 days.
2. Hu-zefa, 25 (?) years, 8 months, 4 days.
3. Babai.
4. Zazai, 37 years, 2 months, 1 day.
5. Neb-ka-Ra, 19 years.
6. Zoser, 19 years, 2 months.
7. Zoser-teta, 6 years.
8. Sezes.
9. Nefer-ka-Ra I., 6 years.
10. Huni, 24 years.

APPENDICES

DYNASTY IV.
(MEMPHITES).

1. Snefru, 24 years.
2. Sharu.
3. Khufu (Cheops), 23 years.
4. Ra-dad-f, 8 years.
5. Khâ-f-Ra (Chephren).
6. Men-kau-Ra (Mykerinos).
7. Shepseskaf.

DYNASTY V.
(ELEPHANTINES).

1. User-ka-f, 28 years.
2. Sahu-Ra, 4 years.
3. Kaka, 2 years.
4. Nefer-ar-ka-Ra I., 7 years.
5. Shepses-ka-Ra, 12 years.
6. Khâ-nefer-Ra.
7. Ra-n-user An, 25 years.
8. Men-ka-Hor, 8 years.
9. Dad-ka-Ra Assa, 28 years.
10. Unas, 30 years.
11. Akau-Hor, 7 years.

DYNASTY VI.
(ELEPHANTINES).

1. Teta III.
2. User-ka-Ra.
3. Meri-Ra Pepi I., 20 years.
4. Mer-en-Ra Miht-em-saf I., 14 years.
5. Nefer-ka-Ra II. Pepi II., 94 years.
6. Mer-en-Ra Miht-em-saf II., 1 year, 1 month.
7. Neit-aker (Nitôkris), a queen.

DYNASTIES VII. AND VIII.
(MEMPHITES).

1. Nefer-ka, 2 years, 1 month, 1 day.
2. Neferus, 4 years, 2 months, 1 day.
3. Ab-en-Ra I., 2 years, 1 month, 1 day.
4. . . . 1 year, 8 days.
5. Ab-en-Ra II.
6. Hanti.
7. Pest-sat-en-Sopd.
8. Pait-Kheps.
9. Serhlinib.

Dad-nefer-Ra Dudumes.

Neter-ka-Ra.
Men-ka-Ra.
Nefer-ka-Ra III.
Nefer-ka-Ra IV. Nebi.
Dad-ka-Ra Shema.
Nefer-ka-Ra V. Khondu.
Mer-en-Hor.
Snefer-ka I.
Ka-n-Ra.
Nefer-ka-Ra VI. Terel.
Nefer-ka-Hor.
Nefer-ka-Ra VII. Pepi-seneb.
Snefer-ka II. Annu.
[User]-kau-Ra.
Nefer-kau-Ra.
Nefer-kau-Hor.
Nefer-ar-ka-Ra II.

DYNASTY IX.
(HERAKLEOPOLITES).

1. Khiti or Khruti I. Mer-ab-Ra

Mâa-ab-Ra.
Khâ-user-Ra.
Âa-hotep-Ra.
Skhâ-n-Ra.
Aah-mes (?)-Ra.
Se-n (?)-mu-Ra.

DYNASTY X.
(HERAKLEOPOLITES).

Mer-ka-Ra.

Ra-hotep-ab Amu-si-Hor-nez-hirtef.

Nefer-ka-Ra VIII.
Khiti II.
Se-heru-herri.
[Amoni?]

According to Lauth, the Turin Papyrus gives 19 kings to the Tenth dynasty, and 185 years.

APPENDICES 275

DYNASTY XI. (THEBAN).

1. Antef I. Seshes-Hor-ap-mâa-Ra Antuf-Âa, prince of Thebes.
2. Neb-hotep Mentu-hotep I.
3. Uah-ânkh [Ter(?)-] seshes-ap-mâa-Ra Antef-Âa II., his son.
4. Seshes-herher-mâa-Ra-Antef III., his brother.
5. Neter-nefer Neb-taui-Ra Mentu-hotep II.
6. Nub-kheper-Ra Antauf, more than 50 years.
7. Neb-khru-Ra Mentu-hotep III., more than 46 years.
8. A'a'h, a queen.
9. Antef V., her son.
10. S-ânkh-ka-Ra I.

According to Lauth, the Turin Papyrus makes the sum of the Eleventh dynasty 243 years, Neb-khru-Ra reigning 51 years.

DYNASTY XII. (THEBAN).

1. Amon-em-hat I. S-hotep-ab-Ra, alone 20 years.
   With Usertesen I., 10 years.
2. Usertesen I. Kheper-ka-Ra, alone 32 years.
   With Amon-em-hat II., 3 years.
3. Amon-em-hat II. Nub-kau-Ra, alone 29 years.
   With Usertesen II., 6 years.
4. Usertesen II. Khâ-kheper-Ra, 19 years.
5. Usertesen III. Khâ-kau-Ra, 3 [8] years.
6. Amon-em-hat III. Mâat-en-Ra, 43 years.
7. Amon-em-hat IV. Mâa-khru-Ra, 9 years, 3 months, 27 days.
8. Sebek-nefru-Ra, a queen, 3 years, 10 months, 24 days.

The Turin Papyrus makes the sum of the Twelfth dynasty 213 years, 1 month, 17 days.

DYNASTIES XIII. (THEBAN) AND XIV. (XOITE).

According to the Turin Papyrus :—

1. Sebek-hotep I. Sekhem-khu-taui-Ra, son of Sebek-nefru-Ra, 1 year, 3 months, 24 days.
2. Sekhem-ka-Ra, 6 years.
3. Ra Amon-em-hat V.
4. S-hotep-ab-Ra II.
5. Aufni, 2 years.
6. S-ânkh-ab-Ra Ameni Antuf Amon-em-hat VI., 1 year.
7. S-men-ka-Ra.
8. S-hotep-ab-Ra III.
9. S-ânkh-ka-Ra II.
10, 11. Names lost.
12. Nezem-ab-Ra.
13. Ra Sebek-hotep II.
14. Ren-seneb.
15. Autu-ab-Ra I. Hor.
16. Sezef-ka-Ra.
17. Sekhem-khu-taui-Ra II. Sebek-hotep III.
18. User-en-Ra.
19. S-menkh-ka-Ra Mer-menfiu.
20. . . . ka-Ra.
21. S-user-set-Ra.
22. Sekhem-uaz-taui-Ra Sebek-hotep IV.
23. Khâ-seshesh-Ra Nefer-hotep, son of Ra-ânkh-f.
24. Si-Hathor-Ra.
25. Khâ-nefer-Ra Sebek-hotep V.
26. [Khâ-ka-Ra].
27. [Khâ-ânkh-Ra Sebek-hotep VI.]
28. Khâ-hotep-Ra Sebek-hotep VII., 4 years, 8 months, 29 days.
29. Uab-Ra Âa-ab, 10 years, 8 months, 29 days.
30. Mer-nefer-Ra Ai, 23 (or 13) years, 8 months, 18 days.
31. Mer-hotep-Ra Ana, 2 years, 2 months, 9 days.
32. S-ânkh-en-s-uaztu-Ra, 3 years, 2 months.
33. Mer-sekhem-Ra Andu, 3 years, 1 month.

APPENDICES

34. S-uaz-ka-Ra Ur, 5 years, . . . months, 8 days.
35. Anemen . . . Ra.
36–46. Names lost.
47. Mer-kheper-Ra.
48. Mer-kau-Ra   Sebek-hotep VIII.
49–53. Names lost.
54. . . . mes-Ra.
55. . . . mât-Ra Aba.
56. Nefer-uben-Ra I.
57. . . . ka-Ra.
58. S-uaz-en-Ra.
59–60. Names lost.
61. Nebasi-Ra.
62. Khâ-khru-Ra.
63. Neb-f-autu-Ra, 2 years, 5 months, 15 days.
64. S-heb-Ra, 3 years.
65. Mer-zefa-Ra, 3 years.
66. S-uaz-ka-Ra, 1 year.
67. Neb-zefa-Ra, 1 year.
68. Uben-Ra I.
69–70. Names lost.
71. [Neb-] zefa-Ra II., 4 years.
72. [Nefer-] uben-Ra II.
73. Autu-ab-Ra II.
74. Her-ab-Ra.
75. Neb-sen-Ra.
76–79. Names lost.
80. S-kheper-en-Ra.
81. Dad-khru-Ra.
82. S-ânkh-ka-Ra III.
83. Nefer-tum-Ra.
84. Sekhem- . . . -Ra.
85. Ka- . . . -Ra.
86. Nefer-ab-Ra.
87. A . . . ka-Ra.
88. Khâ- . . . -Ra, 2 years.
89. Nez-ka- . . . -Ra.
90. S-men- . . . -Ra.
91–111. Names lost.
112. Sekhem- . . . -Ra.
113. Sekhem- . . . -Ra.
114. Sekhem-us . . . -Ra.
115. Sesen- . . . -Ra.
116. Neb-ati-uzu-Ra.
117. Neb-aten-uzu-Ra.
118. S-men-ka-Ra.
119. S-user- . . . -Ra.
120. Khâ-sekhem-[bent]-Ra.

About thirty-seven more names are illegible.

DYNASTIES XV., XVI. AND XVII. (HYKSOS).

According to Josephus, quoted from Manetho:—

1. Salatis, 13 years.
2. Beon or Bnôn, 44 years.
3. Apakhnas or Pakhnan, 36 years, 7 months.
4. Apôphis, 61 years.
5. Iannas or Annas, 50 years, 1 month.
6. Assis, 49 years, 2 months.

. . . .
Ya'qob-hal (Jacob-el).
. . . .
Khian (Iannas) S-user-Set-en-Ra.
. . . .
Apopi I. Aa-user-Ra (reigned more than 33 years).
. . . .
Apopi III. Ra-âa-kenen.

A dynasty of Theban princes was contemporary with the Seventeenth Hyksos dynasty, the last four of whom were independent:

Skenen-Ra Taa I. (revolted against Apopi III.).
Skenen-Ra Taa II. Aa.
Skenen-Ra Taa III. Ken.
Uaz-kheper-Ra Ka-mes and wife Aah-hotep.

DYNASTY XVIII. (THEBAN).

1. Neb-pehuti-Ra Aahmes I. (Amosis), more than 20 years.
2. Ser-ka-Ra Amon-hotep I., his son (Amenophis I.), 20 years, 7 months.
3. Aa-kheper-ka-Ra Dehuti-mes I., his son, and queen Amen-sit.
4. Aa-kheper-en-Ra Dehuti-mes II., his son (more than 9 years), and wife (and sister) Hatshepsu II. Mâ-ka-Ra (daughter of Hatshepsu I.).
5. Khnum-Amon Hatshepsu II. Mâ-ka-Ra, more than 16 years.

APPENDICES 277

6. Ra-men-kheper Dehuti-mes (Thothmes) III., her half-brother, 57 years, 11 months, 1 day (B.C. 1503, March 20, to 1449 February 14, according to Dr. Mahler's astronomical determination).
7. Aa-khepru-Ra Amon-hotep II., his son, more than 5 years.
8. Men-khepru-Ra Dehuti-mes IV., his son, more than 7 years.
9. Neb-mâ-Ra Amon-hotep III., his son (more than 35 years), and wife Teie.
10. Nefer-khepru-Ra Amon-hotep IV. Khu-n-Aten, his son, more than 17 years.
11. Ankh-khepru-Ra and wife Meri-Aten.
12. Tut-ânkh-Amon Khepru-neb-Ra and wife Ankh-nes-Amon.
13. Aten-Ra-nefer-nefru-mer-Aten.
14. Ai Kheper-khepru-ar-mâ-Ra, more than 4 years.
15. Hor-em-hib (Armais) Mi-Amon Ser-khepru-ka, more than 3 years.

DYNASTY XIX. (THEBAN).

1. Men-pehuti-Ra Ramessu I. (Ramesses), more than 2 years.
2. Men-mâ-Ra Seti I. (Sethos) Mer-en-Ptah I., more than 27 years.
3. User-mâ-Ra (Osymandyas) Sotep-en-Ra Ramessu II. (Ramses) Mi-Amon (the Sesostris of the Greeks), B.C. 1348-1281 (according to Dr. Mahler).
4. Mer-en-Ptah II. (Ammenephthes) Hotep-hi-ma Ba-n-Ra Mi-Amon.
5. User-khepru-Ra Seti II. Mer-en-Ptah III.
6. Amon-messu Hik-An Mer-kha-Ra Sotep-en-Ra.
7. Khu-n-Ra Sotep-en-Ra Mer-en-Ptah IV. Si-Ptah and wife Ta-usor.

DYNASTY XX. (THEBAN).

1. Set-nekht Merer Mi-Amon (recovered the kingdom from the Canaanite Arisu).
2. Ramessu III. Hik-an, more than 32 years.
3. Ramessu IV. Hik-Mâ Mi-Amon, more than 11 years.
4. Ramessu V. User-mâ-s-kheper-en-Ra Mi-Amon, more than 4 years.
5. Ramessu VI. Neb-mâ-Ra Mi-Amon Amon-hir-khopesh-ef (called Meri-Tum in northern Egypt).
6. Ramessu VII. At-Amon User-mâ-Ra Mi-Amon.
7. Ramessu VIII. Set-hir-khopesh-ef Mi-Amon User-mâ-Ra Khu-n-Amon.
8. Ramessu IX. Si-Ptah S-khâ-n-Ra Mi-Amon, 19 years.
9. Ramessu X. Nefer-ka-Ra Mi-Amon Sotep-en-Ra, more than 10 years.
10. Ramessu XI. Amon-hir-khopesh-ef Kheper-mâ-Ra Sotep-en-Ra.
11. Ramessu XII. Men-mâ-Ra Mi-Amon Sotep-en-Ptah Khâ-m-uas, more than 27 years.

DYNASTY XXI. (TANITE).

1. Nes-Bindidi (Smendes) Mi-Amon.
2. P-seb-khâ-n I. (Psusennes I.) Mi-Amon Aa-kheper-Ra Sotep-en-Amon.
3. [Nefer-ka-Ra] (Nephelkheres).
4. Amon-em-apt (Amenophthis).
5. ... (Osokhor).
6. Pinezem (?) (Psinakhes).
7. Hor-P-seb-khâ-n II. (Psusennes II.).

[Contemporary with the Twenty-first dynasty was an

illegitimate dynasty of high-priests at Thebes:—

(1.) Hir-Hor Si-Amon.
(2.) Piankhi.
(3.) Pinezem I.
(4.) Pinezem II. with title of "king."
(5.) Men-kheper-Ra and wife Isis-em-kheb.
(6.) Pinezem III.]

DYNASTY XXII.
(BUBASTITE).

1. Shashanq I. (Shishak) Mi-Amon Hez-kheper-Ra Sotep-en-Ra, son of Nemart, captain of the Libyan mercenaries, more than 21 years.
2. Usarkon I. Mi-Amon Sekhem-kheper-Ra.
3. Takelet I. Mi-Amon Si-Isis User-mâ-Ra Sotep-en-Amon, more than 23 years.
4. Usarkon II. Mi-Amon Si-Bast User-mâ-Ra, more than 23 years.
5. Shashanq II. Mi-Amon Sekhem-kheper-Ra.
6. Takelet II. Mi-Amon Si-Isis Hez-kheper-Ra, more than 15 years.
7. Shashanq III. Mi-Amon Si-Bast User-mâ-Ra, 52 years.
8. Pimai Mi-Amon User-mâ-Ra Sotep-en-Amon.
9. Shashanq IV. Aa-kheper-Ra, more than 37 years.

DYNASTY XXIII.

1. S-hir-ab-Ra Petu-si-Bast.
2. Usarkon III. Mi-Amon Aa-kheper-Ra Sotep-en-Amon.
3. P-si-Mut User-Ra Sotep-en-Ptah.

Interregnum.

Egypt is divided between several princes, including Tof-nekht, father of Bak-en-ran-ef. It is overrun by Piankhi the Ethiopian, while Usarkon III. reigns at Bubastis. The son and successor of Piankhi was Mi-Amon-Nut.

DYNASTY XXIV. (SAITE).

Bak-en-ran-ef (Bokkhoris) Uah-ka-Ra, more than 16 years.

DYNASTY XXV.
(ETHIOPIAN).

1. Shabaka (Sabako) Nefer-ka-Ra, son of Kashet, 12 years.
2. Shabatoka (Sebikhos) Dad-ka-Ra.
3. Taharka (Tirhakah) Nefer-Tum-khu-Ra, 26 years.

Interregnum.

Egypt is conquered by the Assyrian king Esar-haddon, and divided into 20 satrapies, B.C. 672-660. Taharka and his successor Urdamanu (Rud-Amon), or Tandamanu (Tuant-Amon), make vain attempts to recover it. Finally, Psamtik, son of Niku (Necho), satrap of Sais, shakes off the foreign yoke.

DYNASTY XXVI. (SAITE).

B.C.
1. Psamtik I. (Psammetikhos) Uah-ab-Ra . . . 664
2. Nekau (Necho) Nem-ab-Ra 610
3. Psamtik II. Nefer-ab-Ra 594
4. Uah-ab-Ra (Apries or Hophra) Haa-ab-Ra . . 589
5. Aahmes II. (Amasis) Si-Nit Khnum-ab-Ra 570
6. Psamtik III. Ankh-ka-n-Ra 526

DYNASTY XXVII.
(PERSIAN).

B.C.
1. Kambathet (Cambyses), Sam-taui Mestu-Ra . . 525
2. Ntariush (Darius I.) Settu-Ra 521

APPENDICES

3. Khabbash Senen Tanen Sotep-en-Ptah, native prince . . . . . . B.C. 485
4. Khsherish (Xerxes) . . . 484
5. Artakhsharsha (Artaxerxes) 465
6. Ntariush (Darius II.) Mi-Amon-Ra 424

DYNASTY XXVIII. (SAITE).

Amon-art-t-rut (Amyrtæus), more than 6 years B.C. 415

DYNASTY XXIX.
(MENDESIAN).

1. Nef-âa-rut I. Ba-n-Ra Mi-neteru, more than 4 years.
2. Hakori Khnum-mâ-Râ Sotep-en-Ptah, 13 years.
3. P-si-Mut User-Ptah-sotep-en-Ra, 1 year.
4. Hor-neb-kha, 1 year.
5. Nef-âa-rut II., 1 year.

DYNASTY XXX.
(SEBENNYTE).

1. Nekht-Hor-hib Ra-snezem-ab Sotep-en-Anhur, son of Nef-âa-rut I., 19 years.
2. Zihu (Teos), 1 year.
3. Nekht-neb-ef (Nektanebo) Kheper-ka-Ra, 18 years.

Egypt reconquered by the Persians, B.C. 349.

II
BABYLONIAN CHRONOLOGY

En sag-saganna, king of Kengi.

Lugal-zaggisi, king of Erech, founds an empire in western Asia cir. B.C. 5000 (?).

KINGS OF LAGAS, cir. B.C. 4000.

Ur-duggina.
Lugal-suggur, vassal of Me-sa, king of Kis.

Gursar.
Nini-khaldu, his son.
Ur-Nina, his son.
Akur-gal, his son.
E-annatum, his son.
En-annadu I., his brother, high-priest.
Entemena, his nephew, high-priest.
En-annadu II., high-priest.

Lugal-usum-gal, vassal of Sargon of Akkad.

KINGS OF KIS.
Me-sa.

Enne-Ugun.

Alusarsid.

Lugal-khassi.

DYNASTY OF AGADE (AKKAD).
Sargon or Sargani-sar-ali, B.C. 3800.

Naram-Sin, his son, B.C. 3750.
Bingani-sar-ali, his son.
Queen Ellat-Gula (?).

FIRST DYNASTY OF UR.
Lugal-kigub-nidudu.
Lugal-kisal-si, his son.

SECOND DYNASTY OF UR.
Ur-Bau, cir. B.C. 2700; his stepson, Nammakhani, high-priest of Lagas.
Dungi I., his son; Gudea and his son, Ur-Nin-girsu, vassal high-priests of Lagas.

DYNASTY OF ERECH.
Sin-gamil.
Sin-gasid.

DYNASTY OF ISIN.
Isbi-girra.
Libit-Istar.
Pur-Sin I.
Ur-Ninip.
Isme-Dagan.
En-annatum, his son, vassal of Gungunum of Ur.

THIRD DYNASTY OF UR.
Gungunum.
Dungi II. (reigns at least 41 years).
Pur-Sin II. (reigns at least 12 years).

APPENDICES

Gimil-Sin (reigns at least 9 years).
Inê-Sin (probably followed by Sumu-abi).

FIRST DYNASTY OF BABYLON, B.C. 2478.

Sumu-abi or Samu-abi, 14 (or 15) years.[1]
Sumu-la-ilu, his son, 36 (or 35) years.
Zabium or Zabu, his son, 14 years.
Abil-Sin, his son, 18 years.
Sin-muballidh, his son, 20 (or 30) years.

Babylonia conquered by the Elamites; Kudur-Laghghamar (Chedor-laomer) king of Elam is suzerain, while Eri-Aku (Arioch) governs southern Babylonia and makes Larsa his capital.

Khammurabi or Ammurapi, the Amraphel of Genesis, 43 (or 55) years (B.C. 2376-2333).

He defeats the Elamites, restores Sin-idinnam to Larsa, and reunites Babylonia.

Samsu-iluna, his son, 38 (or 35) years.
Abesukh (Abishua) or Ebisum, 25 years.
Ammi-ditana, his son, 25 years.
Ammi-zadok, his son, 21 years.
Samsu-ditana, his son, 31 years.

DYNASTY OF SISKU, B.C. 2174.

Anman, 60 years.
Ki-annibi, 56 years.
Damki-ilisu, 26 years.
Iskipal, 15 years.
Sussi, 24 years.
Gulkisar, 55 years.
Kirgal-daramas, 50 years.
Â-dara-kalamma, 28 years.
E-kur-ul-anna, 26 years.
Melamma-kurkurra, 8 years.
Ea-ga . . . 20 years.

THE DYNASTY OF THE KASSITES, B.C. 1806.[2]

Gandis, 16 years.
Agum-si, 22 years.
Agu-yasi, 22 years.
Ussi, his son, 9 years.
Adumetas.
Tazzigurumas.
Agum-kak-rime, his son.

Eight unknown kings.

Kara-indas.
Kadasman-Bel (corresponded with the Egyptian king Amenophis III.).
Kuri-galzu I.
Burna-buryas, his son.
Kuri-galzu II., his son.[3]
Kara-khardas.
Kadasman-kharbe I., his son.

---

[1] The first date is that of a chronological tablet compiled in the reign of Ammi-zadok; the second that of the Dynastic Tablet compiled probably in the reign of Nabonidos. In the latter the reigns of illegitimate kings, Pungun-ilu, Immerum, and Eri-Aku, seem to be included in those of the legitimate rulers of the dynasty. Immerum, the son of Lilium, was a contemporary of Sumu-la-ilu, and perhaps, like Nur-Rimmon and Sin-idinnam in the time of Sin-muballidh and Khammurabi, was vassal king of Larsa in southern Babylonia.

[2] The date is probably from 15 to 20 years too high.

[3] The position of this Kuri-galzu is not certain. One of the Kuri-galzus calls himself "son of Burna-buryas," but since Nabonidos states that a Burna-buryas reigned 700 years after Khammurabi, it is possible that among the eight (or in this case nine) unknown Kassite kings there was a Burna-buryas I., B.C. 1640, whose son was Kuri-galzu I.

APPENDICES

The throne usurped by Nazi-bugas.
Kuri-galzu III., son of Kadasman-kharbe, 35 (?) years.
Nazi-Maruttas, his son, 26 years, B.C. 1378.
Kadasman-Turgu, his son, 17 years.
Kadasman-buryas, 14 years.
Kudur-Bel, 6 years.
Sagarkti-buryas, his son, 13 years (800 years before Nabonidos).
Bibeyasu, 8 years.
Bel-sum-iddin, 1½ year.
Kadasman-kharbe II., 1½ year.
Rimmon-sum-uzur, 30 years (including the 7 years during which the Assyrian king Tiglath-Bir held Babylon).
Meli-sipak, 15 years.
Merodach-baladan I., his son, 13 years.
Zamama-sum-iddin, 1 year.
Bel-sum-iddin, 3 years.

THE DYNASTY OF ISIN, B.C. 1229.

Merodach- . . . 18 years.
Four unknown kings.
Nebuchadrezzar I.
Bel-nadin-pal.
Merodach-nadin-akhi, 22 years.[1]
Merodach- . . . 1½ year.
The throne usurped by Rimmon-baladan.
Merodach-sapik-zer-mati, 12 years.
Nabu-nadin, 8 years.

THE DYNASTY OF THE SEACOAST, B.C. 1096.

Simbar-sipak, 18 years.
Ea-mukin-zeri, 5 months.
Kassu-nadin-akhi, 3 years.

THE DYNASTY OF BIT-BAZI, B.C. 1075.

Ê-Ulmas-sakin-sumi, 17 years.
Bir-kudur-uzur I., 3 years.
Silanim-Sukamuna, 3 months.

THE DYNASTY OF ELAM, B.C. 1055.

An . . . ., an Elamite, 6 years.

THE SECOND DYNASTY OF BABYLON, B.C. 1049.

Nebo-kin-abli, 36 years.
Bir-kudur-uzur II. (?), 8 months, 12 days.
Probably four names missing.

	B.C.
Samas-mudammik	cir. 920
Nebo-sum-iskun	cir. 900
Nebo-baladan	cir. 880
Merodach-nadin-sumi	cir. 860
Merodach-baladhsu-ikbi	cir. 830
Bau-akhi-iddin	cir. 810

Probably two names missing.

	B.C.
Nebo-sum-iskun, son of Dakuri	cir. 760
Nabonassar, 14 years	747
Nebo-nadin-sumi, his son, 2 years	733
Nebo-sum-yukin, his son, 1 month, 12 days	731

THE DYNASTY OF SAPÊ.

	B.C.
Yukin-zera or Khinziros, 3 years	730
Pulu (Pul or Poros), called Tiglath-pileser III. in Assyria, 2 years	727
Ululâ, called Shalmaneser IV. in Assyria	725

---

[1] As Sennacherib makes Merodach-nadin-akhi defeat the Assyrians in B.C. 1107, while the Dynastic Tablet places the death of the Babylonian king in B.C. 1118, there must be a chronological error in the latter.

APPENDICES

	B.C.
Merodach-baladan II., the Chaldæan from the Seacoast	721
Sargon of Assyria	709
Sennacherib, his son	705
Merodach-zakir-sumi, 1 month	702
Merodach-baladan III., 6 months	702
Bel-ebus of Babylon	702
Assur-nadin-sumi, son of Sennacherib	700
Nergal-yusezib	694
Musezib-Merodach	693
Sennacherib a second time	689
Esar-haddon, his son	681
Samas-sum-yukin (Saosdukhinos), his son	668
Kandalanu (Kineladanos)	648
Nabopolassar	626
Nabu-kudurri-uzur (Nebuchadrezzar II.), his son	605
Amil-Marduk (Evil-Merodach), his son	562
Nergal-sarra-uzur (Nergalsharezer)	560
Labasi-Marduk (Laborosoarchod), his son, 3 months	556
Nabu-nahid (Nabonidos)	556
Cyrus conquers Babylon	538

	B.C.
Cambyses, his son	529
Gomates (Gaumata) the Magian usurps the throne, 7 months	721
Nebuchadrezzar III., native king	721
Darius (Dârayavaush), son of Hystaspes	520
Nebuchadrezzar IV., rebel king	514
Darius restored	513
Xerxes I. (Khshayârshâ), his son	485
Samas-erba, rebel king	480
Xerxes restored	479
Artaxerxes I. (Artakhshatra) Longimanus, his son	465
Xerxes II., his son, 2 months	425
Sogdianos, his half-brother, 7 months	425
Darius II. Nothos, his brother	424
Artaxerxes II. Mnêmon, his son	405
Okhos (Uvasu), son of Artaxerxes	362
Arses, his son	339
Darius III. Kodomannos	336
Conquered by Alexander the Great	330

III

ASSYRIAN CHRONOLOGY

Sargon asserts that he was preceded by 330 Assyrian kings, among the earlier of them being Adasi and his son Bel-bani.

HIGH-PRIESTS OF ASSUR.

	B.C.
Isme-Dagon	1850
Samsi-Rimmon I., his son	1820
. . . .	
Igur-kapkapu	(?)
Samsi-Rimmon II., his son	(?)
. . . .	
Khallu	(?)
Irisum, his son	(?)

KINGS OF ASSYRIA.

Bel-kapkapu, "the founder of the monarchy." . .
. . . .

Assur-suma-esir	(?)
Bir-tuklat-Assur, his son, (contemporary of the Babylonian king Kharbe-sipak).	
. . . .	
Erba-Rimmon	(?)
Assur-nadin-akhe I., his son	(?)
. . . .	
Assur-bil-nisi-su	cir. 1450
Buzur-Assur	1440
Assur-nadin-akhe II.	1420

	B.C.
Assur-yuballidh, his son cir.	1400
Bel-nirari, his son	1380
Pudilu (Pedael), his son	1360
Rimmon-nirari I., his son	1340
Shalmaneser I., his son (the builder of Calah)	1320
Tiglath-Bir I., his son	1300
Conquers Babylon and reigns there 7 years	1290
Assur-nazir-pal I., his son, 6 years	1280
Tiglath-Assur-Bel	1275
Assur-narara	1260
Nebo-dan, his son	1250
. . . .	
Bel-kudurri-uzur	1225
Bir-pileser	1215
Assur-dan I., his son [1]	1185
Mutaggil-Nebo, his son	1160
Assur-ris-isi, his son [2]	1140
Tiglath-pileser I., his son	1120
Assur-bil-kala, his son	1090
Samsi-Rimmon I., his brother	1070
Assur-nazir-pal II., his son	1050
. . . .	
Assur-irbi	(?)
. . . .	

[1] A contemporary of the Babylonian king Zamama-sum-iddin. If this is the last king but one of the Kassite dynasty, and not rather one of the unknown kings of the dynasty of Isin, the date of Assur-dan I. will have to be pushed about 40 years further back.

[2] A contemporary of the Babylonian king Nebuchadrezzar I.

APPENDICES

	B.C.
Tiglath-pileser II.	950
Assur-dan II., his son	930
Rimmon-nirari II., his son	911
Tiglath-Bir II., his son	889
Assur-nazir-pal III. his son	883
Shalmaneser II., his son	858
Assur-dain-pal (Sardanapallos), rebel king	825
Samsi-Rimmon II., his brother	823
Rimmon-nirari II., his son	810
Shalmaneser III.	781
Assur-dân III.	771
Assur-nirari	753
Pulu (Pul), usurper, takes the name of Tiglath-pileser III.	745
Conquers Babylon	729
Ululâ, usurper, takes the name of Shalmaneser IV.	727
Sargon, usurper	722
Sennacherib (Sin-akhe-erba), his son	705
Esar-haddon (Assur-akh-iddin), his son	681
Assur-bani-pal, his son	668
Assur-etil-ilani-yukinni, his son	(?)
Sin-sarra-iskun (Sarakos)	(?)
Destruction of Nineveh	606

IV

HEBREW CHRONOLOGY AS CORRECTED BY THE ASSYRIAN MONUMENTS

	B.C.
The Israelitish Exodus out of Egypt in the fifth year of Meneptah, son of Ramses II.	1276
Campaign of Ramses III. in southern Palestine	cir. 1230
Chushan-rishathaim of Aram-Naharaim or Mitanni conquers Canaan	cir. 1225
Saul elected King of Israel	cir. 1020
Accession of David	cir. 1000
Accession of Solomon	cir. 960
Accession of Rehoboam, division of the kingdom	cir. 930
Invasion of Palestine by Shishak I. of Egypt	927

JUDAH.	B.C.	ISRAEL.	B.C.
Rehoboam (17 years).	cir. 932	Jeroboam (22 years)	932
Abijah	915	Nadab	910
Asa	912	Baasha	908
Jehoshaphat	871	Elah	884
Jehoram	846	Zimri, for 7 days	882
Ahaziah or Jehoahaz	842	Omri	882
Athaliah	842	Ahab	874
Joash	837	Ahab and his allies defeated by the Assyrians at Qarqar	853
Amaziah	797		
Uzziah or Azariah	768	Ahaziah	852
Jotham	736	Revolt of Mesha of Moab	851
Ahaz	734	Joram	850
Becomes tributary to Tiglath-pileser	734	Jehu	842
		He pays tribute to Assyria	841
Damascus taken by the Assyrians	732	Jehoahaz	814
		Jehoash	798
Hezekiah	727	Jeroboam II.	783
Invasion of Judah by Sennacherib	701	Zechariah	742
		Shallum	741
Manasseh	697	Menahem	741
Amon	642	Pays tribute to Tiglath-pileser	738
Josiah	640		
Jehoahaz	608	Pekahiah	737
Jehoiakim	608	Pekah	736
Jehoiachin	597	Hoshea	733 or 729
Zedekiah	597	Samaria taken by the Assyrians	722
Jerusalem destroyed by Nebuchadrezzar	586		

V

THE LETTERS OF EBED-TOB (OR EBED-KHEBA), VASSAL KING OF JERUSALEM, TO AMENOPHIS IV., KING OF EGYPT

I. "To the king my lord thus speaks Ebed-Tob thy servant: At the feet of the king my lord seven times seven I prostrate myself. What have I done against the king my lord? They have slandered me before the king my lord, saying : Ebed-Tob has revolted from the king his lord. Behold, neither my father nor my mother have exalted me in this place; the arm of the Mighty King has made me enter the house of my father. Why should I have committed a sin against the king my lord? By the life of the king, I say to the Commissioner of the king my lord : Why dost thou love the Khabiri (Confederates) and hate the (loyal) governors? And yet continually are they slandering me before the king my lord, because I say that the provinces of the king my lord are being destroyed. Continually are they slandering me to the king my lord. But let the king my lord consider, since the king my lord has established the garrisons which have taken the fortresses . . . may the king send help to his country. [May he send troops] to his country! The cities of the king my lord are lost which Elimelech is destroying, even all the country of the king; so let the king my lord send help to his country. I say : I will go down to the king my lord, and shall I not see the tears of the king my lord? but the enemy are strong against me, and I have not been able to go down to the king my lord. So let the king incline towards my face and despatch a garrison to me, and I will go down and see the tears of the king my lord. Since by the life of the king, when the Commissioner departed, I say: The provinces of the king are being destroyed, (yet) thou dost not listen to me. All the governors are destroyed, no governor remains to the king my lord. May the king turn his face to the men and send the troops of the king my lord. No provinces remain unto the king; the Khabiri have wasted all the provinces of the king. If troops come this year, the provinces of the king my lord will be preserved; but if no troops come, the provinces of the king my lord will be destroyed.—To the Secretary of the king my lord, Ebed-Tob thy servant: make a clear report of my words to the king my lord that all the provinces of the king my lord are being destroyed."

II. "'To the king my lord, my Sun-god, thus speaks Ebed-Tob thy servant: At the feet of the king my lord seven times seven I prostrate myself. Behold, the king my lord has established his name at the rising of the sun and the setting of the sun. They have uttered slanders against me. Behold, I am not a governor, a dependent of the king my lord. Behold, I am the king's friend, and I pay tribute to the king, even I. Neither my father nor my mother, but the arm of the Mighty King has established me in the house of my father. [When the governor of the king my lord] came to me, I gave him 13 prisoners (?) and 10 slaves. Sûta (Seti) the Commissioner of the king came to me; I gave 21 slavewomen and 20 male prisoners into the hands of Sûta as a present for the king my lord. May the king give counsel to his country! The country of the king is being destroyed, all of it. Hostilities are being carried on against me. Behold, the mountains of Seir (see Josh. xv. 10) as far as Gath-Carmel have united against all the other governors and are at war with myself. If one looks, shall not one see the tears of the king my lord because war

APPENDICES 289

has been made upon me? While there were ships in the midst of the sea the arm of the Mighty King possessed Naharaim and Babylonia, but now the Khabiri possess the cities of the king (of Egypt). Not a single governor remains (among them) to the king my lord; all are destroyed. Behold, Turbazu has been slain in the gate of the city of Zilû (Zelah), and the king does nothing. Behold, Zimrida of Lachish has been thrown to the ground by (his) servants and murdered. Yaptikh-Addu (Jephthah-Hadad) has been slain in the gate of the city of Zilû, and the king does nothing. . . . Let the king [my lord] send help [to his country], let the king turn his face [to his servants]. Let him despatch troops to the country [of Jerusalem]. [Behold], if no troops come this year, all the provinces of the king my lord will be utterly destroyed. They do not tell to the face of the king my lord that the country of the king my lord is destroyed and all the governors are destroyed. If no troops come this year, let the king send a Commissioner, and let him come to me with allies, and we will die with the king our lord.—To the Secretary of the king my lord, Ebed-Tob thy servant: At thy feet [I prostrate myself]. Make a clear report of these my words to the king my lord that thy faithful servant am I."

III. "To the king my lord thus speaks Ebed-Tob thy servant: at the feet of my lord the king seven times seven I prostrate myself. Behold, has not Malchiel revolted to the sons of Labai and the sons of Arzai to demand the country of the king for themselves? As for the governor who does this deed, why does not the king question him? Behold, Malchiel and Tagi (the father-in-law of Malchiel) are they who have done this, since they have taken the city of Rubutê (Rabbah, Josh. xv. 60). . . . There is no royal garrison. May the king live for ever! Verily Pûru (Pa-Hor) has gone down to him; he has left me and is in the city of Gaza. But let the king remember him and send fifty men as a garrison to defend the country. All the country of the king has revolted. Send Yikhbil-Khamu, and let him consider the country of the king. To the Secretary of the king, Ebed-Tob thy servant: make a clear report of my words to the king: 'Abundant good fortune be unto thee! I am thy servant.'"

IV. "To the king my lord thus speaks Ebed-Tob thy servant: at the feet of the king my lord seven times seven I prostrate myself. [Behold the deed] which Malchiel and Suardatum have done against the country of the king my lord, hiring(?) the forces of the cities of Gezer, of Gath, and of Keilah, and occupying the country of the city of Rubutê (Rabbah). The country of the king has gone over to the Khabiri. And now at this moment the city of the mountain of Jerusalem (Uru-salim), whose name is Bit-Bir (the temple of the god Bir), the city of the king, is separated from the locality of the men of Keilah. Let the king listen to Ebed-Tob thy servant, and let him despatch troops that I may restore the country of the king to the king. But if no troops arrive, the country of the king is gone over to the Khabiri. This is the deed of Suardatum and Malchiel. But may the king send help to his country."

V. *The commencement is lost.*—"And now as to the city of Jerusalem, if this country belongs to the king, why is it that Gaza is made the seat of the garrison for the king? Behold, the country of the city of Gath-Carmel has fallen away to Tagi and the men of Gath. He is in Bit-Sâni, and we have effected that they should give Labai and the country of the Bedâwin (Sutâ) to the Khabiri. Malchiel has sent to Tagi and takes his sons as servants. He has granted all their requests to the men of Keilah, and we have delivered the city of Jerusalem. The garrison whom thou sentest by the hand of Khapi (Apis), the son of Miyaria (Meri-Ra) Hadad-el has taken and has established in his house in Gaza."

VI. "To the king my lord thus speaks Ebed-Tob thy servant: at the feet of the king my lord seven times seven I

APPENDICES 291

prostrate myself. [Let the king listen to] the words [of his servant which] have been conveyed to [him]. ... Let the king know that all the provinces have united in hostility against me, and let the king send help to his country. Behold, the country of the cities of Gezer, of Askalon and of Lachish have given them food, oil, and whatever they wanted; so let the king send help to the troops and despatch troops against the men who have committed sin against the king my lord. If troops come this year, then there will remain both provinces and governors to the king my lord; but if no troops arrive, there will remain no provinces or governors to the king my lord. Behold, this country of the city of Jerusalem neither my father nor my mother has given to me; the arm of the Mighty King gave it to me, even to me. Behold, this is the deed of Malchiel and the deed of the sons of Labai, who have given the country of the king to the Khabiri. Behold, O king my lord, be just towards me as regards the Babylonians; let the king ask the Commissioners whether they have acted violently (?). But they have taken upon themselves a very grievous sin. They have taken their goods and ... let the king ask (them); they had abundance of food, abundance of oil and abundance of clothes, until Pauru the Commissioner of the king came up to the country of the city of Jerusalem, and Adai revolted, together with the garrison and the dependents upon the king. Let the king know that (Pauru) said to me: Adai has revolted from me, do not leave the city. This [year] send me a garrison and a royal Commissioner. Let thy favour be towards me. I have sent to the king my lord 5000 prisoners and ... tribute-bearers. The caravans of the king have been robbed in the field of Ajalon. Let the king my lord know that I am not able to send a caravan to the king my lord according to thy instructions. Behold, the king has established his name in the country of Jerusalem for ever, and he cannot forsake the territory of the city of Jerusalem.—To the Secretary of the king my lord, Ebed-

Tob thy servant. At thy feet I fall : I am thy servant.
Make a clear report of my words to the king my lord, that I
am the vassal of the king. Abundance of good fortune to
thee !—And thou hast performed deeds I cannot enumerate
against the men of the land of Cush. . . . bana is not slain.
There are Babylonians in my house. Let the king my lord
ask in regard to them . ."

LETTER OF SUWARDATUM TO AMENOPHIS IV.

"To the king my lord, my gods, my Sun-god, thus speaks
Suwardata thy servant, the dust of thy feet : at the feet of
the king my lord, my gods, my Sun-god, seven times seven
I prostrate myself. The king my lord directed me to make
war in the city of Keilah ; I made war ; it is (now) at peace
with me ; my city is restored to me. Why does Ebed-Tob
send to the men of Keilah, saying : 'Take silver and march
after me'? And the king my lord knows that Ebed-Tob has
taken my city out of my hand. Again let the king my lord
inquire whether I have taken a man, or an ox, or an ass
from him or his jurisdiction. Again Labai is the con-
spirator who had taken our cities, and now Labai has taken
Ebed-Tob, and they have taken our cities. And the king
knows. To his servant let him grant power, for I did not
know they had done anything until the king had sent an
account of it to his servant."

LETTER FROM LABAI TO AMENOPHIS IV.

"To the king my lord and my Sun-god thus (speaks)
Labai thy servant and the dust of thy feet : at the feet of
the king my lord and my Sun-god, seven times seven I
prostrate myself. I have heard the words which the king
has sent to me, and here am I, and the king apportions his

APPENDICES 293

country unto me. Behold, I am a faithful servant of the king, and I have not sinned, and I have not offended, and I do not withhold my tribute, and I do not refuse the requests of the Commissioner that is set over me. Behold, they have slandered me, and the king my lord will not be hard on my offence. Again it is an offence in me that I have entered the city of Gezer and ordered the city to assemble, saying, 'The king has taken my property and the property of Malchiel.' How could I know what Malchiel has done against me? Again the king has written to Bin-Sumya; he does not know that Bin-Sumya has marched along with the Bedâwin, and lo, I have delivered him into the hand of Adda-dan. Again, if the king sends for my wife, how shall I withhold her; and if the king writes to myself, 'Plunge an iron sword in thy heart and die,' how shall I not perform the commandment of the king?"

VI

THE MOABITE STONE

(*See page* 112)

1. I am Mesha the son of Chemosh-melech, king of Moab, the Dibonite.
2. My father reigned over Moab thirty years, and I reigned
3. after my father. I made this monument to (the god) Chemosh at Korkhah, as a monument
4. of salvation, for he saved me from all invaders, and let me see my desire upon all my enemies. Omri
5. was king of Israel, and he oppressed Moab many days, for Chemosh was angry with his
6. land. His son followed him, and he also said: I will oppress Moab. In my days [Chemosh] said:
7. I will see my desire on him and his house, and Israel shall surely perish for ever. Omri took the land of
8. Medeba (Numb. xxi. 30), and [Israel] dwelt in it during his days and half the days of his son, altogether forty years. But there dwelt in it
9. Chemosh in my days. I built Baal-Meon (Josh. xiii. 17) and made therein the reservoirs; I built
10. Kirjathaim (Numb. xxxii. 37). The men of Gad dwelt in the land of Ataroth (Numb. xxxii. 3) from of old, and the king of Israel built there
11. (the town) of Ataroth; but I made war against the town and took it. And I slew all the [people]
12. of the town, for the pleasure of Chemosh and Moab. I

APPENDICES

    took from thence the Ariel (champion) of (the god) Doda and tore

13. him before Chemosh in Kerioth (Jer. xlviii. 24). And I placed therein the men of Sharon and the men

14. of Me-khereth. And Chemosh said unto me : Go, seize Nebo upon Israel; and

15. I went in the night and fought against it from the break of dawn till noon ; and I took

16. it, and slew all (therein), 7000 men, [boys], women, [girls],

17. and female slaves, and devoted them to Ashtor-Chemosh. And I took from it the Ariels of Yahveh, and tore them before Chemosh. And the king of Israel had built

18. Jahaz (Isa. xv. 4), and dwelt in it, whilst he waged war against me, (but) Chemosh drove him out before me. And

19. I brought from Moab 200 men, all chiefs, and carried them to Jahaz, which I took

20. to add to it Dibon. I built Korkhah, the wall of the forests and the wall

21. of the citadel : I built its gates and I built its towers. And

22. I built the temple of Moloch, and I made sluices of the water-ditches in the middle

23. of the town. And there was no cistern in the middle of the town of Korkhah, and I said to all the people : Make for

24. yourselves every man a cistern in his house. And I dug the canals for Korkhah by means of the prisoners

25. of Israel. I built Aroer and I made the road in [the province of] the Arnon. [And]

26. I built Beth-Bamoth, for it was destroyed. I built Bezer (Deut. iv. 43), for [it was] in ruins.

27. [And all the chiefs] of Dibon were fifty, for all Dibon was subject (to me) ; and I placed

28. 100 [chiefs] in the towns which I added to the land. I built
29. Beth-Medeba (Numb. xxi. 30), and Beth-diblathain (Jer. xlviii. 22), and Beth-baal-meon, and transported thereto the . . .
30. [and the shepherds] of the flocks of the land. And at Horonaim (Isa. xv. 5) there dwelt . . .
31. . . . And Chemosh said unto me : Go down, make war upon Horonaim. I went down [and made war]
32. [and took the city]; and Chemosh dwelt in it in my days. I went up from thence . . .
33. . . . And I . . .

VII

THE TREATY BETWEEN RAMSES II. AND THE HITTITES (*Brugsch's Translation*)

(See page 79)

"In the year 21, in the month of Tybi, on the 21st day of the month, in the reign of King Ramessu Mi-Amun, the dispenser of life eternally and for ever, the worshipper of the divinities Amun-Ra (of Thebes), Hor-em-khu (of Heliopolis), Ptah (of Memphis), Mut the lady of the Asher Lake (at Karnak), and Khonsu the peace-loving, there took place a public sitting on the throne of Horus among the living, resembling his father, Hor-em-khu in eternity, in eternity, evermore.

On that day the king was in the city of Ramses, presenting his peace-offerings to his father Amun-Ra and to the gods Hor-em-khu-Tum, the lord of Heliopolis (On), and to Amun of Ramessu Mi-Amun, to Ptah of Ramessu Mi-Amun, and to Sutekh, the strong, the son of Nut the goddess of heaven, that they might grant to him many thirty years' jubilee feasts, and innumerable happy years, and the subjection of all peoples under his feet for ever.

Then came forward the ambassador of the king and the governor [of his house, by name . . . , and presented the ambassadors] of the great king of the Hittites, Khata-sir, who were sent to Pharaoh to propose friendship with the king Ramessu Mi-Amun, the dispenser of life eternally and for ever, just as his father, the Sun-god [dispenses it] each day.

This is the copy of the contents of the silver tablet which the great king of the Hittites, Khata-sir, had caused to be made, and which was presented to the Pharaoh by the hand of his ambassador Tar-tisubu and his ambassador Rames, to propose friendship to the king Ramessu Mi-Amun, the bull among the princes, who places his boundary-marks where it pleases him in all lands.

The treaty which had been proposed by the great king of the Hittites, Khata-sir, the powerful, the son of Mar-sir, the great king of the Hittites, the powerful, the grandson of Sapalili, the great king of the Hittites, the powerful, on the silver tablet, to Ramessu Mi-Amun, the great prince of Egypt, the powerful—this was a good treaty for friendship and concord, which assured peace [and established concord] for a longer period than was previously the case for a long time. For it was the agreement of the great prince of Egypt in common with the great king of the Hittites that the god should not allow enmity to exist between them, on the basis of a treaty.

To wit, in the times of Mutal, the great king of the Hittites, my brother, he was at war with [Meneptah Seti I.] the great prince of Egypt.

But now, from this very day forward, Khata-sir, the great king of the Hittites, shall look upon this treaty so that the agreement may remain which the Sun-god Ra has made, which the god Sutekh has made, for the people of Egypt and for the people of the Hittites, that there should be no enmity between them for evermore.

And these are the contents :—

Khata-sir, the great king of the Hittites, is in covenant with Ramessu Mi-Amun, the great prince of Egypt, from this very day forward, that there may subsist a good friendship and a good understanding between them for evermore.

He shall be my ally ; he shall be my friend. I will be his ally ; I will be his friend, for ever.

To wit: in the time of Mutal, the great king of the Hit-

APPENDICES

tites, his brother Khata-sir, after his murder, placed himself on the throne of his father as the great king of the Hittites I strove for friendship with Ramessu Mi-Amun, the great prince of Egypt, and it is [my wish] that the friendship and the concord may be better than the friendship and the concord which before existed, and which was broken.

I declare: I, the great king of the Hittites, will hold together with [Ramessu Mi-Amun] the great prince of Egypt, in good friendship and good concord. The sons of the sons of the great king of the Hittites will hold together and be friends with the sons of the sons of Ramessu Mi-Amun, the great prince of Egypt.

In virtue of our treaty for concord, and in virtue of our agreement [for friendship, let the people] of Egypt [be bound in friendship] with the people of the Hittites. Let a like friendship and a like concord subsist in such measure for ever.

Never let enmity rise between them. Never let the great king of the Hittites invade the land of Egypt, if anything has been plundered from it (*i.e.* the land of the Hittites). Never let Ramessu Mi-Amun, the great prince of Egypt, overstep the boundary [of the land of the Hittites], if anything shall have been plundered from [the land of Egypt].

The just treaty which existed in the times of Sapalili, the great king of the Hittites, likewise the just treaty which existed in the times of Mutal, the great king of the Hittites, my brother, that will I keep.

Ramessu Mi-Amun, the great prince of Egypt, declares that he will keep it. [We have come to an understanding about it] with one another at the same time from this day forward, and we will fulfil it, and will act in a righteous manner.

If another shall come as an enemy to the lands of Ramessu Mi-Amun, the great prince of Egypt, then let him send an embassy to the great king of the Hittites to this effect: 'Come and make me stronger than him.' Then shall the great king of the Hittites [assemble his warriors], and the king of the Hittites [shall come] and smite his enemies. But if it should not be the wish of the great king of the Hittites to march out in person, then he shall send his warriors and his chariots that they may smite his enemies. Otherwise [he would incur] the wrath of Ramessu Mi-Amun [the great prince of Egypt. And if Ramessu Mi-Amun, the great prince of Egypt, should banish for a crime] subjects from his country, and they should commit further crime against him, then shall the king of the Hittites come forward to kill them. The great king of the Hittites shall act in common with [the great prince of Egypt].

[If another should come as an enemy to the lands of the great king of the Hittites, then shall he send an embassy to the great prince of Egypt with the request that] he would come in great power to kill his enemies; and if it be the intention of Ramessu Mi-Amun, the great prince of Egypt, (himself) to come, he shall [smite the enemies of the great king of the Hittites. If it is not the intention of the great prince of Egypt to march out in person, then he shall send his warriors and his two-] horse chariots, while he sends back the answer to the people of the Hittites.

If any subjects of the great king of the Hittites have offended him, then Ramessu Mi-Amun [the great prince of Egypt, shall not receive them in his land, but shall advance to kill them] . . . the oath with the wish to say, I will go . . . until . . . Ramessu Mi-Amun, the great prince of Egypt, living for ever . . . that he may be given for them (?) to the lord, and that Ramessu Mi-Amun, the great prince of Egypt, may speak according to his agreement for evermore . . .

[If servants shall flee away] out of the territories of Ramessu Mi-Amun [the great prince of Egypt, to betake themselves to] the great king of the Hittites, the great king of the Hittites shall not receive them, but the great king of the Hittites shall give them up to Ramessu Mi-Amun, the great prince of Egypt [that they may be punished].

APPENDICES 301

If servants of Ramessu Mi-Amun, the great prince of Egypt, leave his country and betake themselves to the land of the Hittites, to make themselves servants of another, they shall not remain in the land of the Hittites [but shall be given up] to Ramessu Mi-Amun, the great prince of Egypt.

If, on the other hand, there should flee away [servants of the great king of the Hittites, in order to betake themselves to] Ramessu Mi-Amun, the great prince of Egypt [in order to stay in Egypt], then those who have come from the land of the Hittites in order to betake themselves to Ramessu Mi-Amun, the great prince of Egypt, shall not be [received] by Ramessu Mi-Amun, the great prince of Egypt, (but) the great prince of Egypt, Ramessu Mi-Amun, [shall deliver them up to the great king of the Hittites.

And if there shall leave the land of the Hittites persons] of skilled mind, so that they come to the land of Egypt to make themselves servants of another, then Ramessu Mi-Amun shall not allow them to settle, he shall deliver them up to the great king of the Hittites.

When this [treaty] shall be known [by the inhabitants of the land of Egypt and of the land of the Hittites, then shall they not offend against it, for all that stands written upon] the silver tablet, these are words which will have been approved by the company of the gods, among the male deities and among the female deities, among those namely of the land of the Hittites, and by the company of the gods, among the male deities and among the female deities, among those namely of the land of Egypt. They are witnesses for me [to the validity] of these words.

[This is the catalogue of the gods of the land of the Hittites:—

Sutekh of the city of] Tunip (Tennib).
Sutekh of the land of the Hittites.
Sutekh of the city of Arnema.
Sutekh of the city of Zaranda.

Sutekh of the city of Pairaka.
Sutekh of the city of Khisasap.
Sutekh of the city of Sarsu.
Sutekh of the city of Aleppo.
Sutekh of the city of . . .
[Sutekh of the city of . . .]
Sutekh of the city of Sarpina.
Astartha of the land of the Hittites.
The god of the land of Zaiath-Khirri.
The god of the land of Ka . . .
The god of the land of Kher . . .
The goddess of the city of Akh . . .
[The goddess of the city of . . .] and of the land of A . . . ua.
The goddess of the land of Zaina.
The god of the land of . . . nath . . . **er**.

[I have invoked these male and these] female [deities of the land of the Hittites; these are the gods] of the land, as [witnesses to] my oath. [With them have been associated the male and the female deities] of the mountains and of the rivers of the land of the Hittites, the gods of the land of Kazawadana (Cappadocia), Amun, Ra, Sutekh, and the male and female deities of the land of Egypt, of the earth, of the sea, of the winds, and of the storms.

With regard to the commandment which the silver tablet contains for the people of the Hittites and for the people of Egypt, he who shall not observe it shall be given over [to the vengeance] of the company of the gods of the Hittites, and shall be given over [to the vengeance of the] company of the gods of Egypt, [he] and his house and his servants.

But he who shall observe these commandments which the silver tablet contains, whether he be of the people of the Hittites or [of the people of the Egyptians], because he has not neglected them, the company of the gods of the land of the Hittites, and the company of the gods of the land of Egypt shall secure his reward and preserve life [for him] and

APPENDICES

his servants, and those who are with him and with his servants.

If there flee away [one] of the inhabitants [from the land of Egypt], or two, or three, and they betake themselves to the great king of the Hittites, the great king of the Hittites shall take them and send them back to Ramessu Mi-Amun, the great prince of Egypt.

Now with regard to the inhabitant of the land of Egypt who is delivered up to Ramessu Mi-Amun, the great prince of Egypt, his fault shall not be avenged upon him, his house shall not be taken away, nor his wife nor his children. He shall not be put to death, neither shall he be mutilated in his eyes, nor in his ears, nor in his mouth, nor on the soles of his feet, so that thus no crime shall be brought forward against him.

In the same way shall it be done if inhabitants of the land of the Hittites take to flight, be it one alone or two or three, to betake themselves to Ramessu Mi-Amun, the great king of Egypt; Ramessu Mi-Amun, the great king of Egypt, shall cause them to be seized, and they shall be delivered up to the great prince of the Hittites.

With regard to him who is delivered up, his crime shall not be brought forward against him. His house shall not be destroyed, nor his wife, nor his children; he shall not be put to death, he shall not be mutilated in his eyes, nor in his ears, nor on his mouth, nor on the soles of his feet, nor shall any accusation be brought forward against him.

That which is in the middle of this silver tablet and on its front side is a likeness of the god Sutekh embracing the great prince of the Hittites, surrounded by an inscription to this effect: 'The seal of the god Sutekh the sovereign of heaven,' and 'The seal of the writing made by Khata-sir, the great and powerful prince of the Hittites, the son of Mar-sir, the great and powerful prince of the Hittites.' That which is in the middle of the frame is the seal of Sutekh the sovereign of heaven.

U

That which is on the other side (of the tablet) is the likeness of the god of the Hittites embracing the great princess of the Hittites, surrounded by an inscription to the following effect: 'The seal of the Sun-god of the city of Iranna, the lord of the earth,' and 'The seal of Puu-khipa, the great princess of the land of the Hittites, the daughter of the land of Qazawadana, the [servant of the goddess Iskhara of] Iranna, the regent of the earth; the servant of the goddess.' That which is in the middle of the frame is the seal of the Sun-god of Iranna, the lord of all the earth."

VIII

THE TRAVELS OF A MOHAR

A Satirical Account of a Tourist's Misadventures in Canaan, written in the Time of Ramses II., the Pharaoh of the Oppression

(*See page* 189)

" I will portray for thee the likeness of a Mohar; I will let thee know what he does. Thou hast not gone to the land of the Hittites, nor hast thou beheld the land of Aupa. The appearance of Khatuma thou knowest not. Likewise the land of Igadai, what is it like? The Zar (Plain) of Sesostris and the city of Aleppo are on none of its sides. How is its ford? Thou hast not taken thy road to Kadesh (on the Orontes) and Tubikhi (the Tibhath of 1 Chr. xviii. 8), neither hast thou gone to the Shasu (Bedâwin) with numerous foreign soldiers, neither hast thou trodden the way to the Magharat (the caves of the Magoras near Beyrout), where the heaven is dark in the daytime. The place is planted with maple trees, oaks, and acacias, which reach up to heaven, full of beasts, bears and lions, and surrounded by Shasu in all directions. Thou hast not gone up to the mountain of Shaua (in the northern Lebanon), neither hast thou trodden it; there thy hands hold fast to the [rein] of thy chariot; a jerk has shaken thy horses in drawing it. I pray thee, let us go to the city of Beeroth (cisterns). Thou must hasten to its ascent, after thou hast passed over its ford in front of it.

Do thou explain the attraction to be a Mohar! Thy

chariot lies there [before] thee; thy [strength] has fallen lame; thou treadest the backward path at eventide. All thy limbs are ground small. Thy [bones] are broken to pieces. Sweet is [sleep]. Thou awakest. There has been a time for a thief in this unfortunate night. Thou wast alone, in the belief that the brother could not come to the brother. Some grooms entered into the stable; the horse kicks out; the thief goes back in the night; thy clothes are stolen. Thy groom wakes up in the night; he sees what has happened to him; he takes what is left, he goes to the evil-doers, he mixes himself up with the tribes of the Shasu. He acts as if he were an Amu (Asiatic). The enemies come, they [feel about] for the robber. He is discovered, and is immovable from terror. Thou awakest, thou findest no trace of them, for they have carried off thy property.

Become (again) a Mohar, who is fully accoutred. Let thy ear be full of that which I relate to thee besides.

The town 'Hidden'—such is the meaning of its name Gebal—what is its state? Its goddess (we will speak of) at another time. Thou hast not visited it. Be good enough to look out for Beyrout, Sidon, and Sarepta. Where are the fords of the land of Nazana? The land of Usu (Palætyrus), what is its state? They speak of another city in the sea, Tyre the haven is her name. Drinking water is brought to her in boats. She is richer in fish than in sand. I will tell thee of something else. Dangerous is it to enter into Zorah. Thou wilt say it is burning with a very painful sting (?) Mohar, come! Go forward on the way to the land of Pa-Kâkina. Where is the road to Achshaph? Towards no city. Pray look at the mountain of User. How is its crest? Where is the mountain of Shechem? Who can surmount it? Mohar, whither must you take a journey to the city of Hazor? How is its ford? Let me (choose) the road to Hamath, Dagara, (and) Dagar-ol. Here is the road where all Mohars meet. Be good enough to spy out its road, cast a look on Yâ . . . When one goes to the land of

APPENDICES

Adamim, to what is one opposite? Do not draw back, but instruct us! Guide us that we may know, thou leader!

I will name to thee other cities besides these. Thou hast not gone to the land of Takhis, Kafir-Malona, Tamnah, Kadesh, Dapul, Azai, Har-Nammata, nor hast thou beheld Kirjath-eneb near Beth-Sopher (Kirjath-Sepher or Debir); nor dost thou know Adullam (and) Zidiputha, nor dost thou know any better the name of Khalza in the land of Aupa, the bull on its frontiers (?). Here is the place where all the mighty warriors are seen. Be good enough to look and see how Qina is situated, and tell me about Rehob. Describe Beth-sha-el (Bethel) along with Tarqa-el. The ford of the land of the Jordan, how is it crossed? Teach me to know the passage in order to enter into the city of Megiddo which lies in front of it. Verily thou art a Mohar, well skilled in the work of the strong hand. Pray, is there found a Mohar like thee, to place at the head of the army, or a *seigneur* who can beat thee in shooting?

Drive along the edge of the precipice, on the slippery height, over a depth of 2000 cubits, full of rocks and boulders. Thou takest thy way back in a zigzag, thou bearest thy bow, thou takest the iron in thy left hand. Thou lettest the old men see, if their eyes are good, how, worn-out with fatigue, thou supportest thyself with thy hand. *Il est perdu, le chameau, le Mohar! Eh bien!*[1] Make to thyself a name among the Mohars and the knights of the land of Egypt. Let thy name be like that of Qazirnai the lord of Aser, because he discovered lions in the interior of the balsam-forest of Baka at the narrow passes, which are rendered dangerous by the Shasu who lie in ambush among the trees. (The lions) measured fourteen cubits by five cubits. Their noses reached to the soles of their feet. Of a grim appearance, without softness, they cared not for

[1] By the use of French words and expressions Brugsch endeavours to represent the Canaanitish terms which the Egyptian writer has affectedly introduced into his work.

caresses. Thou art alone, no stronger one is with thee, no *armée* is behind thee, no Ariel (see 2 Sam. xxiii. 20, Isa. xxix. 1) who prepares the way for thee, and gives thee counsel on the road before thee. Thou knowest not the road. The hair on thy head stands on end; it bristles up. Thy soul is given into thy hands. Thy path is full of rocks and boulders, there is no way out near; it is overgrown with creepers and wolf's-foot. Abysses are on one side of thee, the mountain and the wall of rock on the other. Thou drivest in against it. The chariot jumps on which thou art. Thou art troubled to hold up thy horses. If it falls into the abyss, the pole drags thee down too. Thy *ceintures* are pulled away. They fall down. Thou shacklest the horse, because the pole is broken on the path of the narrow pass. Not knowing how to tie it up, thou understandest not how it is to be repaired. The *essieu* is left on the spot, as the load is too heavy for the horses. Thy courage has evaporated. Thou beginnest to run. The heaven is cloudless. Thou art thirsty; the enemy is behind thee; a trembling seizes thee; a twig of thorny acacia worries thee; thou thrustest it aside; the horse is scratched, till at length thou findest rest.

Explain thou thy attraction to be a Mohar!

Thou comest into Joppa. Thou findest the date-palm in full bloom in its time. Thou openest wide the aperture of thy mouth in order to eat. Thou findest that the maid who keeps the garden is fair. She does whatever thou wantest of her. . . . Thou art recognised, thou art brought to trial, and owest thy preservation to being a Mohar. Thy girdle of the finest stuff, thou payest it as the price of a bad rag. Thou sleepest every evening with a rug of fur over thee. Thou sleepest a deep sleep, for thou art weary. A thief takes thy bow and thy sword from thy side; thy quiver and thy armour are broken to pieces in the darkness; thy pair of horses run away. The groom takes his course over a slippery path that rises in front of him. He breaks thy chariot in pieces; he follows thy foot-tracks. [He finds] thy equip-

APPENDICES 309

ments, which had fallen on the ground, and had sunk into the sand, leaving only an empty space.

Prayer does not avail thee; even when thy mouth says: 'Give food in addition to water that I may reach my goal in safety,' they are deaf and will not hear. They say not yes to thy words. The iron-workers enter into the smithy; they rummage in the workshops of the carpenters; the handicraftsmen and soldiers are at hand; they do whatever thou requirest. They put together thy chariot: they put aside the parts of it that have been made useless; thy spokes are *façonné* quite new; thy wheels are put on, they put the *courroies* on the axles and on the hinder part; they splice thy yoke, they put on the box of thy chariot; the [workmen] in iron forge the . . . ; they put the ring that is wanting on thy whip, they replace the *lanières* upon it.

Thou goest quickly onward to fight on the battlefield, to do the deeds of a strong hand and of firm courage.

Before I wrote I sought me out a Mohar who knows his power, who leads the *jeunesse*, a chief in the *armée* [who goes forward] even to the end of the world.

Answer me not, 'That is good, this is bad;' repeat not to me thy opinion. Come, I will tell thee all which lies before thee at the end of thy journey.

I begin for thee with the palace of Sesostris (Ramses II.). Thou hast not set foot in it by force. Thou hast not eaten the fish in the brook of . . Thou hast not washed thyself in it. With thy permission I will remind thee of Huzana (near El-Arish); where is its fortress? Come, I pray thee, to the palace of the land of Uzi, of Sesostris Osymandyas in his victories, to Saz-el together with Absaqbu. I will inform thee of the land of Ainin (the Two Springs), the customs of which thou knowest not. The land of the lake of Nakhai and the land of Rehoburtha (Rehoboth, Gen. xxvi. 22) thou hast not seen since thou wast born, O Mohar. Rapih (the modern boundary between Egypt and Turkey) is widely extended. What is its wall like? It extends for a mile in the direction of Gaza."

IX

THE NEGATIVE CONFESSION OF THE EGYPTIANS

(*Sir P. Le Page Renouf's Translation*)

(*See page* 186)

The 125th chapter of the Book of the Dead contains the confession which the soul of the dead man was required to make before Osiris and the forty-two divine judges of the dead, before he could be justified and admitted to the Paradise of Aalu :—

" Said on arriving at the Hall of Righteousness, that N (the soul of the dead man) may be loosed from all the sins which he hath committed, and that he may look upon the divine countenances.

He saith:—Hail to thee, mighty God, lord of Righteousness!

I am come to thee, O my Lord! I have brought myself that I may look upon thy glory. I know thee, and I know the name of the forty-two gods who make their appearance with thee in the Hall of Righteousness; devouring those who harbour mischief and swallowing their blood, upon the day of the searching examination in the presence of Unneferu (Osiris).

Verily 'Thou of the Pair of Eyes, Lord of Righteousness,' is thy name.

Here am I; I am come to thee; I bring to thee Right and have put a stop to Wrong.

I am not a doer of wrong to men.
I am not one who slayeth his kindred.
I am not one who telleth lies instead of truth.

APPENDICES

I am not conscious of treason.
I am not a doer of mischief.
I do not exact as the first-fruits of each day more work than should be done for me.
My name cometh not to the Bark of the god who is at the Helm.
I am not a transgressor against the God.
I am not a tale-bearer.
I am not a detractor.
I am not a doer of that which the gods abhor.
I hurt no servant with his master.
I cause no famine.
I cause not weeping.
I am not a murderer.
I give not orders for murder.
I cause not suffering to men.
I reduce not the offering in the temples.
I lessen not the cakes of the gods.
I rob not the dead of their funereal food.
I am not an adulterer.
I am undefiled in the sanctuary of the god of my domain.
I neither increase nor diminish the measures of grain.
I am not one who shorteneth the palm's length.
I am not one who cutteth short the field's measurement.
I put not pressure upon the beam of the balance.
I snatch not the milk from the mouth of infants.
I drive not the cattle from their pastures.
I net not the birds of the manors of the gods.
I catch not the fish of their ponds.
I stop not the water at its appointed time.
I divide not an arm of the water in its course.
I extinguish not the lamp during its appointed time.
I do not defraud the Divine Circle of their sacrificial joints.
I drive not away the cattle of the sacred estate.
I stop not a god when he cometh forth.
I am pure, I am pure, I am pure, I am pure!"

X

LETTERS OF KHAMMURABI OR AMMURAPI (THE AMRAPHEL OF GEN. xiv. 1) TO SIN-IDINNAM, KING OF LARSA (THE ELLASAR OF GENESIS)

I. "To Sin-idinnam thus says Khammurabi: The goddesses of the land of Emudbalum restored your courage to you on the day of the defeat of Kudur-Laghghamar (Chedor-laomer). Because they have supported you among the army of thy hand, turn back the army and let them restore the goddesses to their own seats."

II. "To Sin-idinnam thus says Khummarabi: When you have seen this letter you will understand in regard to Amil-Samas and Nur-Nintu, the sons of Gisdubba, that if they are in Larsa or in the territory of Larsa you will order them to be sent away, and that one of your servants on whom you can depend shall take them and bring them to Babylon."

III. "To Sin-idinnam thus says Khammurabi: As to the officials who have resisted you in the accomplishment of their work, do not impose upon them any additional task, but oblige them to do what they ought to have performed, and then remove them from the influence of him who has brought them."

Sin-idinnam seems to have been the legitimate prince of Larsa, who had been expelled from his dominions by the Elamite invader Eri-Aku or Arioch, and had taken refuge at the court of Khammurabi in Babylon. After the overthrow of the Elamites, Sin-idinnam was restored by Khammurabi to his ancestral principality.

XI

THE BABYLONIAN ACCOUNT OF THE DELUGE

1. Sisuthros spake thus unto him, even to Gilgames:
2. 'Let me reveal unto thee, O Gilgames, the tale of my preservation,
3. and the oracle of the gods let me declare unto thee.
4. The city of Surippak, which, as thou knowest, is built [on the bank] of the Euphrates,
5. this city was (already) old when the gods within it
6. set their hearts to cause a flood, even the great gods
7. [as many as] exist: Anu the father of them,
8. the warrior Bel their prince,
9. Bir their throne-bearer, En-nugi (Hades) their chief.
10. Ea the lord of wisdom conferred with them, and
11. repeated their words to the reed-bed: 'Reed-bed, O reed-bed! Frame, O frame!
12. Hear, O reed-bed, and understand, O frame!
13. O man of Surippak, son of Ubara-Tutu,
14. frame the house, build a ship: leave what thou canst; seek life!
15. Resign (thy) goods, and cause thy soul to live,
16. and bring all the seed of life into the midst of the ship.
17. As for the ship which thou shalt build,
18. . . . cubits shall be in measurement its length;
19. and . . . cubits the extent of its breadth and its height.
20. Into the deep [then] launch it.'
21. I understood and spake to Ea my lord:

22. 'As for the building of the ship, O my lord, which thou hast ordered thus,
23. I will observe and accomplish it.
24. [But what] shall I answer the city, the people and the old men?'
25. [Ea opened his mouth and] says, he speaks to his servant, even to me :
26. [' If they question thee] thou shalt say unto them :
27. Since (?) Bel is estranged from me and
28. I will not dwell in your city, I will not lay my head [in] the land of Bel ;
29. but I will descend into the deep ; with [Ea] my lord will I dwell.
30. (Bel) will rain fertility on you,
31. [flocks] of birds, shoals of fish.'

Lines 32 to 42 are lost.

43. On the fifth day I laid the plan of it (*i.e.* the ship) ;
44. in its hull (?) its walls were 10 *gar* (120 cubits ?) high ;
45. 10 *gar* were the size of its upper part.'

Another version of the account of the Deluge, of which a fragment has been preserved, puts a wholly different speech into the mouth of Ea, and gives the hero of the story the name of Adra-Khasis. This fragment is as follows :—

' I will judge him above and below.
[But] shut [not thou thy door]
[until] the time that I shall tell thee of.
[Then] enter the ship, and close the door of the vessel.
[Bring into] it thy corn, thy goods, [thy] property,
thy [wife], thy slaves, thy handmaids, and the sons of [thy] people,
the [cattle] of the field, the beasts of the field, as many as I appoint . . .
I will tell thee of (the time), and the door [of thy ship] shall preserve them.'

Adra-Khasis opened his mouth and says,

he speaks to Ea [his] lord :
'[O my lord,] none has ever made a ship [on this wise] that it should sail over the land.' . . .

Here the fragment is broken off. The other version proceeds thus :—

46. ' I fashioned its side, and closed it in;
47. I built six storeys (?), I divided it into seven parts ;
48. its interior I divided into nine parts.
49. I cut worked (?) timber within it.
50. I looked upon the rudder and added what was lacking.
51. I poured 6 *sars* of pitch over the outside ;
52. [I poured] 3 *sars* of bitumen over the inside ;
53. 3 *sars* of oil did the men carry who brought it . . .
54. I gave a *sar* of oil for the workmen to eat ;
55. 2 *sars* of oil the sailors stored away.
56. For the [workmen?] I slaughtered oxen ;
57. I killed [sheep?] daily.
58. Beer, wine, oil and grapes
59. [I distributed among] the people like the waters of a river, and
60. [I kept] a festival like the festival of the new year.
61. . . . I dipped my hand [in] oil :
62. [I said to] Samas (the Sun-god): ' The storeys (?) of the ship are complete ;
63. the . . . is strong, and
64. the oars (?) I introduced above and below.'
65. [Those who should be saved?] went two-thirds of them.
66. With all I had I filled it; with all the silver I possessed I filled it;
67. with all the gold I possessed I filled it;
68. with all that I possessed of the seed of life of all kinds I filled it.
69. I brought into the ship all my slaves and my handmaids,
70. the cattle of the field, the beasts of the field, the sons of my people, all of them did I bring into it.

71. The Sun-god appointed the time and
72. utters the oracle : 'In the night will I cause the heavens to rain destruction ;
73. enter the ship, and close thy door.'
74. That time drew near whereof he uttered the oracle :
75. 'On this night will I cause the heavens to rain destruction.'
76. I watched with dread the dawning of the day ;
77. I feared to behold the day.
78. I entered into the ship and closed my door.
79. When I had closed the ship, to Buzur-sadi-rabi the sailor
80. I entrusted the palace with all its goods.
81. Mu-seri-ina-namari (the waters of the morning at dawn)
82. arose from the horizon of heaven, a black cloud ;
83. the storm-god Rimmon thundered in its midst, and
84. Nebo and Merodach the king marched in front ;
85. the throne-bearers marched over mountain and plain ;
86. the mighty god of death lets loose the whirlwind ;
87. Bir marches causing the storm (?) to descend ;
88. the spirits of the underworld lifted up (their) torches,
89. with the lightning of them they set on fire the world ;
90. the violence of the storm-god reached to heaven ;
91. all that was light was turned to [darkness].
92. In the earth like . . . [men] perished (?)

Two lines are lost here.

95. Brother beheld not his brother, men knew not one another. In the heaven
96. the gods feared the deluge, and
97. hastened to ascend to the heaven of Anu.
98. The gods cowered like a dog who lies in a kennel.
99. Istar cried like a woman in travail,
100. the great goddess spoke with a loud voice:
101. 'The former generation is turned to clay.
102. The evil which I prophesied in the presence of the gods,
103. when I prophesied evil in the presence of the gods,
104. I prophesied the storm for the destruction of my people.

105. What I have borne, where is it?
106. Like the spawn of the fish it fills the deep.'
107. The gods wept with her because of the spirits of the underworld;
108. the gods sat dejected in weeping,
109. their lips were covered . . .
110. Six days and nights
111. rages the wind; the flood and the storm devastate.
112. The seventh day when it arrived the flood ceased, the storm
113. which had fought like an army
114. rested, the sea subsided, and the tempest of the deluge was ended.
115. I beheld the deep and uttered a cry,
116. for the whole of mankind was turned to clay;
117. like the trunks of trees did the bodies float.
118. I opened the window and the light fell upon my face;
119. I stooped, and sat down weeping;
120. over my face ran my tears.
121. I beheld a shore beyond the sea;
122. twelve times distant rose a land.
123. On the mountain of Nizir the ship grounded;
124. the mountain of the country of Nizir held the ship and allowed it not to float.
125. One day and a second day did the mountain of Nizir hold it.
126. A third day and a fourth day did the mountain of Nizir hold it.
127. A fifth day and a sixth day did the mountain of Nizir hold it.
128. When the seventh day came I sent forth a dove and let it go.
129. The dove went and returned; a resting-place it found not and it turned back.
130. I sent forth a swallow and let it go; the swallow went and returned;

131. a resting-place it found not and it turned back.
132. I sent forth a raven and let it go ;
133. the raven went and saw the going down of the waters, and
134. it approached, it waded, it croaked and did not turn back.
135. Then I sent forth (everything) to the four points of the compass ; I offered sacrifices ;
136. I built an altar on the summit of the mountain.
137. I set libation-vases seven by seven ;
138. beneath them I piled up reeds, cedar-wood and herbs.
139. The gods smelt the savour, the gods smelt the sweet savour ;
140. the gods gathered like flies over the sacrificer.
141. Already at the moment of her coming, the great goddess
142. lifted up the mighty bow which Anu had made according to his wish (?).
143. 'These gods,' (she said), 'by my necklace, never will I forget !
144. Those days, I will think of them and never will forget them.
145. Let the gods come to my altar ;
146. (but) let not Bel come to my altar,
147. since he did not take counsel but caused a flood and counted my men for judgment.'
148. Already at the moment of his coming, Bel
149. saw the ship and stood still ;
150. he was filled with wrath at the gods, the spirits of heaven, (saying) :
151. 'Let no living soul come forth, let no man survive in the judgment !'
152. Bir opened his mouth and says, he speaks to the warrior Bel :
153. 'Who except Ea can devise a speech ?
154. for Ea understands all kinds of wisdom.'

APPENDICES 319

155. Ea opened his mouth and speaks, he says to the warrior Bel:
156. 'Thou art the seer of the gods, O warrior!
157. Why, O why didst thou not take counsel, but didst cause a deluge?
158. (Let) the sinner bear his own sin, (let) the evil-doer bear his own evil-doing.
159. Grant (?) that he be not cut off, be merciful that he be not [destroyed].
160. Instead of causing a deluge, let lions come and minish mankind;
161. instead of causing a deluge, let hyænas come and minish mankind;
162. instead of causing a deluge, let there be a famine and let it [devour] the land;
163. instead of causing a deluge, let the plague-god come and minish mankind!
164. I did not reveal (to men) the oracle of the great gods,
165. but sent a dream to Adra-khasis and he heard the oracle of the gods.'
166. Then Bel again took counsel and ascended into the ship.
167. He took my hand and caused me, even me, to ascend,
168. he took up my wife (also, and) caused her to bow at my side;
169. he turned to us and stood between us; he blessed us (saying):
170. 'Hitherto Sisuthros has been mortal, but
171. henceforth Sisuthros and his wife shall be like unto the gods, even unto us, and
172. Sisuthros shall dwell afar at the mouth of the rivers.'
173. Then he took us afar, at the mouth of the rivers he made us dwell.

XII

THE BABYLONIAN EPIC OF THE CREATION

Tablet I.

When the heaven above was not yet named
or the earth beneath had recorded a name,
the primæval (*ristû*) deep was their generator,
Mummu-Tiamat (the chaos of the sea) was the mother of
   them all.
Their waters were embosomed together, and
the corn-field was unharvested, the reed-bed was ungrown.
When the gods had not yet appeared, any one of them,
by no name were they recorded, no destiny [was fixed].
Then the great gods were created,
Lakhmu and Lakhamu issued forth [the first],
until they grew up [when]
Ansar and Kisar (the upper and lower firmaments) were
   created.
Long were the days, extended [was the time, till]
the gods [Anu, Bel, and Ea were born],
Ansar [and Kisar gave them birth].

 . . . . . .

The deep [opened] its mouth [and said,]
to [Tiamat], the glorious, [it spake]:
While their path . . .
I will overthrow their path . . .
Let lamentations arise, let complaining [be made]
[When] Tiamat [undertakes] this [work]

 . . . .

Their way shall be difficult . . .
[Then] the god Mummu answered [his] father the deep :

  . . . .

Their way [shall be overthrown],
the light shall be darkened, let [it be] as the night !
The deep [heard] him and [his] countenance was lightened ;
evil planned they against the gods.

  . . . .

Tiamat, the mother of the gods, lifted up herself against them,
gathering her forces, madly raging.
The gods united themselves together with her,
until (all) that had been created marched at her side.
Banning the day they followed Tiamat,
wrathful, devising mischief, untiring (?) day and night,
prepared for the conflict, fiercely raging,
they gathered themselves together and began the battle.
The mother of the deep (?) (*Khubur*), the creatress of them all,
added victorious weapons, creating monstrous serpents,
with sharp fangs, unsparing in their attack.
With poison for blood she filled their bodies.
Horrible adders she clothed with terror,
she decked them with fear, and raised high their . . .
' May their appearance . . .
Make huge their bodies that none may withstand their breast !'
She created the adder, the horrible serpent, the Lakhamu,
the great monster, the raging dog, the scorpion-man,
the dog-days, the fish-man and the (Zodiacal) ram,
who carry weapons that spare not, who fear not the battle,
insolent of heart, unconquerable by the enemy.
Moreover that she might create (?) eleven such-like monsters,
among the gods, her sons, whom she had summoned together,
she raised up Kingu, and magnified him among them :
' To march before the host, be that thy duty !

Order the weapons to be uplifted and the onset of battle!'
That he might be the first in the conflict, the leader in victory,
she took his hand and set him on a throne:
'I have uttered the spell for thee; exalt thyself among the gods,
assume dominion over all the gods!
Highly shalt thou be exalted, thou that art alone my husband;
thy name shall be magnified over [all the world]!'
Then she gave to him the tablets of destiny, and laid them on his breast:
'Let thy command be obeyed, let the word of thy mouth be established!'
When Kingu had exalted himself, and made himself like Anu (the god of heaven),
she determined for the gods her sons their destiny:
'The opening of your mouth shall quench the fire;
The exalted of Kidmuri (*i.e.* Kingu) shall dissolve its flame.'

. . . .

TABLET II.

(Begins with a speech of Ansar to Merodach.)

'Tiamat our mother has risen up against us,
gathering her forces, madly raging.
The gods have united themselves together with her,
until (all) that has been created marches at her side.
Banning the day they have followed Tiamat,
wrathful, devising mischief, untiring (?) day and night,
prepared for the conflict, fiercely raging,
they have gathered themselves together and begun the battle.
The mother of the deep (?), the creatress of them all,
has added victorious weapons, creating monstrous serpents,
with sharp fangs, unsparing in their attack.

APPENDICES 323

With poison for blood she has filled their bodies.
Horrible adders she has clothed with terror,
she has decked them with fear, and raised high their . . .
'May their appearance . . .
may their bodies be huge so that none may withstand their breast!'
She has created the adder, the horrible serpent, the Lakhamu,
the great monster, the raging dog, the scorpion-man,
the dog-days, the fish-man (Aquarius), and the (Zodiacal) ram,
who carry weapons that spare not, who fear not the battle,
insolent of heart, unconquerable by the enemy.
Moreover that she may create (?) eleven such-like monsters,
among the gods, her sons, whom she has summoned together,
she has raised up Kingu and magnified him among them.
'To march before the host,' (she has said,) 'be that thy duty!
Order the weapons to be uplifted and the onset of battle!'
That he may be the first in the conflict, the leader in victory,
she has taken his hand and seated him on a throne :
'I have uttered the spell for thee ; exalt thyself among the gods,
assume dominion over all the gods!
Highly shalt thou be exalted, thou that art alone my husband ;
thy name shall be magnified over [all the world]!'
Thereupon she has given him the tablets of destiny and laid them on his breast :
'Let thy command be obeyed, let the word of thy mouth be established !'
When Kingu had exalted himself, and made himself as Anu,
she determined for the gods her sons their destiny :
'The opening of your mouth shall quench the fire ;
the exalted of Kidmuri shall dissolve its flame !'

[When Merodach heard this, his heart] was grievously
 troubled,
he . . . . . . and his lips he bit;
. . . . . his heart grew angry
. . . . . . his cry.
. . . . . . [he determined on] battle.
[Then spake he to] his father (Ea): 'Be not troubled;
. . . . . . thou shalt become the lord of the deep.
. . . . . . with Tiamat will I contend.'

. . . .

Merodach [heard] the words of his father,
in the fulness (?) of his heart he said to his father.
'O lord of the gods, offspring (?) of the great gods,
if indeed I am your avenger,
Tiamat to overpower and you to rescue,
make ready an assembly, prepare a banquet (?).
Enter joyfully into Ubsugina (the seat of oracles) all together.
With my mouth like you will I give the oracle.
What I create shall never be changed,
the word of my lip shall never go back or be unfulfilled!'

TABLET III.

Thereupon Ansar opened his mouth,
to [Gâgâ] his [messenger] he uttered the word:
'O angel [Gâgâ] who rejoicest my heart,
[to Lakhmu and Lakh]amu will I send thee;
[the command of my heart] thou shalt gladly hear (?):
'Ansar, your son, has sent me,
the wish of his heart he has caused me to know.
Tiamat our mother has risen up against us,
gathering her forces, madly raging.
The gods, all of them, have united themselves unto her,
all whom she has created march at her side.
Banning the day they have followed Tiamat,

APPENDICES

wrathful, devising mischief, untiring (?) day and night,
prepared for the conflict, fiercely raging,
they have gathered themselves together and begin the fray.
The mother of the deep (?), the creatress of them all,
has given them victorious weapons, creating monstrous serpents
with sharp fangs, unsparing in the onset.
With poison for blood she has filled their bodies.
Horrible adders she has clothed with terror,
she has decked them with fear, and raised high their . . .
'May their appearance . . .
May their bodies grow huge so that none may stand before them !'
She has created the adder, the horrible serpent, the Lakhamu,
the great monster, the raging dog, the scorpion-man,
the dog-days, the fish-man and the ram,
who carry weapons that spare not, who fear not the conflict,
insolent of heart, unconquerable by the enemy.
Moreover that she may have eleven such monsters,
among the gods, her sons, whom she has summoned together,
she has raised up Kingu and magnified him among them :
'To march before the host, be that thy duty !
Order the weapons to be uplifted and the onset of battle !'
That he may be first in the conflict, the leader in victory,
she has taken his hand and set him on a throne :
'I have uttered the spell for thee, exalt thyself among the gods,
assume dominion over all the gods !
Highly shalt thou be exalted, thou that art alone my husband ;
thy name shall be magnified over [all the world] !'
Then she gave him the tablets of destiny, and laid them on his breast :

'Let thy command be obeyed, let the word of thy mouth
  be established!'
When Kingu had exalted himself and made himself as
  Anu
she determined for the gods her sons their destiny:
'The opening of your mouth shall quench the fire,
the exalted of Kidmuri shall dissolve its flame.'
I sent forth Anu, but he would not meet her;
Ea was terrified and turned back.
Then I bade Merodach, the counsellor of the gods, your
  son;
to attack Tiamat his heart urged him.
He opened his mouth and spake unto me:
'If I am indeed your avenger,
Tiamat to overpower, you to rescue,
make ready an assembly, prepare a banquet (?).
Enter joyfully into Ubsugina, all together.
With my mouth, like you, will I then pronounce an
  oracle,
what I create shall never be changed;
the word of my lip shall never go back or be unfulfilled.'
Hasten therefore and determine at once for him his
  destiny
that he may go forth and meet your mighty foe!'
Lakhmu and Lakhamu heard this and lamented,
the gods of heaven, all of them, bitterly grieved:
'Foolish are they who thus desire battle (?);
nor can we understand the [design] of Tiamat.'
Then they came together and marched . . .
the great gods, all of them, who determine [destinies].
They came before (?) Ansar, they filled [his abode],
they crowded one on the other in the gathering . . .
they sat down to the feast, [they devoured] the food;
they eat bread, they drank [wine],
with sweet honey wine they filled themselves,
they drank beer, and delighted their soul (?)

APPENDICES

...... they ascended into their [seats],
to determine the destiny of Merodach their avenger.

Tablet IV.

Then they set him on a princely throne ;
before his fathers he seated himself as ruler.
' Yea, thou art glorious among the great gods,
thy destiny has no rival, thy name (?) is Anu ;
from this day forward unchanged be thy command,
high and low entreat thy hand !
Let the word of thy mouth be established, thy judgment never be violated,
let none among the gods overpass thy bounds !
as an adornment has (thy hand) founded the shrine of the gods,
may the place of their gathering (?) become thy home.
O Merodach, thou art he that avenges us,
we give unto thee the sovereignty over the multitudes of the universe.
Thou givest counsel, let thy word be exalted ;
may thy weapons be victorious, may thine enemies tremble !
O lord, be gracious to the soul of him who putteth his trust in thee,
but pour out the soul of the god who has hold of evil.'
Then place they in their midst a robe ;
they spake to Merodach their first-born :
' May thy destiny, O lord, excel that of the gods ;
command destruction and creation, and so it shall be done.
Set thy mouth that it may destroy the robe ;
bid it return and the robe shall be restored !'
He spake and with his mouth destroyed the robe ;
he spake to it again, and the robe was re-created.
When the gods his fathers beheld (the power) of the word of his mouth,

they rejoiced, they saluted Merodach the king,
they bestowed upon him the sceptre, the throne and reign,
they gave him a weapon unrivalled, consuming the hostile:
'Go,' (they said,) 'and cut off the life of Tiamat,
let the winds carry her blood to secret places.'
(Thus) the gods, his fathers, determined for Bel his destiny,
they showed his path, and they bade him listen and take the road.
He made ready the bow and used it as his weapon;
he made the club swing, he fixed its seat;
then he lifted up the weapon which he caused his right hand to hold;
the bow and the quiver he hung at his side.
He set the lightning before him,
with glancing flame he filled its body.
He made also a net to enclose the dragon Tiamat.
He seized the four winds that they might not issue out of it,
the south wind, the north wind, the east wind (and) the west wind;
he made them enter the net, the gift of his father Anu.
He created the evil wind, the hostile wind, the storm, the tempest,
the four winds, the seven winds, the whirlwind, the unending wind :
he caused the winds he had created to issue forth, seven in all,
confounding the dragon Tiamat, as they swept after him.
Then Bel lifted up the Deluge, his mighty weapon :
he rode in a chariot incomparable, (and) terrible.
He stood firm, and harnessed four horses to its side,
[steeds] that spare not, spirited and swift,
[with sharp] teeth, that carry poison,
which know how to sweep away [the opponent].
[On the right] . . . mighty in battle,

APPENDICES

on the left they open . . .
. . . . . . before thee.
[Bring to the feast] the gods, all of them,
[let them sit down and] satisfy themselves with food,
[let them eat bread], let them drink wine,
[let them ascend to their seats?] and determine the future.
[Go now,] Gâgâ, approach before them,
deliver unto them [the message I entrust to] thee:
' Ansar, your son, has sent me,
the wish of his heart he has caused me to know.
Tiamat, our mother, has risen up against us,
gathering her forces, madly raging.
The gods, all of them, have united themselves unto her,
even those who created you march at her side.
Banning the day they have followed Tiamat,
wrathful, devising mischief, untiring (?) day and night,
prepared for the conflict, fiercely raging,
they have gathered themselves together and begin the battle.
The mother of the deep (?), the creatress of them all,
has given them victorious weapons, creating monstrous serpents,
with sharp fangs, unsparing in their attack.
With poison for blood she has filled their bodies.
Horrible adders she has clothed with terror,
she has decked them with fear, and raised high their . . .
' May their appearance,' (she has said) . . .
' Let their bodies grow huge so that none may stand before them !'
She has created the adder, the horrible serpent, the Lakhamu,
the great monster, the raging dog, the scorpion-man,
the dog-days, the fish-man and the ram,
who carry weapons that spare not, who fear not the fight,
insolent of heart, unconquerable by the enemy.
Moreover that she may have eleven such monsters,

among the gods, her sons, whom she has summoned together,
she has raised up Kingu and magnified him among them.
'To march before the host, be that thy duty!
Order the weapons to be uplifted and the onset of battle!'
That he may be the first in the conflict, the leader in victory,
she has taken his hand and set him on a throne:
'I have uttered the spell for thee,' (she has said); 'exalt thyself among the gods,
assume dominion over all the gods!
Highly shalt thou be exalted, thou that art alone my husband;
thy name shall be magnified over [all the world]!'
Thereupon she has given him the tablets of destiny, and laid them on his breast:
'Let thy command be obeyed, let the word of thy mouth be established!'
When Kingu had exalted himself and made himself like Anu
she fixed for the gods, her sons, their destiny ·
'The opening of your mouth shall quench the fire;
the exalted of Kidmuri shall dissolve its flame.'
I sent forth Anu, but he would not meet her;
Ea was terrified and turned back.
Then I sent forth Merodach, the counsellor of the gods, your son;
to attack Tiamat his heart urged him.
He opened his mouth and said unto me:
'If I indeed am your avenger,
Tiamat to overpower and you to rescue,
make ready an assembly, prepare a banquet (?).
Enter joyfully into Ubsugina all together.
With my mouth like you will I pronounce the oracle.
What I create shall never be changed,
the word of my lip shall never go back or be unfulfilled!'

Hasten therefore and determine for him at once his destiny,
that he may go forward and meet your powerful foe!'
Then went Gâgâ and completed his journey
unto Lakhmu and Lakhamu the gods, his fathers,
he prostrated himself and kissed the ground at their feet,
he bowed himself and stood up and spake unto them:
. . . . . . clothed with fear;
with lustre and terror he covered his head.
He directed also his way, he made his path descend,
to the place where Tiamat [stood] he turned his countenance;
with his lip he kept back . . .
his finger holds the . . .
On that day they extolled him, the gods extolled him,
the gods, his fathers, extolled him, the gods extolled him.
Then Bel drew near, eager for the struggle with Tiamat,
looking for victory over Kingu her husband.
When she beheld him, her resolution was destroyed,
her understanding was overthrown, her plans confounded.
And the gods, his helpers, who marched beside him
beheld (how Merodach) the prince amazes their eyes.
He laid judgment on Tiamat, yet she turned not her neck;
with her hostile lips she uttered defiance:
' Let the gods, O Bel, enter on battle behind thee,
[behold,] they are gathered together to where thou art!'
Bel [launched] the Deluge, his mighty weapon;
against Tiamat, who had raised herself (?), thus he sent it.
' Thou wert mighty [below,' he cries,] ' exalted above,
yet thy heart [has urged thee] to begin the strife,
[to lead the gods from] their fathers to [thy side];
[thou hast gathered them around thee] and raisest thyself
  [against us],
[thou hast made] Kingu thy husband
[and hast bestowed on] him divine power.
. . . . . . thou hast devised evil,

[against the] gods, my fathers, hast thou directed thy
  enmity.
[May] thy host be fettered, thy weapons be restrained !
Stand up, and I and thou will fight together.'
When Tiamat heard this,
she uttered her former spells, she repeated her command.
Tiamat also cried out vehemently with a loud voice.
From her roots she rocked herself completely.
She uttered an incantation, she cast a spell,
and the gods of battle demand for themselves their arms.
Then Tiamat attacked Merodach the counsellor of the
  gods;
in combat they joined ; they engaged in battle.
Then Bel opened his net and enclosed her ;
the evil wind that seizes behind he sent before him.
Tiamat opened her mouth to swallow it ;
he made the evil wind to enter so that she could not close
  her lips.
The violence of the winds tortured her stomach, and
her heart was prostrated, and her mouth was torn open.
He swung the club ; he shattered her stomach ;
he cut out her entrails ; he divided her heart ;
he overpowered her and ended her life ;
he threw down her corpse ; he stood upon it.
When Tiamat who marched before them was conquered,
he dispersed her forces, her host was overthrown,
and the gods her allies who marched beside her
trembled and feared and turned their backs.
They fled away to save their lives ;
they clung to one another, fleeing helplessly.
He followed them and broke their arms ;
he flung his net and they are caught in the snare.
Then filled they the world with their lamentations ;
they bear their sin and are shut up in prison,
and the elevenfold creatures are troubled with fear.
The host of spirits (?) who marched beside them (?)

APPENDICES

he throws into fetters and [binds] their hands,
and [tramples] their opposition under him.
And the god Kingu who [had been made leader over] them,
he bound him also and did to him as to the [other] gods.
And he took from him the tablets of destiny [that were on] his breast;
he sealed them with his pen and hung them from his own breast.
From the time he had bound and overmastered his foes
he led the illustrious foe captive like an ox,
bringing to full completion the victory of Ansar over his antagonists.
The warrior Merodach (thus) performed the purpose of Ea.
Over the gods in bondage he strengthened his watch, and
he turned backwards Tiamat whom he had overpowered.
Then Bel trampled on the body of Tiamat;
with his club that spares not he smote her skull,
he broke it and caused her blood to flow;
the north wind bore it away to secret places.
Then his fathers beheld, they rejoiced and were glad;
they bade peace-offerings to be brought to him.
And Bel rested; his body he fed;
he strengthened his mind (?), he formed a clever plan,
and he stripped her like a fish of her skin in two halves;
one half he took and with it overshadowed the heavens;
he stretched out the skin, he appointed watchers
bidding them that her waters should not issue forth;
he lit up the sky, the sanctuary rejoiced,
and he set it over against the deep, the seat of Ea.
Then Bel measured the form of the deep;
as a palace like unto it he made E-Sarra (the upper firmament).
The palace of the upper firmament, which he created as heaven,
he caused Anu, Bel and Ea to inhabit as their stronghold.

Tablet V.

He made the stations of the great gods;
he fixed the stars, even the twin-stars, to correspond with them;
he ordained the year, appointing the signs of the Zodiac over it;
for each of the twelve months he fixed three stars,
from the day when the year issues forth to its close.
He established the station of Jupiter that they might know their bounds,
that they might not err, that they might not go astray in any way.
He established the station of Bel and Ea along with himself.
He opened also the gates on either side,
the bolts he strengthened on the left hand and on the right,
and in their midst he set the zenith.
He illuminated the Moon-god that he might watch over the night,
and ordained him for a guardian of the night that the time might be known,
(saying): 'Month by month, without break, make full thine orb;
at the beginning of the month, when the night begins,
shine with thy horns that the heaven may know.
On the seventh day, halve thy disk;
stand upright on the Sabbath with the [first] half.
At the going down of the sun [rise] on the horizon;
stand opposite it [on the fourteenth day] in full splendour (?).
[On the 15th] draw near to the path of the sun;
[on the 21st] stand upright against it for the second time.'

. . . .

APPENDICES

Tablet VI. (?)

The gods in their assembly created [the beasts],
they made perfect the mighty [monsters];
they caused the living creatures of the [field] to come forth,
the cattle of the field, the wild beasts of the field, and the creeping things of the [field];
[they fixed their habitations] for the living creatures [of the field]
[and] adorned [the dwelling-places] of the cattle and creeping things of the city;
[they created] the multitude of creeping things, all the offspring [of the earth]!

. . . .

XIII

A SUMERIAN ACCOUNT OF THE CREATION FROM THE CITY OF ERIDU

The glorious temple, the temple of the gods, in the holy place (of Eridu) had not yet been made;
no reed had been brought forth, no tree had been created;
no brick had been made, no roof had been formed;
no house had been built, no city had been constructed;
no city had been made, no dwelling-place prepared.
Nippur had not been built, E-kur (the temple of Nippur) had not been constructed.
Erech had not been built, E-Ana (the temple of Erech) had not been constructed.
The deep had not been created, Eridu had not been constructed.
The glorious temple, the temple of the gods, its seat had not been made.
All lands were sea.
When within the sea there arose a movement,
on that day Eridu was built, E-Sagila was constructed,
E-Sagila where the god Lugal-du-azaga dwells within the deep.
Babylon was built, E-Sagila was completed.
The gods and the spirits of the earth were created all together.
The holy city (Eridu), the seat of the joy of their hearts, they proclaimed supreme.
Merodach bound together a reed-bed on the waters;

dust he made, and he poured it out on the reed-bed.
That the gods might dwell in a seat of the joy of their hearts,
he formed mankind.
The goddess Aruru created the seed of mankind along with him.
He made the beasts of the field and the living creatures of the desert.
He made the Tigris and Euphrates and set them in their place;
he declared their names to be good.
The *ussu*-plant, the *dittu*-plant of the marshland, the reed and the forest he created.
He created the verdure of the plain,
the lands, the marshes, and the greensward also,
oxen, and calves, the wild ox and its young, the sheep and the lamb,
meadows and forests also.
The he-goat and the gazelle brought forth (?) to him.
Then Merodach heaped up an embankment at the edge of the sea;
. . . . . . as it had not before been made,
. . . . . . he caused it to exist.
[Bricks] he made in their place,
. . . . . . roofs he constructed;
[houses he built], cities he constructed;
[cities he made], dwelling-places he prepared;
[Nippur he built], E-kur he constructed;
[Erech he built], E-Ana he constructed.

. . . .

Printed by BALLANTYNE, HANSON & CO.
At the Ballantyne Press

www.ingramcontent.com/pod-product-compliance
Lightning Source LLC
Chambersburg PA
CBHW021155230426
43667CB00006B/406